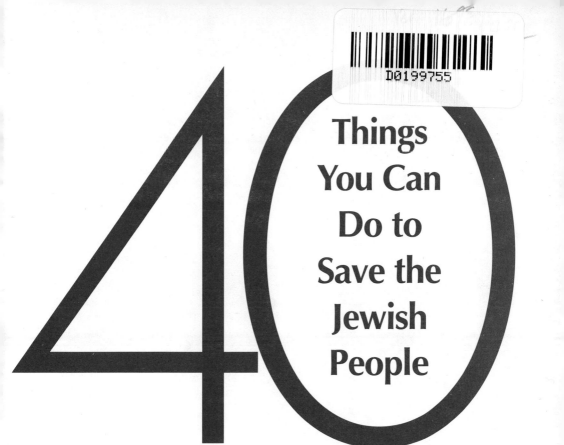

40

Things You Can Do to Save the Jewish People

Some really practical ideas for parents who want to raise "good enough" Jewish kids to insure that the Jewish people last at least another generation

40

Things You Can Do to Save the Jewish People

*Some really practical ideas for parents
who want to raise "good enough" Jewish kids
to insure that the Jewish people last
at least another generation*

Joel Lurie Grishaver

Alef Design Group
Los Angeles

Library of Congress Cataloging-in-Publication Data

Grishaver, Joel Lurie.
40 things you can do to save the Jewish people / Joel Lurie Grishaver.
    p.   cm.
    "Some really practical ideas for parents who want to raise "good enough" Jewish kids to
insure that the Jewish people last at least another generation."
    ISBN 1-881283-04-6 : $16.95
    1. Jewish religious education --Home training.   2. Judaism--Study and teaching--
    United States.   3. Jewish families--United States--Religious life.
I. Title.   II. Title: Forty things you can do to save the Jewish people.
BM570.G66   1993
296.7'4--dc20   93-2587
                                                    CIP

This manuscript has been carefully and *patiently* copyedited by Carolyn Moore Mooso. In addition to copyediting,
we thank Carolyn for creating the dictionary entries on page 146 and the glossary.

Alef Design Group
4423 Fruitland Avenue
Los Angeles, California 90058
(213) 582-1200
MANUFACTURED IN THE UNITED STATES OF AMERICA

For My Mother

and My Sister Judy

for having taught me the Torah of our
family recipes and stories.

40 Things
You Can Do to Save the Jewish People

A Jewish Home

Jewish Nationalism

Jewish Education

Bar/Bat Mitzvah and Teenagers

Dating & Marriage

Final Wisdom

Appendices

Basic Principles

How Much Can I Get Away With and Still Go to Heaven?

I am regularly heard to say, "I would give anything to weigh 168 pounds again." The truth is, I wouldn't and I haven't.

In my life I have weighed over 230 pounds. Less than a year ago I weighed as little as 202 pounds. But, these days I am weighing around 212. There is a price to pay to lose weight. It means not eating. It means lots of discipline. It means taking my exercise program seriously. I care enough about my health and my appearance not to let myself get too fat, but all my desires to again wear a medium sweater, to have a flat stomach, and even to feel physically better aren't yet enough motivation to let the skinny person inside me find the discipline to endure the suffering needed to wear away the fat. The truth is, like almost everyone else I know, I want it both ways. I want to be skinny and I want butter. I want to look like a hunk and I want to sleep in and not go to the gym. I want to lose the gain without the pain! That in essence is the meaning of a bumper sticker I saw the other day when I was down in Orange County: "HOW MUCH CAN YOU GET AWAY WITH AND STILL GO TO HEAVEN?"

My business partner, Alan, has one of those metabolisms which can burn anything. But even so, he doesn't get as hungry as I do. In our daily game of "chicken," where all of us try to see how long we can last before someone has to give in and suggest lunch—he outlasts me and Jane every day. Lunch doesn't seem to matter to him. Then, no matter what he does eat, nothing sticks. I, on the other hand, have to deal with the constant balancing of my desire for food and my desire for hunkhood. In the end, I have to try for a compromise—because I can't have it both ways. We are all playing "HOW MUCH

CAN YOU GET AWAY WITH AND STILL..." That is the essence of living in America. Jewish life here is very much the same.

Jewish life in America began with such a compromise, balancing the obligations of the Jewish tradition with the best route to economic success. The first Jews who came here left their synagogues and families and rabbis and communities behind in order to find freedom and wealth. It wasn't that they were fleeing their Jewish obligations—it was just that they were responding to an immediate call rather than "answering to a higher authority." It was a commitment to a new life now, Jewish life later. First they came and set up stores and peddling routes and businesses. Then, they sent for their families. Later, when they felt the need, first cemeteries, then *B'nai Brith* lodges, then synagogues and (much later) Jewish schools were established.

Our Jewish lives, too, are imprinted on those patterns. We struggle to live in both worlds, yet we share our ancestors' sense of what comes first. First we pay the piper, then we blow shofar. While we know (when we are honest) that we can't be in synagogue and at the play-off game at the same time, we still want it both ways. Ironically, there is a power in that ambivalence, a power which will be lost if we ever give up wanting to hear the shofar or be in synagogue. Our lives have been organized: peddling route first, then family, then the synagogue. As much as we all want our own "Jewish living" version of weighing 168 pounds, and as much as we talk about it, we are only going to give up so much. Each of us has our own point of compromise.

This is a book by a Jew who also wants it both ways—written for families who want it both ways, too. If we really wanted to raise Jewish kids—and if that was our only want—we would be much tougher on ourselves and on our kids. But that is not our only want—it is only one strong desire. This is a practical book about improving the odds. It is a collection of simple practical techniques which invite positive, fun, meaningful Jewishness to inhabit larger portions of our unrestricted American lives. It is a book about: "HOW MUCH CAN WE GET AWAY WITH AND STILL RAISE "JEWISH ENOUGH" CHILDREN WHO WILL IN TURN RAISE OTHER JEWISH CHILDREN?"

The Rabbis of the Talmud also drew on the wisdom of folk practice. In the Talmud, they sometimes used a problem-solving technique called *Tze u'Lomed*—"Go and study." When they couldn't reason out the right ritual practice, when logic and deductive Talmudic reasoning couldn't do the job— they went out and examined the Jewish lives people were actually leading. Sometimes visionary idealism is the best path; sometimes, it is the wisdom of

3

real life. As with many things, it is a question of balance. (The rabbis had a name for that, too, they called it *Midah k'Neged Midah*—literally, "Measure for Measure," but for our purposes, "Equilibrium," or "Proper Measure.") The idea of *Tze u'Lomed* tells us that sometimes, the people do know best.

This is a *Tze u'Lomed* book. Very little of it came from my mind or my imagination. It is the story of my parents, their friends, my students, their parents, my friends, and their children—all the people I have gone and watched as they've struggled with the real problems of day-to-day Jewish living. Slowly, in my mind, over the past few years, often when I am driving late at night, I've been busy assembling a new Talmud for contemporary Jewish life. I call my imaginary project *Talmud 2000*. It is made up of conversations real and reconstructed—it is my own montage of truths and practices I've assimilated, reconstituted in a form that seeks to teach more than all of the original settings. Throughout this book, you'll see excerpts from *Talmud 2000*, the Talmud of my imagination. Here, in this fantasy Jewish talk-show of my inner struggles, the wisest practitioners of day-to-day Judaism will share the best wisdom and insight, as we again try to repackage and balance Judaism so it can thrive through its next transformation.

Use this book for inspiration. Take the "40 Things" as examples, models, starting points—not a complete list or program. By the time you're done reading, I'm convinced that you'll be convinced that you could have formulated a better list. Go ahead and do it! That is the real purpose of this book—to be a starting point.

1 Never Think that Any One Thing Will Work

The most frequent mistake made in Jewish child-rearing is asking the question: "What one thing will make the most difference in my child's Jewish future?" Know from the start that the formula for Jewish identity is a blend of many key experiences and connections. There is no one key.

Do not make the same mistake that many Jewish institutions make—never place a single bet. The big phrase they use is "bang-for-the-buck." They tend to do a little bit of research and then place all their money on one horse to win.

They ask, "Is it better to invest in early childhood education or high school youth groups, day schools or summer trips to Israel?" They think that they can find a "silver bullet"—the one experience which will make the most difference in "Jewish Identification. They've forgotten that Jewish life is a blend, that it takes a long time to age (in the right oak barrels). They are striving for a fine wine, grown from only one grape and turned out in a few weeks. It is a good desire—but it is unrealistic.

Here is the truth. You want it all:

Column A

You want to establish a Jewish home with Jewish learning and practice.

You can pick your celebrations. You can choose how you want to manifest the performance of mitzvot (for our purposes, mitzvot are Jewish actions). And, you can find your own ways as a family for

5

acquiring and celebrating Jewish learning. But to be an effective Jewish home you need at the very least: (1) Jewish rituals, (2) Jewish obligations, and (3) a process of ongoing Jewish growth.

Column B

You want to provide a Jewish education which goes from preschool through at least an active involvement in Hillel in college. (Personally, I want to insist on Jewish studies in college—but I've decided that the better part of valor is to make that an ideal rather than an expectation.) After that, you need to accept the fact that they are Jewish on their own—or that they are not yet (and may never be) Jewish on their own.

You can pick you own flavors of Jewish schooling. Preschools offer hot and cold running child-centeredness in dozens of styles and forms. Jewish schools come in day schools and supplemental schools. Either form can be Community, Reform, Reconstructionist, Conservative, Orthodox or nondescript. What research does tell us is, the more the better. Some researchers have argued "the more hours the better" (with 3,000 hours being suggest as a minimum ideal—something only day schools can easily reach). Other studies have suggested that it is the number of years of consistent involvement which make a difference (with seven years being the suggested minimum).

Here is the simple trade-off. Most supplemental schools (afternoon Hebrew schools) suffer from acute minimalism—they don't teach enough because the time is too limited. Most day schools suffer from claustrophobia—they are too small. After six or eight years in the same classroom with the same kids, day schools tend to culminate in prison-break scenes where kids struggle free and scramble over the barbed wire fence. Either way, you have to pay your money—and take your chances.

No one knows for sure. But here are three truths. (a) The more Jewish education, the better. (b) The less Jewish education the more risky the enterprise. And, (c) my own unresearched truth: Any Jewish education that makes it through the senior year of high school is infinitely more likely to produce a dynamically informed, involved, and committed Jew than is any kind of Jewish education that ends just when pubic hairs are first beginning to grow.

Here is **Joel's First Law of Jewish Survival:** Every year of Jewish education which takes place after bat or bar mitzvah is worth three or more years of anything which takes place earlier.

Column C

You want involvement in Jewish recreation. (In the latest jargon this is called non-formal education. It used to be informal education, but the jargon changed.)

This can and should include Jewish summer camp (day, then sleep-away), an active and positive Jewish youth group, and a high school Israel trip.

Do not settle for formal Jewish education alone. (Formal = School.) You need Jewish social opportunities, a Jewish dating pool, a circle of Jewish friends, and a place to practice, create, explore, play with, and evolve Jewishness. Schools provide skills, information, and insight. Camps, youth groups and then later, an Israel trip, provide a **context**.

However, do not be fooled into thinking that with strong non-formal involvement you can let your child skip the pains of Hebrew school. This is the basic truth. You can't master Hebrew in three weeks at camp. You don't learn Jewish history at three youth conventions a year, etc. You can deepen those understandings, but Jewish learning takes a **foundation**. That is what schooling builds.

When formal and non-formal balance each other, the system hums.

Column D

Finally, **you want affiliation**. Choose at least two from this list:

a synagogue, a _havurah_, a Jewish community center, a Jewish organization, a Jewish federation.

The research is beginning to suggest that those who choose "religious" affiliation (i.e. synagogue membership) have a better chance of raising "Jewish enough" kids—many more of their children tend to become involved, affiliated, identified and committed Jews than those who choose the secular Jewish trail. (The research, however, doesn't tell us whether it is the "chooser" or the "choice" which is the critical factor.)

Know only two truths about this column:

7

(1) You can't be Jewish alone. It may work when your kids are young. Your family may be able to "make *Shabbes*" alone for a while—but as the kids grow it takes Jewish friends and then Jewish dates to extend your Jewish family into the next generation. (2) American culture is religious. (9 out of 10 Americans believe in God, 8 out of 10 pray regularly, 7 out of 10 identify themselves as regular "church"-goers.) Sooner or later, everyone goes to church, except us. Just about everyone believes in God, except us. That is what all the surveys say. Statistically, we Jews are the great exceptions, the only real believers in secular ethical culture. Ultimately, the foundations of Jewish life are embedded in a religious culture, too.

It is possible to build Jewish life on a different bedrock, to secularize its structures. But, in the long run, it is much harder (not much easier) to do so. Believe it or not, it takes much more effort to constantly retranslate all of Jewish culture to filter out religion. All of the basic Jewish systems which run on autopilot—family holiday celebrations, synagogue gatherings, Torah learning—involve religious elements. You can amputate the religious (some kibbutzim have succeeded for a generation or two) but it demands reinventing each wheel.

I have often thought that the job of keeping Jewish life alive in America is a lot like being a zookeeper. Zookeepers build artificial habitats. Almost no animal in a zoo lives in its natural habitat. Likewise, it is just about impossible to reproduce the actual environment from which the animal came. It is the zookeeper's job to figure out, when it comes time to build an animal habitat, how much has to be identical, how much can be approximated, and how much can be ignored. We Jews who are living in America are building an artificial environment in which to raise and breed Jews. Just as is true of pandas, it is difficult to get Jews to mate with each other.

Judaism works better when there is a total Jewish environment. If everything is closed on Saturday, Shabbat is much easier. If everyone is eating matzah, keeping Passover is not an issue. As zookeepers, we are on a great adventure, transplanting Jewish life to a new frontier. However, in doing so, we accept great risk.

I also think a lot about the fallacy of "Jewish cloning." Cloning seems to be an important—if unspoken—metaphor in the War for Positive Jewish Identification, as well. Everyone seems to think it is possible to make new Jews out of skin-scrapings; they imagine that there is a single injection or procedure which will make the difference. The newest research and articles on "Jewish identification" and "in-marriage" have a clinical feel. They miss the impact of the smell of warm ḥallah. They keep on looking for "the one factor." They want to find the "Jewish gene" which can be spliced into a person with minimum effort in order "Judify" them, or perhaps make them susceptible to Jewishness. It doesn't work that way. Jewish life is Jewish life. It is part of every "gene;" it is the whole genetic configuration. It is not a "retrovirus" but the interplay of the myriad factors that determine who we are as entities. We've all been brainwashed by all those medical movies where the doctor stays up all night (in endless sweaty cross-dissolves) for weeks and invents a miracle cure. It doesn't always work that way. Jewish identity is the kind of thing you solve through proper diet, exercise, a combination of treatments— and often by drinking plenty of fluids. Ultimately, dynamic Jewish life, the kind of Jewish lives that in turn produce their own Jewish kids, are nurtured, not bred. It is not a question of finding a single element, but of building a life path.

This is the very bottom line. This Chinese menu of Jewish child-rearing comes with no guarantees. It may not work. But it has the best chance of making a difference. Balance and continuity are the keys. Can you leave out an element? Sure! Can it still work? Absolutely! Can you go your whole life and never get the mumps? Sure!

2 Always Tag All Four Bases

This metaphor is "too cute" but it works. You build Jewish identification most effectively when you tag all four bases: National (ethnic)—feeling like a member of a people, Communal (religious)—feeling connected to a community of faith, Familial (family)—experiencing Jewishness as the glue which holds your family together, and Personal (spiritual)—where Judaism meets your personal (inner) needs. The best Jewish practice hits a "home run;" it goes all the way around the diamond—and scores. Most of the time we only hit singles and doubles—touching one or two of these bases. The secret is to spread it around—trying to reach each of these four touchstones as often as possible. The mistake most "one-way" Jews make is that they keep hitting the same singles.

> Judaism/Jewishness is spun around four centers: National, Communal, Familial, and Personal. They operate as independent but related points of connection—not concentric circles of identification. I see neither a hierarchy nor a direct progression, but rather an interdependent network.

a. *National* **Judaism is ethnic and political.**

Listen to this story: This kid, one of my former students, had no Jewish genes—nothing about him was genetically Jewish. His mother was a Jew by choice. She converted as a teenager when her mother (a non-Jew) converted and married a second husband, a Jewish man. The kid's father was also born a non-Jew. He converted to marry the kid's mother. (Dad's father was or still is a "Klan" member.) I had the kid in Hebrew school and he often disrupted class, claiming that he

10

had been given a choice between the two religions. It was not uncommon for Christian symbols to pop up as doodles and in his art projects. I never knew whether this was a confused exploration or simply an act of Hebrew school defiance. I suspect that it was a little bit of both. Sometimes, he even wore a St. Christopher medal—it was a great manifestation of tough anger.

However, I will never forget that day during the Gulf War when, in the middle of the afternoon services, the rabbi came in and announced that the first SCUDs had hit Tel Aviv. The kid began to really cry—he was just sobbing. All of a sudden this real tough little guy—a junior gangster—was bawling his eyes out for his distant relatives and his people. That is the power of National Jewish identification.

National Judaism comes from the bagel and chicken soup place. No matter how much we dilute the Jewish people through intermarriage, no matter how many generations past *tzimmes* and *kishke* we get, something of National Jewish identification remains. No matter how much we try to define Judaism as a religion, the national, ethnic thing always makes a comeback. Here are some manifestations.

1. Just about all Jewish kids know how many Jewish kids are in their class at school. I've never figured out how they know—because it is almost never discussed. It is a "radar" kind of thing. And, it speaks volumes about the national level of Jewish identification.

2. National Judaism is knowing the story that once during the World Series, Sandy Koufax refused to pitch on Yom Kippur. Every Jewish kid knows that story—even if they don't know who Maimonides or Mickey Marcus were. National Judaism is the special connection we have with Barbara Streisand, Albert Einstein, Bugsy Siegel, Golda— and a hundred other personalities.

3. National Judaism is the way my mother checks out the obituaries and the election ballot for Jewish names.

4. National Judaism is that moment at Yom Kippur services or when you are at Seder and you have that sense that every Jew in the world—every Jew all over the world—is in the same place doing essentially the same thing. It is a really powerful feeling.

5. National Judaism is the power in visiting Israel for the first time, all those experiences: facing the void of the Holocaust, marveling at the

11

innovations of kibbutzim, standing in awe and envy at heroic Masada with its mythic expression in the modern Israeli Army, and the wonderful irony in finding a place with Jewish cops and Jewish hookers.

National Jewish identification is durable, but on its own it isn't very deep. It has worked well for those immersed in a total Jewish existence in Israel (though many Israeli educators and even political leaders are now questioning whether or not on its own it is enough). It has never transferred all that well to the diaspora as a Jewish way of life—except in the Zionist glory days when establishing the State of Israel was a big deal. But it does have its moments.

National Judaism doesn't tend to come with a lot of content or very many practices, but it is tenacious. It is the "stiff-necked" part of who we are as Jews; it is hard to get rid of. All the most recent studies suggest that a national (or secular, ethnic, cultural) Jewish identity is very hard to pass on. It tends to be sterile, because it lacks ritual and an entry point into the spiritual. Alone, it tends not to build committed Jews who do Jewish stuff all the time and in-marry; but all the same, National Jewish identification is all but indestructible. There are a lot of half-Jewish truck drivers out there who proudly wear their Jewish stars. That makes it very powerful.

The Talmudic rabbis recognized the importance of this "national" Jewishness and they labeled it with the phrase "*Kol Yisrael Arevim Zeh ba-Zeh*" ("All Jews are intertwined one with the other"). They understood that a primal, subrational Jewish connection should be the foundation of every Jew's identity.

b. *Communal* Judaism is a source of both friendship and support.

To understand the role of communal Judaism, just pretend that Walnut Grove, the *Little House on the Prairie* place, was Jewish: your sense of self would be nurtured by the Doctor, the Preacher, the Teacher, the swimming hole by the bridge, a couple of good friends, Sunday after-"shul" picnics and softball games, and even the line of credit at Olsen's Emporium.

For 100 years or more, American Jewry has tried to ensure its survival in the communal arena. We have built a Judaism of institutions, though in the past 10 years, we've hedged our bet and begun to celebrate the family. As usual, we want it all from a single solution—not an interactive drug therapy. And in doing so, we've made a big, two-part mistake.

The first mistake was assuming that an institution is a community. Institutions can be communities—but just sharing the same locker room at the JCC doesn't mean you have a relationship. Locker rooms can be places of community, even of Jewish community, even of authentic Jewish community, but they can also be just facilities. The same is true of attending a synagogue Purim carnival; it doesn't mean that anyone will be at your house fixing lunch while you are busy burying your mother. That is the difference between institutions and communities. Too often, our Jewish institutions have downgraded our interactions from communal relationships to chance encounters coincidental to a programmatic calendar.

The second mistake was thinking that a strong family can do without a community. Alvin Schiff, the former director of the Board of Jewish Education of Greater New York, made just that mistake. He wrote a major report on the sorry state of the Hebrew School, in which he suggested that because Hebrew Schools are all failing, the solution is to replace Hebrew Schools with family educators who visit and educate families in their homes. In the original model, authentic Judaism, families and communities were supposed to work together. Think of Mayberry. Aunt Bee and Sherrif Andy Taylor were important to who Opie became, but he also needed Homer, Floyd, Barny, Goober, and Gomer.

Communal Judaism was originally designed to be organized around synagogues where people went every day. Once, synagogues were communities, not institutions. Jews prayed there three times a day, hung out with their friends there, solved society's problems there, studied there, and celebrated their lives there. Later, like almost everything else American, community "membership" degenerated into "affiliation," so that "belonging" has been reduced to "paying dues." Today you can either *affiliate* or just *pay your dues*, not only to synagogues, but *havurot,* JCCs, Federations—and lots of other Jewish institutions.

A Personal Reflection: Last week I called a lawyer in Boston in order to get the rights to a passage from a book. He is a seventyish man who had been a member of the Temple Sinai Brotherhood with my father. I knew his name—I must have talked to him sometime before in my life, but I can't remember. He was just a name on an old temple roster. It has been twenty years or more since I have been at Temple

13

Sinai. Most of the community I knew and loved has been eroded away in the politics of rabbinical firings, the creation of splinter congregations, and the inevitable plague of endless mobility. Yet, when David Lurensky and I talked, and conjured the memories of Rabbi Cohan, Harry Wheeler, Evelyn Borovsky Roskin, Miriam Kallen, Tommy, and a dozen others—a whole universe reopened its doors to me and said, "You belong."

Community is the thing that was operating when Rabbi Cohan and his wonderful wife, Sally, visited me in the hospital on my twelfth birthday when my appendix exploded. Rabbi Cohan came once and did the official "cheek pinch" and "hair tousle" clerical visit; Sally came back every day, each time with a different box of candy—and we had great conversations. They don't build *rebbetzins* like that anymore.

Harry Wheeler was my father's "best friend." To my knowledge they never hunted, fished, bowled, or played cards together. They never hung out. My parents never "went out" with the Wheelers—I don't think I was ever even in their house. Yet, every time I picked up the phone and Harry was there, his response was always, "Tell your father his best friend is on the phone." There was no bravado in that appellation. It expressed a truth. Because Harry and my father did share one very strong connection—the fellowship of the temple brotherhood. They cooked scrambled eggs for three hundred together at brotherhood breakfasts, ran fundraisers together, endured endless meetings and cups of coffee together, all of which cemented their bond. That, too, is the power of community.

Evelyn Borovsky Roskin was the temple's musical director. She was a fat woman who sweated too much, wore way too much red lipstick, and could have been a nightmare aunt. But to me, she was a queen. I love music. I cannot sing at all. She found a place for me in her junior choir. Later, when it was time for me to become a bar mitzvah, she worked with me for endless hours and produced the only occasion when I've ever sung on key. My mother even has a tape to prove it. My father borrowed a tape recorder from Harry Wheeler and hid it (with permission) under the *bimah* to make it. I owe the success of my first solo Jewish performance to Evelyn Borovsky Roskin and her sense of professionalism, dedication and community.

Miriam Kallen was the congregation's spinster aunt. She was a famous local educator, the sister of two even more famous educators—Horace, a major philosopher, and Deborah, an Israeli educational pioneer. She was an adoptive grandmother in my family and several others. She frequently shared our Shabbat and festival tables. I was occasionally a guest in her home. It was a wonderful, dusty place filled with medieval looking furniture and floor-to-ceiling books. There were magazines piled everywhere. I can remember that she always served me Swanson's chicken pot pies. I never really liked them, but I loved having dinner at her house—both the books (especially one by Frank Lloyd Wright) and her attention. I am who I am today, because Miriam once dared me to consider the rabbinate. My relationship with Miriam was a gift of my membership at Temple Sinai.

Tommy was the Italian janitor who was the temple custodian. He, too, was a member of the temple community. He was a short, bald man, who constantly chomped the remnants of a cigar, who said little and smiled a lot. He had a room in the temple basement. He didn't live there, but there was a cot and some furniture—a place for him to hang out. When I was ten or eleven, Tommy stopped kicking me out of his room. It was the "in" place to hang out—all the big kids did, or at least the cool ones. It was better than being let into the inner room at Studio 54. More than I can ever explain, hearing jokes and stories in Tommy's room, filled with his cigar smoke, was an important part of going to Shabbat services and belonging to the Jewish community.

That point when you walk into a synagogue and sixteen people say hello to you, and each one has her or his little interaction with you—knowing you well enough to know you—is when you feel the communal connection. It is when you know you belong—and that your family is more than just an island unto itself.

Once, a long time ago, the rabbis of the Talmud, the ones who designed the basic forms of the Judaism we now practice (or don't practice) came up with a morning exercise program called *Birkot ha-Shahar*. It wasn't quite Jane Fonda; it was a spiritual wake-up process, in which a series of blessings were said in connection with ordinary wake-up activities. There were blessings for hearing the rooster, stretching, putting your feet on the floor, getting dressed and so on. Each of these blessings made a double connection, both reminding the sayer of the gifts which God had bestowed and setting an ethical agenda of the ideals that should be fulfilled in the coming day. It was a great plan and it didn't work. Like most home exercise programs, people couldn't stay on it. Then the rabbis worked out a modification—they left it as a mitzvah for Jews to do alone when they actually woke up in the mornings, but also added it to the collective ritual when Jews got together for morning services. In those days, the rabbinic in-crowd all went to services every day. We, who have dieted alone, failed and then joined Weight Watchers—we, who have bought exercise devices to use at home and then joined a gym to improve our workout frequency—understand the power of community. So did the rabbis. The story of *Birkot ha-Shahar* teaches us that communities sustain our rituals and help us to remain Jewish despite any personal ambivalence or doubt.

c. *Familial* Judaism has the power and the ambivalence of intimacy.

Everyone, at least everyone I know, has two families. One is our real family, our birth family. It is the one in which we feel stuck. Our real families frustrate and anger us, they embarrass us, they challenge our individuality and maturity—yet we know that they are always there. Each of us also recruits and adopts a "pseudo-family," a group of friends who feel like family. We celebrate our holidays with this psuedo-family (when we can get away with it), we confide our inner lives to our psuedo-families—telling them all the things our real families wouldn't understand. We share vacations and joys with our pseudo-families; yet, we live with a deep insecurity (a hidden, inner knowledge) that ultimately our pseudo-families can drift away on the winds of mobility, lifestyle change, economic evolution, or just disappear because of the currents of time. It is the very rootedness of our real families which generates much of the tension. We live with the dual knowledge that they will always be there for us—no matter what—and that we can never escape them—no matter what. Likewise, it is the very ad hoc status of our pseudo-families which allows the intimacy and safety—and in turn, the deeper sense of ultimate loneliness. Pseudo-families, in an ironic sense, offer all the freedom and angst of a one-night stand.

Family isn't all it used to be—yet it can still accomplish all the same things, no matter what its shape, definition or form. The great pain which adds to our anxiety is that family's greatest truth is no longer there. It used to be true that—no matter what—families were always there. Families have always been

16

places of tension and support, fighting and great love, tender nurture and debilitating conflict—all the great opposites. But, despite all the tensions—families worked, because families were always there. Today, we have a new sense that family is as family does—and to get the power of family we often have to work hard to sustain our connections. Sometimes we must even "recruit" our families.

Until recently, the tendency of North American Jewry has been to follow the *Birkot ha-Sha<u>h</u>ar* principle and move things from the home to the synagogue. The sukkah is one obvious example. So is public "baby naming," and so are a lot of other home customs. The tendency right now is to return things to the home—to revalidate the home as a setting for Jewish practice and reauthorize the performance of major ritual functions by family members. It is a critical step, but if we overcompensate, as we usually do—we will be equally threatened.

d. *Personal* Judaism comes from the inner place.

Personal Jewish identity is personal. That makes it the hardest to talk about, because you never know exactly when it develops or what went into it. But, it is our end goal.

> In one of his autobiographical books, Elie Wiesel explores the question of "What is a good Jew?" He has one of the characters, obviously himself, talk it over with a rabbi. The rabbi asks the kid, "Are you a good Jew?" The kid answers, "I don't know!" Later the Rabbi says, "I think a good Jew is a person who, when asked if he is a good Jew, sincerely answers, 'I don't know.'"

The lesson here is that Judaism touches us in many ways at different points in our psyches and our souls. The best chance for us and our children to find a sustainable Jewish existence, one which will survive all the compromises, is to try to constantly tag all four bases: *national, communal, familial,* and *personal.*

To slip into another metaphor, we need to have a healthy diet of Jewish experiences—that is the way we grow strong Jewish identities. Just as the dietician will tell you to build good health by eating from the four basic food groups, Jewish Identity is best built by combining strong and positive experiences in each "zone." Once again, we want it all and can't have it all. Often we will have to make choices. We will have to decide: Do we have a great

Shabbat family dinner or go to temple? On a busy weekend, can the kids skip Sunday School because we went to Cousin Arlene's bat mitzvah? We know that most of us will compromise—just as most of us will cheat, at least a little, on every diet. We know, in truth, that ultimately it is the overall calorie count that matters—if we cheat (but not too much) it will just take a little longer. But, poor diets can destroy rather than aid our health. The same is true of compromised Jewish lives. When we compromise and edit, as we all will do, it is critical to learn the lesson of our forebears, the founders of the American Jewish community, and never to eliminate or completely ignore any of these categories—even if one of them sings to us most loudly. To grow strong Jewish identities, we need to live well balanced if not total Jewish lives—eating adequately from all four nutritional groups, touching all four bases.

Batter up.

3 Start a Jewish Expectations Photo Album

Before your child begins her or his Jewish education, take a photo album and label the pages with the pictures you hope to take over the next 15 years. Then, slowly proceed to share the album and take the pictures.

Last Sunday I was talking to some students when Hillel said: "I only go to Hebrew High because my parents make me, and to see my friends." This was a real kid named Hillel, not the college program, not the school, not the rabbi who almost froze on the roof and then later stood on one foot. I even know Hillel's parents. A couple days later I spoke to his father, Bill, and told him that I was happy to see that Hillel had outgrown his social autism towards adults—that he had even talked to me. I shared Hillel's message, the archetypal, "I only go to Hebrew High because my parents make me, and to see my friends."

Bill laughed and said, "That's funny, because we've never talked about it. But if he had ever objected, we would have insisted. The interesting thing is that he works hard to see his friends; he's the one who makes all the arrangements to get to USY events."

Instantly, I knew that a great lesson was in the making. Listen to the juxtaposition: "*because my parents make me*" with "*we've never talked about it.*" That was wonderful—Hillel's parents "*made him*" even though they had "*never talked about it.*" I loved it. It became Joel's next law:

Joel's Second Law: The best way of making a child fulfill a Jewish obligation is by preempting the need to talk about it—to establish so clear an expectation that it isn't even worth bringing up.

Next, I began to think about how to gently and effectively set those expectations so they wouldn't feel oppressive. In that process I remembered a phone conversation with my friend Carol. She said:

Today Rob and I went to vote together; it was his first time. I took a picture of him as he entered the voting booth.

To which Harlene Appelman said (when I read this to her), "That's a great idea."

Then I remembered something Carol had told me over a year ago:

Today was Rob's first day of college. I took a picture of him before he left home. It was exactly like the picture I took of him 13 years ago when he first went to the Jewish day school. Except he weighed 200 pounds more.

To which Harlene Appelman also said, "That is wonderful."

When the spark jumped and Carol's pictures were connected to Bill's successful setting of Hillel's expectations—a plan was born. So here is a gentle, inobtrusive way of setting expectations which your child will probably never dare to question.

1. Buy a photograph album.

2. Take a label-maker, a calligraphy pen, lots of stickers—whatever works for you—and label all the pages before you start to take any pictures. The labels should be the photographs you hope to take as your child grows. There are no rules about what non-Jewish events could be included (and possibly "Judified"). In fact, there are no rules about what Jewish events should be included. If I did it today, this would be my list.

a. First Day of Jewish School

b. Consecration

c. First Time Saying the Four Questions

d. First Jewish Day Camp

e. First Jewish Sleep-Away Camp

f. First Junior Youth Group Event

g. Bar/Bat Mitzvah

h. First Day at Hebrew High School

i. First Day as a Teaching Aide in the Hebrew School

j. First Senior Youth Group Event

k. Confirmation

l. Trip to Israel

m. First Day as a C.I.T at a Jewish Camp

n. Hebrew High School Graduation

o. First Day of Jewish Studies in College

p. First Job as a Jewish Teacher, Counselor, or Youth Group Advisor

q. Junior Year in Israel

r. Etc.

3. The trick is not just to actually take the pictures, but to share the book with your child on a regular basis. Every time you add a picture, you should read the whole book together, talking about what it will be like— while you ooze with the pride you expect to feel.

This "Kodak moment" was brought to you courtesy of the photogenic opportunities of the Jewish tradition. If you understand Carol's commitment to picture taking, her desire to preserve important moments, you have internalized an important Jewish insight: *She-he-heyanu* saying.

Joel's Third Law: The *She-he-heyanu brakhah* is Judaism's way of saving "Kodak moments" in our hearts. Every time you want a picture to save the moment, whether or not you snap the shutter, say this *brakhah* and add it to the album in your heart.

Extensions and Other Creative Paths, Etc.

Our goal here is to "make our kids" do the Jewish things we hope will make a difference "without ever talking about it." This means gently setting expectations, but not doing it in a way that turns into a game of "I dare you to make me." Here are some creative and non-intrusive (organic, if you will) suggestions.

1. My friend and frequent inspiration, Shelly Whizin, made an album for her husband Bruce's sixtieth birthday. Not only were there photos and other clippings—but a whole collage. She added dozens of stickers and rubber stamps, glitter and ribbons, and turned the whole thing into a work of art. She wrote poetry and pasted quotations on every page. Feel free to do the same, proactively or retroactively. It might be fun to "do the book" when your child is still an infant, and then add the photos as time goes by. (Remember with photo albums you can always add or eliminate pages.)

2. When I first met Carol and her husband Joel (ל״ז), all three of us became instant fast friends. We loved each other almost before we knew each other—because we were working on a project together. My birthday came up a month into the relationship. They didn't know what to get me, but they wanted to do something, and they wanted the relationship to grow (outside of the work we all were doing). Carol made a coupon book good for "one free trip to Seattle" and filled it with "opportunities" like touring, eating out, seeing movies, and even sitting by the fire. The coupon book of Jewish opportunities could be wonderful: a new outfit for Consecration, a sleeping bag before you go to Camp Ramah, a bag of Tootsie Rolls for your first shul-in, a silver dollar when you say the four questions for the first time, etc.

3. My mother used to put my sister and me to bed with Patty Putt-Putt and Peter Putt-Putt stories respectively. These were original characters who served as our alter egos in all the adventures and problem-solving experiences our childhoods mandate. They did all the things we dreamed of doing but could not (yet) do. They managed to solve all the problems we never dreamed could have a solution (yet). They were our personal healing and playing reality. There was a lot of prescription in those stories. My mother used Peter and Patty to do a lot of modeling. It was a great way of sneaking in expectations between rides on flying rocket sleds that went "putt-putt-putt."

4. Years ago Craig Taubman, my friend, teacher, personal muse, fellow "two a.m. hot dog boiler" (in the days when we were both broke), used to do an

exercise with groups called "A Letter to My Unborn Child." It was a kind of modification of an older Jewish idea called an "Ethical Will." It was a sharing of hopes and expectations. Right now, we're editing a book from Rabbi Richard Israel. It, too, has a letter to an unborn child, his daughter, followed by letters written to her at critical points in her development. Heartfelt letters can often be critical ways of sharing dreams. If we don't talk about them, if we don't say it, our kids may never know.

5. My business partner Jane came up with the idea of having kids write themselves cards (or dictate the text for cards to you) for events that are still years in the future—and then you mail them at the appropriate moments. This is a literary time capsule thing. So on the first day of Jewish preschool, the child sends her/himself a Consecration card, a Bar or Bat Mitzvah card, a Confimation card, and a postcard to her/himself in Israel.

Warning. Timing is everything. In their book, *Rituals For Our Times*, Evan Imber-Black and Janine Roberts use two television shows to make a point.

One is a *Cagney and Lacey* episode in which the parents give Harvey Jr. a set of eighteenth-birthday gifts which affirm their expectations that he is about to go to college. It ends in a door-slamming, "I'm-never-going-to-talk-to-you-again" fight, when Harvey Jr. announces that he has joined the Marines.

In contrast, a different gift-giving emerges in an episode of *The Wonder Years*. Karen, the teenage daughter, and her father are in conflict. It is a former Marine confronting his peace-activist daughter, it is the myth of college versus a year of adventure and freedom roaming in a VW micro-bus, it is "Ward Cleaver meets the Sixties"—head on. After all the fighting, at the end of the episode, he gives her a birthday gift, his old worn Marine kit bag and says, "It's for college or if you go somewhere—either way you have to have something to put your stuff in and this one got me through some pretty rough times."

I'll quote the Torah of Kenny Rogers more than once in this book:

You gotta know when to hold 'em, know when to fold 'em...

Just remember this: Expectations are much better set long before they are actual—not just a few steps ahead of the critical moment of enforcement.

I never promised you it would be easy—remember, we want it both ways. We want them to be free, and we want them to freely choose exactly what we want.

Shabbat

4 Always Remember Shabbat— Even When You Don't Keep It

Frequently we are forced (because of our ambivalent priorities) to choose between celebrating Shabbat and doing something else we consider really important. Even if we make the non-Shabbat choice, we should do the other thing in a *Shabbesdik* way.

Okay. It is Friday afternoon and you have just checked into your hotel room in Orlando, Florida—at Disney World. It has been a hell of a day: airports, luggage, rental cars—and nudgy kids. You check into the hotel and hit the pool. Then comes the big decision point—it is soon to be Friday night. Will you make it *Erev Shabbat* or Friday night?

If you were a traditional, follow-the-rules kind of Jewish family, you would change into your good clothes and proceed to celebrate Shabbat for the next twenty-six hours. (Yes, for the record, even the Orthodox, who keep kosher and observe Shabbat—they, too, take their kids to Disney World and Disneyland. They just plan ahead and still follow all the Jewish rules). This could be you (but probably not).

Most Jewish families don't celebrate Shabbat even when they are at home (most weeks). They just have Friday. So, for them, Friday and Saturday at Disney World is a non-issue. They put on their gaudy vacation clothes, buy some of those glow-in-the-dark necklaces they sell all over the park at night—and really enjoy the electrical parade.

Even if you are a Shabbat-making family, this week, with your kids chomping at the bit to ride Space Mountain, you're highly likely to take a vacation from Shabbat, too. You can argue, "After all, we're spending quality family time together—God will forgive us." You buy your glow-in-the dark necklaces, some Mickey Mouse *kippot*—the kind with ears and your name written on them—and really enjoy the electrical parade.

This is our proactive option. When you leave the pool, take your shower, relax and then put on the vacation duds. But, while you're getting unpacked, take the candlesticks and candles out of the suitcase. You can all gather around the dresser in the "parents'" room, light candles, kiss, maybe sing a Shabbat song—and then head out to your encounter with Space Mountain.

The bottom line here is that by "keeping" this one small part of Shabbat (at least) you've taught yourself and your familiy an important lesson: Judaism is always with us—we always take it with us when we go on vacation, and we never take a vacation from it.

When I brought this excerpt to class, one of my adult Talmud students explained it to me. He is just a good Jewish parent who goes to adult education while his son is at Hebrew High. But he understood something none of the scholars who were my formal Jewish teachers ever taught me.

> Ira Smith taught: **Why are the Ten Commandments repeated in the Torah, once in Exodus 20 and once in Deuteronomy 6?** I think it is to teach us the difference between "remembering" and "keeping." In Exodus 20 we are told: "Remember the Sabbath day, to have it holy." In Deuteronomy we are told, "Keep the Sabbath day, to have it holy." The idea could be, that even if you are not "keeping" all the rules of Shabbat, Shabbat can have a kind of holiness if it is always part of your consciousness.

Ira's insight is brilliant. He understands something the rabbis also know, but do not state so succinctly. If you follow all the Shabbat laws, then you may not touch a hammer on Shabbat. The idea (one of the fences around Shabbat) is that if you can't touch the hammer, there is no possibility of using it to do work. So the hammer, and all tools, "have cooties" on Shabbat and may not be touched—they are called *muktzeh*. *Muktzeh* is a "tool taboo" which was

27

imposed to protect the "work taboo." But, later, after having etched all those rules, the rabbis ask, "What happens if you really have to move the hammer?" The answer given in Jewish law, is "use your elbow." They explain that if you have to touch or move something on Shabbat (and in a sense, not keep Shabbat) you should do it in a way that makes it impossible to forget that it is still Shabbat and special conditions apply. Therefore in the "breaking" of a Shabbat rule, the sense of Shabbat is still kept. Or, as Ira has taught us, we are "remembering" Shabbat, even when we are not "keeping" it.

> **Joel's Fourth Law:** Said in the name of Ira Smith: Even when you feel that you can't be *shomer(et) mitzvot*, a keeper of mitzvot (Jewish actions), always be *zokher(et) mitzvot*, one who remembers (and teaches) that those mitzvot exist.

Here is another truth; the more Shabbat ritual, the more likely it is to have an impact. Let's put it this way:

> When your family is in Orlando, if you did your homework and found a synagogue and went there Friday night or Saturday morning, it could teach an important lesson—Jews are everywhere. It could also build the foundation of some new life-long friendships.

When I was in college, a couple of my roommates and I were fond of road trips. When there was a break, we would take off for a couple of days of camping and visiting friends on other campuses. We were living together in a private Jewish house (it was the sixties so we called it a "Jewish commune") and it became our practice to stop and hunt up a synagogue twice a day. We would hit a small town, hunt the phone book, find the synagogue and often surprise the ten or so old men who were gathered there for morning or evening services. We got a lot of great receptions and a bunch of free meals out of it. They loved meeting young and committed Jews and we loved hearing the stories of their Jewish lives.

> But, let's assume that having lit candles and kissed each other, you still push on to Disney World. Once you're there, you're going to eat dinner, right? If you can get bread and wine, you can make it a Shabbat dinner. Your quick and quiet blessings won't bother anyone, but they will make a powerful Jewish memory and message. And, if you can't get the wine—Jewish law says that you can make *Kiddush* on any beverage or food except for water.

Two of my most powerful Jewish memories both have to do with unusual Shabbat celebrations.

Once, with a youth group I was advising in the Chicago area, I and a bunch of the kids went camping. It wasn't a formal youth group event. It was over a weekend, so Shabbat was there to confront. I had packed the candles, wine, and ḥallah, but they were embarrassed about performing our strange national ceremonies in a public campground. Before sundown we took a walk around and found an Orthodox family who had come to camp out for the whole Shabbat. They had taken great care to surround their campsite with an *eruv*, a ritual fence, so that they could carry on Shabbat, a heat source which would keep their water and food hot so they wouldn't have to kindle a flame on Shabbat, etc. It had a powerful impact on us, and their family and our group welcomed Shabbat together. Those candles burning in the wood are an important part of who I am as a Jew.

Likewise, later, I was the youth advisor for a Reform synagogue in the Los Angeles area which made a practice of an annual Saturday trip to Disneyland. I didn't like the idea of Disneyland on Shabbat, but there was little I could do to stop it. So, I took a lesson from an old camp director, teacher, and friend, Jerry Kaye, and brought a tin of cinnamon and a short Havdalah candle in my pocket. Saturday night, with soda in hand, I gathered my youth group in the park at the end of Main Street, USA, and discreetly made Havdalah while we waited for the electrical parade. No one minded. A lot of people were impressed and a few asked questions. We even gathered a dozen or so Jewish families around us. A good time was had by all—then the music, lights and fireworks started.

Our two lessons are: Always take your Jewish practice with you—and the more the merrier.

Jewish Vacation Opportunities

There are both "Jewish Vacations" and "Vacations with Jewish Elements." Jewish Vacations are Israel and the Lower East Side, Eastern Europe and the Touro Synagogue in Newport. There is just about nowhere you can go (except maybe certain mountain ranges in North Dakota) where there isn't something Jewish to see, do, eat, or meet. By the way, even if you don't visit something Jewish in North Dakota you can still light Shabbat candles and make *ha-Motzi*.

1. Make a point to take some Jewish vacations. Every possible Jew should get to eat Gus's Pickles (the Lower East Side), see a concentration camp (Eastern Europe), put a note into the *Kotel* (Israel), etc.

2. Find out what is available and Jewish wherever you are. I've made little old men open wonderful little synagogues in Athens, in Cheltenham,

England, in little cities in northern Texas, and several other places, and have had great experiences each time. In all cases the synagogue was worth seeing and the little old man was worth meeting. There are Jewish museums and Jewish cemeteries—all kinds. I've never been there, but I hear wonderful stories of a synagogue in Curaçao with wonderful white sand floors. Did you know that there is a Jewish children's museum in Wilmette, Illinois?

3. Collect stuff from your Jewish visits. Postcards are good. So are slides, snapshots, or even videos. Revisit your Jewish vacations.

4. And, the central message of this chapter, do the regular Jewish stuff on your vacation.

An Epilogue: Two Stories

One of my Talmud students brought me this problem, his own *Talmud 2000* question.

> A teenage daughter asks permission to go to Club Med in Mexico with her best girlfriend during spring break. The parents say, "Yes." It's a little expensive, but there are no conflicting family vacation plans. Later, when they do a calendar check, they find that Seder falls during the week she will be gone. They *want* to ask her not to go, but she has already been *given* permission—they won't make it an order. Instead, they *urge* her to change her mind (because it is important to them that Seder be a whole-family thing, and because it is important to them that she "do" Seder). She is moved but not convinced. They search for a compromise. The brilliant solution they come up with is this: The daughter will be given a box of matzah and told to "eat it" during the week. The question of what else she will eat or not eat is left open-ended and not discussed. She rejects the solution, saying, "I hate matzah," but then offers her own compromise, "I'll take a Haggadah with me and read from it while I'm there." Her compromise was accepted. The question: Did they do the right thing?

The Moral of the Story: The Jewish calendar was designed to be a window through which we viewed time and staged our lives. We shouldn't fall into Passover; we should build to it. But, that isn't the way most of us live our lives. The big mistake was obviously "not checking the calendar" but the more profound problem was not feeling the tidal pull of the calendar and

30

"knowing" when Passover would be... That's a good polemic, but not necessarily the real-life solution.

If we do the box scores we learn the following:

* The parents were not into Passover enough to check out the dates of spring vacation—even though they regularly conflict. Deduct one point.

* Once they do *grok* the problem, they try for a mid-course correction. Give them a point. You'll have to evaluate the point total for "urging" rather than "commanding" on your own.

* Their daughter rejects their intervention—deduct another point.

* They then try for a compromise which keeps the Jewish tradition from "losing altogether." Add five points. However, you may deduct as many points as you feel appropriate (zero to three) for the nature of the compromise.

* The daughter then rejects even the minimalist compromise. Deduct more points.

* But then the daughter cares enough to suggest her own compromise, feeling the need to "remember" Passover in some way. Add some points.

* If we were objective, we would want both the matzah and the Haggadah. It's a deconstruction of Judaism to make a choice between them (like choosing between giving up all of your blood or all your bones) but still it is interesting that the daughter chose "Jewish meaning" over "Jewish eating." Evaluate this choice. Total your points and give a final "survivability quotient."

This was a real life Jewish dilemma in which a friend, student and teacher of mine—a good, committed, caring Jew—sincerely struggled to be both a "fair parent" and a "force for Jewish continuity." Real life is sloppy—and doesn't lend itself to clear paradigms except in self-help books. I don't know the full meaning of this story, I only know that the second story feels better.

I used the Club Med Passover "dilemma" in a workshop and heard this story from Susie Dworetz in return.

In 1990 our family scheduled a spring vacation to Carlsbad Caverns. Then we realized that the vacation included the first Seder night. We called our temple and the federation, but learned that the nearest organized Jewish community was more than 100 miles away. We went anyway, but when we got to town, I opened the phone book to the medical section and started calling doctors. Eventually I found a Jewish doctor who invited us to Seder.

Now this, too, is a rich and wonderfully ambivalent story with a beautiful ending. Write you own pithy summation line to this entire epilogue.

5 Have Shabbat Candles Mean Something

The act of lighting and blessing candles on Friday night is not enough—to be effective you have to do it with both feeling and meaning.

As I am writing this book, we are busy celebrating the journey of Columbus and remembering the Spanish Inquisition. It is a '92 kind of thing. Lots of Jewish money has been spent celebrating and studying Sephardic (Spanish) Jewish culture.

The great discovery, amid all this frenzy, is the presence of hundreds of Marrano families among the oldest Hispanic families in the American Southwest. Marranos are Jews who did not flee Spain when every Jew was offered the choice of leaving, converting, or dying. To retain their money and their family homes, many Jews elected to stay and make their Judaism less obvious. We understand those decisions, because many of our ancestors made the same choice—downscaling their Jewish traditions in exchange for economic advancement. Marranos are hidden Jews, hidden since the Inquisition.

Over the years we have learned that some of these families have been in hiding so long that they have forgotten what they are hiding. There have long been stories of Spanish Catholic families who had strange family rituals. Several such families used to light candles inside deep pitchers every Friday night. They had long since forgotten both the reason and the connection to Shabbat—they just knew that it was a secret family practice, an obligation they had to pass on.

In his book, The Masks Jews Wear, Eugene Borowitz suggests that American Jews have become Marranos. He means it in the sense that our Jewish practice has become more and more secretive. I think he is also right in that we are also preserving lots of customs and rituals whose meanings are long lost.

A Jewish couple had Friday night dinner at a Spanish-surnamed family's house in Albuquerque. As they sat down to dinner, the wife walked up to a portrait of Jesus which was on the wall and turned it backwards—facing the wall. The Jewish family protested, explaining that wasn't necessary. The Hispanic couple then explained that this was a family custom—they did it every Friday!

Joel's Fifth Law: Do not let your Jewish rituals become Marrano customs. Make sure they are not hidden and make sure they have meaning.

My colleagues at the Whizin Institute for Jewish Living, Steve and Sibyl Wolin, the authors of *The Resilient Self*, have done a great deal of research into alcoholics' families. I've learned a lot from listening to them teach. They've found that children of alcoholics who establish families with strong rituals tend not to pass on the alcoholism, whereas families without such rituals tend to do so in much greater numbers. In other words, rituals are a definitional factor in healthy families. In another study (conducted by one of their colleagues) which the Wolins are fond of citing, it is suggested that children who come from families with meaningful rituals have much higher self-esteem and do much better in school. The lesson is there to learn: the little bit of discipline and effort involved in lighting Shabbat candles once a week can change lives. If you make sure that this is a powerful and meaningful moment for everyone in the family, you are even more likely to bring the magic (or even the holiness) in.

Candlelighting is a big deal. Open up almost any how-to-be-Jewish manual and you will find that it devotes serious space and verbiage to the subject of lighting Shabbat candles. Topics will include candlelighting times, the proper form of the blessing, the way to hold and wave your hands—and if you're lucky, some wonderful quotations to read. They are right to concentrate on Shabbat candles, but usually they only tell you part of the trick. The words, the timing, and the choreography are important—but they are not the whole story. Making candlelighting meaningful is the other part of the trick—the "magic" if you will.

Shabbat and its definitional ritual, Shabbat candles, are the quintessential expressions of family Judaism. That is why they are so important.

The Midrash says that after Sarah died, Isaac went into deep depression. For him, life seemed to be over. When the servant brought Rebekkah, he felt better, but he still wasn't happy. He led her into his mother's tent and she moved in. When Friday came, she baked hallah. Before sundown, she lit candles. When Isaac smelled the hallah and saw the glow of the Shabbat candles, he felt much better. The sense of Jewish continuity made a difference. Then, they could live happily and Jewishly ever after.

Shabbat candles tend to form a definitional boundary, indicating that the family has chosen to actively manifest their Jewishness together. They are a clear sign of a Jewish home. There are other ways of doing that—but the weekly observance of Shabbat represents the clearest and easiest practice. The act of lighting Shabbat candles is the simplest and least demanding way of indicating that Shabbat is actively in your life. Simply put, a family that "makes" Shabbat every week—at least by lighting candles—sets itself apart from "holiday-only" Jews who tend to live their Jewishness on an exclusively "national" (ethnic) level, manifesting their Jewishness only at the High Holidays, Hanukkah, and Pesah. The difference is easy to see. Shabbat candles set them apart—defining this family, your family, as a force for making Jewishness an ordinary part of their lives. Ahad ha-Am was an important secular Zionist philosopher who taught: "More than Israel has keep the Shabbat, the Shabbat has kept Israel." Even though his central focus was "culture" and not "religion," "nation" and not "God's will"—he understood what lighting Shabbat candles and other Shabbat rituals did for Jews. We should learn the same lesson.

Now for the story of candles in general. Candles are always meaningful. They hypnotize us and capture our imagination the way that ocean waves do. You sit and watch and think. Partially it is the light. Partially it is the flicker of the flame with its ever-changing but repetitive form. But, the act of initiating Shabbat can be much more. It comes with ancient words—and in its modern practice (because once kindling Shabbat candles was a private meditation for women), kisses and hugs. Dr. Ron Wolfson, my friend, teacher, and part-time boss, likes to tell the story of taking his daughter Havi to an Italian restaurant when she was a little more than a year old. She was belted into a car-seat carrier and they placed her on the red-and-white checked tablecloth, facing the red patio candle in the white plastic mesh. As soon as she saw the flame, she began waving her hands in imitation of her mother's weekly candlelighting ballet. That is the power of flames.

35

Often, in families who have learned the secrets of "group process," candle-lighting time is a moment of formal "sharing." They go around the table talking about "One good thing which happened to me this week...," or "One hope which I have for next week...," etc. It is an activity which adds meaning to some families' practice. However, it is a process which will not work at all for other families. I've seen and heard of a lot of good family fights and hurt feelings when one parent wanted to "process" Shabbat feelings and other family members were less than supportive. When Ron Wolfson and I were working on his first book, *The Art of Jewish Living: The Shabbat Seder*, we interviewed a woman named Karen Vinocor, a single mother. She said something I have always remembered: "The best part of Shabbat for me is when I bless my children. I get to hug them and kiss them and they have to stand there and take it, whether they like it or not." Every time I have been at a Shabbat table and seen a 9- to 14-year-old boy (it is almost always the boys) resist his mother or father's hugs or kisses, I think of Karen and realize that another kind of meaningful event is also taking place. Deep meaning is not always shared verbally or even acknowledged at the moment it is felt.

However, if you are going to make the effort to make Shabbat an important part of your family's life together, find a way to make it meaningful—the extra effort is worth it. The same is true of every Jewish ritual.

Additional Activities

1. Robin Feldman tells a great story of a couple in her Jewish Holiday Workshop class who brought in their practice Shabbat candles—one was pink and one was orange. Their explanation was simple: Their first-grader loved pink, their preschooler adored orange. It is a wonderful echo of an older custom where Jewish mothers would light one candle for each of their children—every week.

   By the way, two is not a mandatory number. Single people light one candle. Married people should light at least two, but you can light as many as you want. The general idea (and empty nesters please hear this) is that you can always add candles, but you shouldn't ever decrease the number.

2. My friend and personal advisor in many such matters, Melanie Berman, says: "And boys should be encourage to light candles, too, so that they are accustomed to doing so as well. Eventually, they may well be the ones who need to do so in their own households." She also says, "And girls have to make kiddush, so that they can know how to do so, when they are on their own (and feel valid doing so if they wind up as single mothers some day)."

3. I've told you about Miriam Kallen in a previous chapter. She was one of our regular guests when I was growing up, an adoptive elder in our family. When I was reading *New Traditions: Redefining Celebrations for Today's Families,* by Susan Abel Lieberman, I relearned what she added to our family. Rituals often seem awkward when one person does them alone. It is very hard for me to make Shabbat or even light Hanukkah candles when I am alone, but I usually find a way to do it. Company helps. Rituals are "performed." They are "performances." It is often easier to discover your way of voicing and enacting them when you have an audience. Inviting guests can enhance celebrations; they contribute not only by what they bring, but simply by just being there.

4. Sally Shafton, a laywoman who became one of the world's first para-rabbinics, is another friend and teacher. She would have her children study the weekly Torah portion and then present it to the family and guests each Shabbat. They would do it in song, skit, lecture, game, poem, poster—whatever—and do it with a lot of pride, joy, and even laughter.

6 Always Insist that Shabbat Come First

Even if you let your kids do something else on Friday night, insist that they participate in your family Shabbat dinner first.

I am personally convinced that God, in God's infinite wisdom, intentionally scheduled Shabbat so that it would conflict with high school basketball games, critical football games, and all important dances and parties. It was exactly the same insight which led to the scheduling of Hebrew School just when it would overlap with every single after-school sport and club, and which made Sunday School have to go head-to-head with soccer games.

When Mordechai Kaplan (the founding ideologue of Reconstructionist Judaism) reworked the biblical concept of the "chosen" people into the "choosing" people, he was no fool—he had realized that we are constantly being forced to "choose" Judaism every time we confront the calendar.

One of my fantasy *Talmud 2000* discussions addresses this question. It is an assemblage of conversations I've heard from lots of parents of teenagers (primarily mothers) about what to do when their teenagers want to express their free will and therefore question the predetermination of a weekly family Shabbat ritual.

MISHNAH: Friday night is supposed to be a family time. How? They should spend it in synagogue and at home. One said: "First at home and then in synagogue." One said: "First in synagogue and then at home."

Solomon the Ritual Slaughter (Solomon Shechter) said: "At sundown they should be at shul to welcome the Sabbath, then they should walk (or drive directly) home to bless, dine, sing, talk, and study as a family. It is to be an evening of quality time. They can come to the synagogue the next morning."

The Two Wise Ones (Isaac Mayer Wise and Stephen S. Wise) taught: "Families should welcome the Shabbat around the dining room table with ceremony and joy, then in the eighth hour join the community and expand their celebration. Friday is the one time when most of the community can be together."

The Sages taught: "The more the family celebrates Shabbat, the more it is to be praised."

Rashi's Commentary: Conservative practice emphasizes Saturday morning services when the Torah is read. On Friday night, the preferred mode is a brief sundown service then a long evening at home. Many Conservative synagogues do not even offer a "late" service on Friday night. The Reform movement emphasized Friday night, making it the major service of the week. Often, if there is no Mitzvah Event, many Reform synagogues do not offer Saturday morning services at all. What they agree upon is that Shabbat is supposed to be quality family time.

GEMARA: We know that it is good to have a family Shabbat together when the children are little, but where do we learn it is at all possible to keep the kids either at home or in synagogue when they become teenagers?

Sarah: "I made it a rule that the family was to be home on Friday night. I would never let them go out. But, the girls were allowed to have any guests they wanted. Lots of their friends came to love Shabbat at our house, perhaps even more than our daughters. The only exceptions were the few times I let them make Shabbat with someone else's family."

Helen: "They have to be home for Shabbat dinner; that is the rule in our house. Then, they can go out and do whatever they want. Shabbat comes first, then they can go out. Sometimes, we'll have dinner a little bit earlier than usual, or eat it more quickly than would be ideal in order to accommodate some special event, but they know that Shabbat is essential and that it comes first. That is our practice and that is our message."

Susan: "From the time the kids were little, we made Friday night a major production number. Not only did we have the best food, but we sang and did skits. Later, when the kids were older, we made sure that they each had their parts to do and felt that it was important. By the time they were teenagers, our home was always filled with guests and activities—most of the time, Shabbat was a major 'happening' and that made it the place they wanted to be. There were a few fights when big conflicts came up. Almost always we said, 'No!' Once or twice we gave in. But it was almost never a problem—we wanted them home, they wanted to be home, and that is the way it was."

Bonnie: "Friday night was never a problem in our house, almost never. Our kids were happy to be there with us and our friends. Saturday morning wasn't a problem either. We went to shul and our kids went too, to be with their friends. Our big conflict was Saturday afternoon. It happened when Oren was old enough to be in Little League. We made a decision which many people will think was a strange one for a Conservative rabbi's family—we let Oren play in his Shabbat afternoon games, but he and the whole family walked there together. We wouldn't drive there, even though he could ride his bicycle to the field (because it was inside the *eruv*). We had to bend a little, but we found a way to fit Little League into our Shabbat."

Joyce: "We went for a principle of most 'Shabbatot.' There were just some experiences that 'weren't worth fighting over.' We made Shabbat a regular part of our kids' lives from the time they were little, but we didn't want them to come to hate it or being Jewish. We wouldn't let them hang out at the mall or just go to the movies, but homecoming, the school play, band exchange, and few other events became the 'exceptions' which proved the Shabbat rule."

Bruce (the one father who entered the conversation): "We believe in tough Shabbat love. We tell our kids that we are going to make Shabbat every single week and we want them to be there. But, if they can't do that, we will still make it without them. Hopefully, someday, they'll come back to the table. Meanwhile we will both miss them and enjoy our Shabbat."

Fran: "We used to make Shabbat every week. It was a big family thing. But, when David died, I just couldn't face it any more. The kids were fourteen and sixteen and I didn't know what to do with the empty chair. I didn't want to put anyone else in it, and I couldn't stand seeing it empty. So, I gave it up. Now that I want it back, my kids have set other patterns. I just don't know how to get it back."

The right answer: The one which works for your family.

> In Ron Wolfson's *The Art of Jewish Living: The Shabbat Seder*, a doctor named Larry Neinstein says: "We always sing at least one Shabbat song. Whether we sing more than that is highly dependent on when I come home, how stressed out I am. If I am in a good mood and relaxed, then we may sing for a while; if I'm stressed out, it's *Bim Bam* and 'Let's eat'!" We all have weeks when we need it to be "*Bim Bam* and 'Let's eat.'" So do our kids. Knowing when to make those compromises is important; knowing when they've been made too many weeks in a row is critical.

The trick with Shabbat, or any other Jewish practice, is to always have it as a place holder in your life. You have to make sure that it is always there—even when you or your kids can't enter into it fully, because, once Shabbat is gone, once the rhythm is broken, it may never return again. In that sense, Shabbat always has to come first. Believe it or not, a strong Jewish identification is being built every time you know that what you are doing is compromising the "real" way Shabbat should be—when it stops feeling like a compromise, then you have to worry. That is when Shabbat is starting to slip away.

> This is **Joel's Sixth Law**: It is always better to know that you are *compromising* an important Jewish practice because at the moment you "need" to do something else, than to *pretend* that the Jewish tradition consists only of things you want to do.

By the way, the problem is called "teenagers" not "Shabbat." Listen:

> Adolescents may refuse to participate or be available for family rituals for a period of time. This is usually a developmental stage, corresponding to a teen's wish to go with friends, or to separate from the ways the family does things for a while. Some families respond by joining their teenager and dropping most familiar rituals, and developing a minimized ritual style. This often occurs when family rituals have been shaped primarily for the children, and the adults have neglected their need for meaningful rituals of their own....Discovering that your rituals have become minimized as children have grown and moved on is a useful signal that adult relationships need some attention. (Imber-Black and Roberts, *Rituals For Our Times*, pages 59-60)

> Therefore, **Joel's Seventh Law**: Never do Jewish things for your children's sake. In the end, this will only serve to make Judaism childish

and something all of you outgrow (years before dating and marriage come along). Rather, do Jewish things for yourself and then find a way to involve your kids.

Epilogue

Conflict and compromise over traditional practice go back a long way. When you do compromise, don't do so easily or lightly. Remember, lots of Jews fought for the right not to have to give in and go to the ball. To the best of my understanding, Hanukkah is really a celebration of a civil war over leisure-time activities. It was Jewish practices vs. Greek leisure-time activities. It was the same battle we face. The priests, the guys who officially ran the Jewish religion, had lots of Greek hobbies. They liked going to the gymnasium, the theatre, and the baths. Meanwhile, the Hasidim (the forerunners of the first rabbis) thought that Jews should spend their spare time studying Torah and sheltering the homeless—and doing mitzvah stuff like that. It was a classic Hebrew School vs. Soccer Practice kind of thing; only then it was being part of the group who was writing the Talmud vs. naked discus throwing and wrestling. When the two factions got into a fight on the "playground," they got taken to the principal's office and Antiochus, the local "Greek" monarch, settled things his way. He said, "Forget about which is the right way to worship your God—instead, I'll be your god and tell you precisely how to worship me." It was then that Mattathias Maccabee took things into his own hands and the fighting started. In our hearts, each of us is still fighting.

> **This is the bottom-line strategy:** Your life will be filled with constant conflicts between Jewish activities and other things you want or need to do. It will always look like an either/or choice, a Hanukkah war choice.

> **Joel's Eighth Law** is this: When you have to make choices, the Jewish tradition must never lose. It can compromise, but it must never lose.

That is not the answer "good" Jews will give. A "good" Jew always believes that Judaism comes first, that Judaism must always win. I believe that too, just not so strongly. If I am honest, I don't and I can't live that way. (Maybe I'm weak!) Making sure that Judaism never loses is the path of the "good enough" Jew. "Good enough" Jews survive and tend to raise "good enough" Jewish children. "Good enough" is not the most authentic path, but it is one well worn by our ancestors.

Some Practical Applications

1. Even though it is not an *official* mitzvah, we all know that Jewish kids are supposed to go to Sunday School except for vacations. Once, when we skipped "real" school in order to reach Chicago in time for some family event, my parents showed me just how important Jewish education was by allowing me to go to Sunday School at my mother's childhood temple the Sunday I was there. I was in second or third grade and it was a Sunday I will never forget. At a school assembly we sat on benches in the unfinished social hall and sang some songs (about half of which I knew), and the principal read us a *K'ton-ton* story, the first I had ever heard. (*K'ton-ton* is a Jewish Tom Thumb.) It was a great day.

   Think of the model; take your kid to Sunday/Hebrew School when you go on a trip. You'll have to call and make the arrangements, but it is a great lesson both for your kids and for the class they wind up in.

2. *Kashrut* is one of folk Judaism's compromise points where the "God will forgive me" principle often takes over. We all know that Jews are supposed to keep kosher. Kosher means that you follow all the rules which have been evolved in the Torah, Talmud, and later Law Codes. There should only be one way of keeping kosher, but we know better than that—

   a. Orthodox Jews have a bunch of levels of kashrut. It is a great game of *frum* machismo to say "My *kashrut* is stricter than yours." *Glatt kosher* is only one manifestation of hyper-kashrut available.

   b. We unorthodox Jews have our own levels of kashrut, too—the most famous of which is "Biblical *kashrut*." Biblical *kashrut* (avoiding shellfish and pork products, but not caring about the mixing of milk and meat) is the perfect example of a folk creation. It is not sanctioned by any movement. It is not found in any book of Jewish law, modern or ancient, since Talmudic times (yes, I know it is in the Bible)—but lots of Jews keep it. It is a compromise kashrut position which gives meaning and direction to those who choose it. It acknowledges that Jewish life includes food boundaries while opening up lots of dining opportunities. There are many ways you can compromise *kashrut* and still learn some of its lessons.

   c. Food laws may not be your thing, but I will recommend that you evolve your own food boundaries. If food restrictions don't work for

43

you, how about positive incentives? Make a commitment to eat hallah every Shabbat or matzah on Passover. Find some way to remember that "Jewish" covers what you eat and don't eat. Forgetting that is
much worse than whatever you put in your mouth.

3. I have a friend who drinks one cup of coffee every Yom Kippur morning.
It is something he doesn't want to do—but feels he has to do. He consid-
ers himself a caffeine addict. He fears the headaches which would follow
because of withdrawal. The good news is, he (1) repents the coffee during
his confessional, and (2) upholds the rest of the fast. It is a lot better than
drinking the cup of coffee and then giving up.

The bottom line is this: Even when we give up on being "perfect Jews" or
even "good Jews," we should still have a target to strive to be "good enough
Jews."

7 Let Your Kids Drink Wine as Soon as They Can Make Kiddush on Their Own

Make the privilege of having a sip of wine on Friday night (and other Jewish holidays) a reward for learning how to say the proper *brakhah*.

This lesson I learned from my friends Barbara and Jim Zeidman. This was their family practice: "When the kids were old enough to say the kiddush on their own, we let them drink wine."

The way I've been told the story is that it wasn't a well thought out plan, it was just a momentary solution which lasted. You can see the scene. It was a chaotic Shabbat dinner with these three antsy kids each wanting their moment of glory—each wanting their own moment of attention—and none of whom was willing sit still. There were two working parents who had each had his and her own hard day at work. But, with some badgering and pushing, and some caring and some cajoling, a Shabbat table came together. They sat and began their table ritual, three one-line *brakhot*: candles, then wine, then hallah. In the midst of that ritual, the kids started asking for a sip of wine. As a stopgap measure, they were told, "When you can say the kiddush on your own—you can drink wine." In that instant, a weekly ritual became a life-cycle challenge, an accomplishment.

Learn from the model and learn from the way the spontaneous can be Jewishly profound.

Open up a book of Jewish "Zen" wisdom called *Pirke Avot* (5.24)(a minor tractate from the Talmud) and you will find the early rabbis' version of the ages of a Jewish person.

45

5 = Time to Study Bible
10 = Time to Study Mishnah
13 = Time to Perform All Mitzvot
15 = Time to Study Talmud
18 = Time for Marriage
20 = Time to Earn a Living
30 = Time for Power
40 = Time for Wisdom
50 = Time for Giving Counsel
60 = Old Age
70 = White Hair
80 = Rare Old Age...

When we look at this list, we realize that the world has changed since 60 C.E. and so has Jewish life (and the age of marriage isn't the only critically different factor). The rabbinical list was originally a list of personal obligations. It was a list of things you "had" to do. Most American Jews have learned the American Express lesson that "membership has its privileges." We like to talk about "what we get to do..." That was the lesson the Zeidmans had internalized and applied that Shabbat evening. They saw "wine drinking" as a privilege which could be earned—in the same way a bat or bar mitzvah has become a privilege for which one works—even though this is 180 degrees from the original intent.

The truth the Zeidmans teach us—by making wine drinking a privilege which comes as a payoff for learning how to say the *brakhah* over wine—is that using the understandings of our era, we need to make Judaism something into which we are always growing, something that continually offers new challenges, responsibilities and privileges.

I was once sitting at a meeting where we were discussing Jewish programs for families with toddlers. At that meeting someone joked, "It would all be much easier if Judaism had something to say about toilet training." It got a big laugh. Then my friend, teacher, and personal inspiration, Harlene Appelman, the founding Czarina of Jewish Family Education in Detroit, said: "It does! It says that you have to be toilet trained before you can wear *tzi-tzit*." *Tzi-tzit* are the fringes found on a *tallit*, the wearing of which the Torah makes into a mitzvah/privilege/obligation for adult Jews. Even though it is not an actual obligation until one is thirteen, the tradition encourages beginning mitzvah challenges as soon as possible. It is sort of a Tom Sawyer thing—based on the "not just any boy can whitewash a fence" principle.

Traditional Jewish practice has its set times for first wearing *tzi-tzit*, trying to ask the four questions at Seder, lighting your own <u>h</u>anukkiyah, fasting through all of Yom Kippur, etc. Usually they are connected not to age, but to accomplishment. The lesson is simple: that which will one day become an *obligation* is best begun as a *challenge* to earn a *privilege*.

We live in an era when we need to construct a new version of the "ages" found in *Pirke Avot*. If we are smart, like the Zeidmans, they will be personal and actual, rather than institutional. It should not just be:

    3 = Jewish Mommy and Me
    4 = Jewish Preschool
    6 = Day School or Sunday School
    9 = Jewish Sleep-Away Camp
    13 = Hebrew High School
    16 = Summer Trip to Israel
    18 = Join Hillel

It should be more than a list of enrollment dates (though they should be included, too.) So, let's play *Talmud 2000* and learn the lessons of "Jewish toilet training." Figure out the milestones of growth in your modern Jewish family. What are the stages of a modern Jewish life cycle? What privileges and what obligations are attached to each stage? It could be a great "evening program"—a game the whole family could play. It would even look great on the mantle.

Applications

What is so perfect about the Zeidmans' "get to drink wine when you can say kiddush" model is that it gives a mundane reward for a Jewish action.

1. Among the classic "accomplishments" which match up with rewards in the Jewish tradition: Fasting on Yom Kippur (in what year did you first get past lunch?), Shofar blowing, Leading *Ein Keloheynu* (Conservative shuls) or *Shir ha-Kavod* (Orthodox shuls), Leading the Four Questions, etc. In my temple, my rabbi invites everyone who has a shofar to come up on the *bimah* and blow the final *t'kiyah gedolah* on Yom Kippur. Rabbi Larry Kushner does the same thing. He calls it the Big Band Beth El sound. In his case, every 11th-grade graduate of the Congregational

School is given a shofar. Joining the horn section is a privilege of graduation. Think of other ways of adding incentives to your *mitzvot*. (Not just any boy can blowtorch a stove to make it *kosher l'Pesaḥ*.)

2. In a chapter in a book I wrote last year, one about bar mitzvah, I made a similar suggestion (which will in fact appear in this book as part of **Number 36: Joel's Bar Mitzvah Advisory**.) There, I tell parents, based on a commentary on the *Pirke Avot* passage found above, that from the day of the bar or bat mitzvah the rules for punishment in the family should change. From that moment on, modes of discipline should shift from the parents' imposing order, to the child's manifesting self-control. In other words, grounding and docking and being sent to your room should stop— and the new young adult's taking responsibility to change and fix the problem should begin. This makes bar or bat mitzvah an *accomplishment* which grants a real *privilege*, the *obligation* to be responsible for one's self.

3. My own favorite example of another possibility is this fantasy. Before I would let any child of mine get a driving permit, I would demand of that child that she or he master the third chapter of *Bava Kamma* in the Mishnah. The Mishnah is the first layer of the Talmud. The third chapter of *Bava Kamma* is all about collisions. Even though it deals with what happens when two potters with pots balanced on their heads run into each other by accident, it is a perfect example of what could be Jewish Driver Education, a study of your responsibilities if you get into accident.

   Don't worry, I don't know the official statistics, but in a survey of my friends, 12 out of 9 newly licensed Jewish teenage drivers will dent or otherwise injure a family car within the first two years of driving. You do have something to look forward to. If they've studied texts about responsibility in advance—you'll be one leg up.

4. Now go and develop your own list. Think about the points in your child's life (Jewish and not so Jewish) where an *accomplishment* can earn a corresponding *privilege* or *responsibility*.

P. S.

Be sure you learn the other great lesson from the Zeidman story: Use spontaneous opportunities for Jewish growth and commitment when they pop up. It was the middle of the Gulf War when Barbara called me. Kent, 12, was in front of the television set, treating news reports like basketball scores. Barbara thought he was too happy about the victory, too unconcerned for those who were dying. She asked me about a midrash she had once heard where God stopped the angels from rejoicing when the Egyptians were drowning in the Red Sea. We went over it, then she studied it with her son. That is real "laser-targeted" Jewish education—the kind that only "smart" Jewish parents can provide.

8 Do Not Make Them Go to Services; Create Reasons They'll Want to Go

The battle over "having to go to services" is best won when there are friends, events, and opportunities at the synagogue which draw your child there—and combat the natural resistance.

When I was young, I asked my father, "If you don't believe in God, why do you go to synagogue so regularly?" My father answered, "Jews go to synagogue for all kinds of reasons. My friend Garfinkle, who is Orthodox, goes to talk to God. I go to talk to Garfinkle."

Harry Golden

A True Story: It is Yom Kippur morning. The family enters the synagogue. The eldest son tells his parents that he is going to talk to his friends on the steps for a while before he comes in. He never shows up. The family assumes that he is sitting with his friends. But then, as the synagogue clears, the eldest son is nowhere to be seen. A little panicked, the parents begin to drive around the neighborhood and find him in the playground, playing some hoop. His blue blazer is thrown over the fence, the grey slacks and black shoes have been left in the dust. Eldest son is dressed in his basketball togs. A couple of questions determine that they had been hidden in his *tallit* bag, his bar mitzvah *tallit* bag. What is the family to do? Yell? Laugh? Both?

A Second True Story: It is Erev Yom Kippur and I am having dinner with another set of friends. The fourteen-year-old middle child announces that he is not going to services tonight. Middle child is angry and depressed—typically fourteen. The mother, with an embarrassed smile, says: "He's going tomorrow; about that he has no choice." Then, she informs middle child that there is to be no television and no telephone if he stays home. Once he leaves the room, she smiles and says, "Hormones! I'll be so glad when he is through with them." I smile silently. Then she adds, "It just wasn't worth fighting over..." I indicate my understanding—but I really don't understand. This is a temple-going family. They are always there together.

Know that both of these are great Jewish families. They go to services regularly. They are involved and active members of the community. The parents serve on multiple boards. One child went to a day school, the other went to Hebrew School and Jewish summer camps. Both families observe Shabbat and the holidays. It doesn't make any sense.

So with hands thrown up in the air (because pulling out their hair isn't worth it) both sets of parents ask two questions: (1) Where did we go wrong? and (2) What can we do about it? (Even though both of our stories are Yom Kippur stories, the problem is one which manifests itself every Shabbat— that's why it is in the Shabbat section.) The answers come with a parade of memories.

When I was little, we made Shabbat and then my parents went to temple. I stayed home with Betty Mahoney, the Catholic baby-sitter. I only went with them to services when it was a special event. Special events were holidays, life cycle events, and children's services. Birthday blessings were a big thing.

By the time I was ten, I began to go with them frequently. It was an "act like an adult" thing. I liked it. My father—next to whom I got to sit—used to fill his suit pocket with butterscotch candies. I liked them. I also liked to take off the wrappers and then look at the service through amber-colored glasses. My father and I shared this little crime of eating in services. I liked that, too. It was a kid kind of thing.

By the time I was twelve, I was an atheist and had stopped going to services. I had my reasons: I no longer believed in them, I hated getting dressed up, and they were boring. My family still forced me to go for the big events, not only the High Holidays, but important guest speakers, Sisterhood Shabbat, and the like. It was a family mitzvah—an obligation which my mother decreed.

By the time I was fourteen or fifteen, I was going to services a lot again—except when there were school events. I was now into my Jewish period—a rabbi-in-training (thanks to Miriam Kallen). But the best part of Friday night was going out to Howard Johnsons. After services, after *Oneg Shabbat* and hanging out in Tommy's room, half the temple, including the Rabbi, would go out to Howard Johnsons and take over the back room. We would order ice cream and talk and tell stories. **A Good Time Was Had By All**. Good times are powerful motivation.

In my sixteenth or seventeenth year, a youth group president, either Dicky Silver or Jeff Goldfarb (I no longer remember which of them it was) had an inspiration. Because he wanted the Sinaiites (the youth group) to be at services, he began to schedule post-service house parties on Friday night. First we would all go to temple, then to someone's house, roll up the rug and dance the night away. **A Good Time Was Had By All** there, too.

Here is the lesson: when your kid is already a rebellious teenager, there is just about nothing you can do but hope that it is just a passing stage. Most of this has already been set in motion. That which you have already done about Shabbat (or any Jewish practice), sits as a seed in his or her heart and memory, waiting to germinate and evolve into an adult Jew.

There are, however, things you can try in the meantime:

* You can make your kid go to services as often as you dare (you'll have to decide how often the fight is worth it).

* You can try to establish a reward system for her and/or him. These are not little prizes you give or stars on a chart which add up to a prize. When you are a teenager, "reward" is not likely to be defined as a chance to sit with the family or eat a butterscotch candy—and it is not likely to be the quest for a deeper spirituality. It could be, but it isn't likely. From about age fourteen until whatever year in the mid-twenties that being a teenager is now officially over, what is most likely to get a teenager to go to synagogue is the chance to see and be with friends.

If your kid is still ten years old or younger, you have a great chance of solving the "I don't want to go to services" problem by preempting it. Otherwise, you'll be playing catch-up.

a. Make sure that you child has friends in the synagogue and that the synagogue has a social group of which your child is a part.

b. Let your child sit with his or her friends at services (sometimes they can sit with you, sometimes your child can sit with one of their parents). Now hear this, I am not recommending the "let them roam free to stuff paper towels in the bathroom sinks and then leave the water running" route...

c. Encourage your child to use Shabbat services and the holidays as a chance to socialize with his or her friends. Model the behavior, then encourage its adoption. Depending on your Shabbat observance, when your kids are in the junior high school range go out afterwards with other families, or have people over. (If you go out to a restaurant, let the kids have their own table—if you go over to someone else's house, they'll find a room on their own). When your kids are older, let them go out together afterwards, or roll up the rug at your house and have the first party.

Applications

1. What is good for the goslings is also good for both the goose and the gander. Make sure that you have your own rewards for going to *shul*. If you can pick a shul that has a service which really moves you half the time, you've got a real find. Often, prayer will work for one partner, but not the other. She or he needs a reward, too. Make sure you meet Garfinkle and have a chance to talk with him. Make your synagogue a place where you belong—where you are rewarded just by attending. That is not a question of program—it is a question of acquaintance and friendship.

2. Most synagogues are good at greeting you and welcoming you once or twice—they are not so good at actually helping you fit in. Community membership is something you have to earn. If you don't bond after some effort, you may have to look for a different place which will reward you.

3. Learn about prayer. The siddur is not an obvious book. Even if you can *read* the Hebrew—even if you can *understand* the prayer book, the meaning of Jewish prayer is not automatically accessible. Going from the meaning to the interior process of worship is another leap. Some people do so intuitively, most need guidance, some never dare to jump. Read a book or

53

two—or take a class. It will probably make a lot of difference. (Call me, or ask a Jewish teacher or rabbi in your area—any one of us will make some recommendations.)

4. What is true for services is also true of other Jewish obligations which are often both stressful and rewarding. Help to build up the rewards in every Jewish meeting you have to attend, facing "Super Sunday" or other fund-raising experiences—and every family gathering.

9 Shirley— Just Bring Home a Pizza

Know what is the "essence" of a Jewish practice and what is the popular "form" of its expression. You must seek the essence; you don't always have to fulfill the form. In other words, sometimes the sense of a Shabbat dinner together (when everyone had to work and is tired) can be better conjured over a pizza than a formal dinner with cloth napkins.

At times Vicky Kelman expresses truths which are insights of total genius. I am proud that she has been among my friends; I am proud to claim her as one of my teachers. This is entirely one of her stories. I have just borrowed it and retold it here.

It was a Shabbat camp, a family camp, which Vicky was running. It was the middle of some session where parents were talking about the difficulties of Jewish life. One woman, Shirley, talked about the problems of being a single mother and managing to get Shabbat on the table after a full day of work. She said, "My son and I have a wonderful Shabbat morning. He goes to Saturday school at temple, I go to services. We can make the Sabbath day happen—but I can't seem to get Friday night together. "

Vicky empathized with the image of picking up a young son from day care, rushing home, and trying to get a white-table-cloth-and-napkin event together—even if was only to be dinner for two by Shabbat candlelight. Vicky had a moment of epiphany. She looked at this woman and said, "Shirley—just bring home a pizza." Then she explained that the essence of

Shabbat—a peaceful dinner together—is more important than the formal conventions.

Vicky's lesson is about Shabbat, and about more than Shabbat. Vicky's revelation was not to put off Shabbat, not observe less Shabbat, not to limit the ceremonies because it was difficult, but to find an easier path to the authentic. That is her genius. The true meaning of Shabbat is rooted in the candles, the hallah, the kiddush wine, the singing, the peaceful time at the table—the freedom from work, the sense of shalom. It is not connected to cloth napkins, brisket, chicken soup with noodles and all of those things. The formalities often help to set the mood. They often enhance the sense of the sacred, adding to the power of the rituals—but they are the shell, not the spark.

One of those M.O.T. folk sayings which has always been there is: "It's hard to be a Jew." If you don't know what M.O.T. is—deduct 10 points from your score in the "National (Ethnic)" column. (M.O.T. = Member of the Tribe.) We sometimes take this "macho" attitude about how difficult it is to be a Jew, like a fraternity brother convincing a pledge that a painful stunt he has to perform in order to be part of the group will be good for him. You know the ritual words: "I did it, we all did it, so you can do it." We often, now, invoke them just before we make our children enter the car pool to Hebrew School Hell. (More on that later.) This "hard to be a Jew" thing comes from the same place as a parent telling a child, "When I was your age I used to walk to shul—ten miles—through the snow." This is a deep truth:

> Challenges are good when they can be overcome. That is the "Outward Bound" lesson—the good feeling at the top of the cliff or the bottom of the zip line. We like to overcome our fears and discover how boundless our resources really are.
>
> Challenges are not good when they are so overwhelming that they disable you. There are the "Outward Bound" failures who sit crying, devastated, at the bottom of the ladder, totally paralyzed by fear. Sometimes our, "It's hard to be a Jew" attitude and traditions do that too.

Here is where ancient Jewish wisdom helps us. Jewish mystics tell a story about an original cosmic accident. God had prepared the world with vessels which were going to hold God's light—so it wouldn't be too bright and people wouldn't get too close. Somehow, it didn't work. God was too intense, the vessels weren't strong enough. Crash! The vessels shattered and both sparks of God's light and the shattered shards of the shells which were supposed to contain them, fell to earth together. That is our world; our job is to regather the sparks, sorting them from broken husks of shell.

That is Vicky Kelman's lesson here, spark and shell. It is good that it is "hard to be a Jew." One could have told Shirley that the effort to make a Friday night into Shabbat, would add pride and commitment to her life—that it would be worth it. One could have taught her the Marlynn Dorff practice: "Set your Shabbat table on Thursday night!", explaining: "That's why God invented Tupperware™ and microwaves." But, that wasn't this moment. Ron Wolfson often tells families who are making Shabbat for the first time to serve hot dogs—not because they are easy, but because kids will love them. This isn't "Hot dogs make Shabbat a party," though there is a time for that. It isn't "Pizza is informal"—like, "Why can't I go to services in my jeans—they're more comfortable than a stupid tie." This is spark and shell, preserving the Shabbat emotional, ritual, and historic experience, while just simplifying the menu. Sorting spark and shell takes judgment; we often don't know which is which. Consider the impact if we made the same statement about a Passover Seder being too much work, "Don't worry, Shirley. Bring in a pizza!" Think of the cliff—it is almost always better to conquer it if you can. Accept an alternate route to the top only if you can't make it directly up the face—yet.

Carrots in the Soup: An Epilogue

I've promised not to reveal this source:

> This friend of mine fakes the chicken soup served on Jewish holidays. This friend gets endless compliments on the homemade soup—but it isn't home made. This is the way it is done:

> Big cans of Swanson's chicken broth are emptied into a pot. Some carrots and celery are cut up. A very little bit of schmaltz (chicken fat) is stirred in, so there will be grease circles on the top, and some separately cooked chicken is shredded in. Next, it is reseasoned to taste. Finally, a carrot is run through the food processor and pureed. It is stirred into the soup, lending a little sweetness and changing the color to a soft gold with a slight orange hue.

This is the point. Even when you are making your Judaism easier, because you need to, a little effort can still make it feel authentic. Homemade chicken soup is often in the eye of the beholder.

Joel's Ninth Law: Give yourself permission to simplify your Jewish practice when you absolutely need to (trim "shell" not "spark"), but always try to make it taste authentic when you do.

These days it has been given a name: "holiday stress." Finally, we've acknowledged that it is very hard, if not impossible, to plan and pull off a meaningful, memorable "good time had by all." To a large degree, as my friend Carol points out, this is because we want them to be perfect. Making a holiday celebration "perfect" is like trying to travel at the speed of light—it is something we should approach, not expect to achieve. Perfect is beyond hard. Perfect = stress. We need to give ourselves permission to make a good-enough Shabbat, good-enough Seder, and good-enough Hanukkah, etc. After all, we've all experienced our own Thanksgiving from Hell—I know mine is a great story. Lots of people have created lots of holiday hells for themselves and for their guests by striving for perfection. Hell! In your heart, just order a pizza—then add whatever fixings and rituals you want.

Holiday Celebration

10 | Make Kiddush and *ha-Motzi* on Thanksgiving

It is important to treat Thanksgiving as a Jewish ritual meal and thereby blend Jewish and American values into a single expression.

When I was in college, I made friends with a wonderful coed named Hildy whose family was one of the very few Orthodox families who lived in Lewiston, Maine. I loved the two or three visits I made to spend Shabbat with them. They were wonderful people and I loved being in Maine, especially in autumn when the leaves were turning.

Because they were Orthodox, Shabbat was by the book. Electricity was not used—lights were either left on or off. Nothing was carried outside the house—we wore our *tallitot* to shul and back. It was a really peaceful and wonderful time. It was a wonderful juxtaposition of authentic Judaism—following all the rules—and small-town American life. It was sort of "Paul Revere does Shabbat."

I remember doing the dishes with Hildy on one of those Saturday nights (because no one would run the dishwasher 'til after Havdalah), when she made a comment I'll never forget. She said, "I love Thanksgiving because it's the only time during the year when we use our electric carving knife." This was a family who ate in the dining room with crystal, china, linen, and silver every week. It was a family

which made a big deal out of every Jewish holiday—all of which they celebrated for the requisite two days. This was a family whose life was filled with
celebrations—the irony was that only one day a year could they use their electric carving knife. What impressed me, however, was that they had a Jewish
connection with Thanksgiving.

That year I went back to my own home for Thanksgiving and insisted that
my mother buy a hallah and set out the kiddush cups. Thanksgiving had
always had its own rituals. There was a Pilgrim boy candle and a Pilgrim girl
candle and a plaster turkey which had always shared the table since the family had visited Plymouth Plantation when I was eight or nine. There was the
cornucopia (I didn't know what this wicker horn was really called 'til I went
to graduate school) which overflowed with the same gourds every year, plus
new nuts, figs, and grapes. My father always made a Robert Young-ish "Thank
You, God" grace-like speech. But, we had never thought to make it Jewish—
we had never thought to remember that when the Pilgrims were gathering that
first fall harvest in their new land, they went back to the Bible and found their
own way of bringing the Sukkot ritual alive. Thanksgiving is nothing more
than a Pilgrim version of a creative Sukkot celebration—add the popcorn and
cranberries, take out the *lulav* and *etrog*, and you get the picture.

The moment I figured out from Hildy's family (whom I suddenly knew
without asking made kiddush and ate hallah at Thanksgiving) that
Thanksgiving wasn't just an American holiday, my world changed. I was no
longer involved in a thousand discussions about Jewish American or
American Jew. There was no question of priorities—the answer was simple.
From then on, I've made kiddush before eating turkey.

To be fair to my parents, we always had chopped liver as an appetizer on
Thanksgiving. I've since learned that many Jewish families do. It's not just a
question of having a limited number of recipes—rather, it was an ethnic version of the same insight. When a Jewish family (at least an Ashkenzic Jewish
family) celebrates with a meal, chopped liver is part of the process (soup and
"fish" are the other options). I've since learned that many Italian American
families begin Thanksgiving with antipasto—and I guess Chinese American
families do it with a *pou-pou* platter... But, kiddush adds another dynamic—
it shows not only a melding of food, but of spirit.

Application

Rav Kook was a famous Israeli Rabbi, mystic, and teacher. He said that it was the job of the Jew:

L'Hadesh et ha-Kadosh u-l'Kadesh et he-Hadash.

To re-NEW the SACRED and to SANCTIFY the NEW.

That is the lesson to be found in making kiddush on Thanksgiving. We've long learned to videotape our *b'nai mitzvah* events and use an electric guitar to pray—now we need to let the Pilgrims make a Hebrew *brakhah*.

Interesting Extensions

1. My father, the engineer, spent many evenings of my childhood sitting with me while I copied over my homework. He tried hard to convince me that homework, learning—algebra—was important, and perhaps in his understanding, sacred. The shared time kept my grades from sinking me into the world of burger flipping, and did convey the importance of study. (Look Ma, I'm writing another book!) It could have been simply conveyed if we began every homework session with a *brakhah*:

    Barukh Atah Adonai, Eloheinu Melekh ha-Olam, Asher Kidshanu b'Mitzvotav, v'Tzivanu la'Asok b'Divrei Torah.

    Praised are You, Adonai, Ruler of the cosmos, The One-Who-Gave us sacred mitzvot, and made it a mitzvah for us to involve ourselves in the study of Torah.

    It would have been a powerful way to convince me that comprehending the "distributive property" and the proper use of the "adverb" were holy acts. In a way, my father did that, but a *brakhah* would have been a powerful statement.

2. Jews have translated Happy Birthday into Hebrew—*Yom hu-Ledet Same-ah*—but we need to do more. Here are some *Talmud 2000* questions: "What *brakhah* should be said about a birthday?" "What midrashim should be written about Adam's Birthday? What did Deborah get as a birthday gift? What did Bathsheba give Solomon?, etc. What should be birthday mitzvot? Is there a specific *tzedakah* custom which should be created? (Here is the kernel of a secret we will reveal later: Until we make all birthdays Jewish events, we'll never succeed in down-scaling bar and bat mitzvah.)

3. Next: "What Torah portion should we read on the Fourth of July?" Probably the Deuteronomy one which goes, "Proclaim liberty throughout the land..." Now hunt for the haftarah.

11 Make Your House Smell Jewish

Find sensory ways to make your house feel Jewish. Smell is one very powerful sense (but not the only one.)

My sister used to work for a company that sold aerosol spray air freshener. One of her best developments was a flavor called "new car." You sprayed it in your car and your car again had that "new car" smell. It wasn't as good as new—but you still got to experience it as new. Their market testing didn't pan out—so they never made it. These days my sister is in aftershave and underarm deodorant. But the absolute truth is, a gefilte fish air freshener may be a great way to save the Jewish people.

There is a short movie called *Gefilte Fish* which Jewish family educators love to show. It is about twenty minutes long and it involves three generations of Jewish women telling the camera how each of them makes gefilte fish:

The grandmother shows off her chopping bowl and chopping knife. She makes hers by hand—doing every single step in an intimate and personal way.

Her daughter, the mother, is a working woman. She uses a food processor. If you listen to her closely, between the explanations of how she does it, she is apologizing for using the technology. It is as if she feels that something is being lost through her lack of personal, intimate, and direct contact with the fish.

Finally, we get to the granddaughter. She is a college kid, perhaps a graduate student, and her tongue-in-cheek presentation of making gefilte fish involves opening a jar and putting the fish on a piece of lettuce.

The subliminal message of the film is that because the mother didn't take the time to personally hock and mash the fish, her daughter, the third generation, completely lost the art and the tradition of the making of "fish." Because the film is used as a trigger film for lots of Jewish discusions, it frequently provokes the over-simple truth: "As goes gefilte fish, so goes the Jewish people."

We live in a decade during which our food has gone from fresh to canned to frozen to take-out. Successive generations of food preparers have found their own kinds of convenience. I come from a family of working women. My mother's mother helped to run a store. When times were good, she had a maid—when times were bad, when the depression hit, Grandma Lurie worked in the store and did everything at home herself. My Nana Grishaver was an iron woman who raised two boys on her own, working full time and keeping house. The best story about my Nana is that she—this little four-foot-something woman—once bought an iron bunk bed in downtown Boston and then carried it home on her back, first on the M.T.A. and then up Summit Avenue to the house on Atherton Road. That is a feat I could never accomplish. I have nowhere near that strength, but at least according to family legend, Nana Grishaver did. Then, she cooked supper.

As soon as my sister was old enough not to need someone at home, my mother went back to work. She, too, was always a working woman. As the fifties went, we were a "fast-food" family. Frozen hadn't come in yet, so it was a lot of broiled meat and canned vegetables. My family was proper enough to do it with four courses every night. A typical meal was a half grapefruit appetizer or a glass of tomato juice, a lettuce and tomato salad, steak, canned green beans and instant mashed potatoes, then a dessert like canned peaches or applesauce out of a jar. Serious cooking was reserved for weekends and holidays. I did not suffer.

Here are my culinary confessions:

(1) I do not cook at all—my kitchen skills are limited to boiling, "nuking," and grilling.

(2) My father was a much better cook than my mother. Even so, neither of them knew how to make gefilte fish. My whole family came from Western Europe; they didn't know from gefilte fish.

(3) Today, my sister is a much better cook than my mother. Judy works hard during the week and does instant food or take-out most nights—but, when she cooks, she really cooks.

(4) My mother's cooking is simple, but absolutely good—do not think that she ever was a bad cook, she isn't—she just doesn't have the same urge to "*potchke*" as Judy or Dad.

(5) Even though the family didn't know from "fish" we were big on chopped liver. My father used to make it—attaching the grinder to the Mix-master. No, we didn't hand grind it—it wasn't totally "hand made"—but we didn't food process it, either. When my father died, both my mother and my sister carried on the chopped liver tradition—and the famous Grishaver Dutch Butter Cookies. I eat both—I make neither.

(6) When I was twelve or thirteen, we began to feel a need for "fish" at our Jewish events. In hindsight, it was our need to assimilate to the peer pressure of our Eastern European neighbors. My mother then went to the store and bought some. From then on, we always had "Mother's" fish at Jewish moments. It was a family joke. We went from no fish, to "Mother's Gefilte Fish" out of the jar. Who made the gefilte fish?—Mother did!

(7) When my mother remarried, my mother's husband was not thrilled with "Mother's Gefilte Fish". So, my mother learned a new secret—she learned to reboil the manufactured fish in her own broth. That is the closest anyone in the family has ever come to making our own—our story is not "handmade," "processed" and then "out of a jar." We're going the other way.

According to my friend Harlene Appelman, smells are the earliest and strongest memories. She is working on a book called *Making Jewish Memories*, and this is one of the "truths" she's learned in her research. She tells me that according to the scientists, if you want to imbed a memory, you

66

should do it with smell. Harlene tells parents to bake ẖallah and fill the house with "fish" smells—and let the aroma of Jewishness be part of the warm, nurturing, sense of home all children will want to sustain and replicate as they grow. Smells are important memories.

As a basic concept, making your house smell Jewish by hand making Jewish foods and crafts for Jewish celebrations and practices is a good idea. Both your sweat and the aroma convey a message.

My friend Carol has a different story. She has always been big on making Jewish memories for her two boys. Left on her own, Carol will never choose the cooking option. But, when it comes to Jewish events—Carol goes full bore. When the boys were young, no Friday went by without the smell of yeast announcing fresh ẖallah on the way. Prior to Passover her house smells of "fish" for a couple of days. Now, here is the secret I should not reveal. Carol fakes her fish. She buys it half-made from the butcher—hard core New York kosher fish. It comes frozen; she boils and slices it—and gains two and a half days of authentic "fish" aroma without having to mash and dice.

That is the secret, but here is the truth. When she starts the fish, her sons Geoff and Rob get one whiff and head for the hills. Carol is a great cook, but they claim to hate the kinds of food she makes. Carol has always done the "authentic" Jewish thing—even if she finds useful short cuts—and they claim to like none of it. They are a crew who once sneaked out to McDonalds during the intermission at a family Seder. Carol has done everything right: all the rituals, all the family events, all the aromas—and every time she starts one of these recipes, they start to kid her.

And now it is time for you to vote: What *is* the truth?

a. Carol is a complete failure—all her efforts have backfired.

b. Carol has been a complete success—all the kidding and complaining are just her kids' ways of showing love.

c. The jury is still out—we have to wait ten or fifteen years before we have any idea what all this means.

In fifteen years I'll give you the real answer. So what was the point of this whole drill? Here are the lessons to learn:

1. Homemade Judaism is a great idea. Filling your house with Jewish smells is both a good literal practice as Harlene suggests and a good metaphor. Ask yourself this: Does your house ever feel, look, or smell Jewish? Or is

it just an American home that sometimes thinks or orders-in Jewishly? That difference is important. The more Jewish the flavor of the house, the more likely you are to transfer a strong Jewish identification.

2. Just because we have stated one truth about Jewish smells, that doesn't mean it is the only truth. Look at my family. Just because you don't hand make your "fish" doesn't mean you won't raise Jewish children, or that they won't wind up hand making or boiling fish on their own. If all that was important was the food and the smell, you could just open a jar of "Mother's" and spray the house with my sister's "fish" smell aerosol air defreshener. Things are not that simple.

3. I find it interesting that none of the strong women I know ever call the movie *Gefilte Fish* sexist—even though it places culinary responsibility and guilt directly on the women. I suspect it slides in under their "feminist" radar and directly attacks their Jewish mother's guilt. My father is proof that men can make a Jewish house smell like a Jewish home, too— even if I am a failure. The truth is, my sister has carried on his tradition. Good for you, Judy!

4. Sadly, there are no guarantees. Judaism is a way of life, not a formula. Geoff and Rob tell that story. Even so, we never know the final outcome. Ways of life involve people and people have tendencies, not certainties. The sad truth is this—you can do everything right as a Jewish parent, follow the program the whole nine yards, and your kids may not respond. The other truth, however, is that they just may not have responded, yet.

In my kitchen I keep a jar of chicken soup base. You add it to boiling water and get chicken stock. It isn't chicken soup yet—you have to doctor it (cut the carrot and celery and add the noodles or *k'neidlakh*). I've never quite mastered the art of making great chicken soup out of chicken soup base (though I am told it is not hard). At times, when a cold or flu makes me wish that I still lived with my mother, instant chicken soup base comes in handy. It isn't what I really *want*. I used to stop for these great chicken noodles at the Atomic Cafe (ל״ז) before it closed—they were different from, but just as good as mother used to make. But now I settle for chicken stock because rarely (when I want it) will I have either the carrot or the energy to slice the carrot. Instant chicken stock is an approximation—a chemical foundation that a skilled chef can build on. In my own hands it makes salty flavored hot water that is usually too strong—because I tend to overdo it. I don't feel much better about canned chicken soup or frozen-in-the-bag chicken soup. I just get by—and the house never smells from it.

There is no such thing as Instant Jewish Identity stock. But, it is possible to assemble a relatively quick base of essential affiliations, involvements, items, and celebrations. Even starting with this assembled Jewish Identity base—your handmade stock—you don't yet have soup. To turn stock into soup, you have to be willing to *potchke*. It takes the willingness to boil the noodles and slice the carrot. Done well, it comes really close to homemade. Otherwise, it is essentially the hot, salty water I live with, when I really need either the Atomic Cafe (ז״ל) or my mother. I don't wish hot salty water on anyone else, but that is what simple answers make. You have to cut the carrot and hope.

12 Make a Big Deal Out of Purim

It is much better to overemphasize Purim than to worry about Halloween.

This year the premiere Conservative Jewish day school in Los Angeles wound up with a great fight between parents at an open house. It was the great Halloween controversy.

This day school has learned that day schools have to be more than good regular schools which also teach Judaica—they have to promote Jewish life. To that end, they run parent programs, family events, some community worship experiences and, like most congregational schools, they occasionally take the kids away to camp for a non-formal weekend experience.

For whatever reason, this day school scheduled a junior high school Shabbat retreat on a weekend during which Halloween would fall on Saturday night. The retreat, which started on Thursday, was scheduled to have Havdalah at sundown and then have the kids home early on Saturday evening.

At the open house, an informal gathering turned into a game of "How Dare You?"

A Parent: "How dare you schedule a weekend over Halloween—what are you going to do about it?"

Another Parent: "How dare you set Halloween against Shabbat—why are you sending your child to a day school?

Another Parent: "How dare you let your child celebrate Halloween at all? It is a Christian holiday; Jewish kids shouldn't celebrate it!"

Another Parent: "I want my daughter to feel good about being Jewish. Judaism shouldn't make them feel bad. How dare you suggest that I deprive them of a holiday that is as innocent and naive as Halloween? It isn't Christmas!"

And so it went. If you were one of these parents, would you tell your day school to:

a. Reschedule the weekend?

b. Hold the weekend without change?

c. Insure that the kids will be back early enough to have a Halloween experience?

d. Extend the night and run a Halloween experience under the school's safe direction?

e. Expand the quality and impact of the school's Purim celebration?

You know the Mark Twain quote, the one about his father getting smarter as he got older. That is what writing this book taught me about my parents. In hindsight, despite all the things I yelled at them when I was a teenager, they have now evolved into a world class set of Jewish parents.

For Halloween, we carved a pumpkin and left a bulb glowing in it all night (candles were deemed too dangerous so my father rigged this battery thing). It went right in the front window where we should have kept our <u>H</u>anukkah menorah—if we had know about the mitzvah of advertising the miracle. When we were little, we got to buy those store-bought costumes with the plastic and elastic masks. When we were older, we threw together something. Soon, however, costumes weren't cool—and they were given up or minimalized. Whatever the dress, my family "did" Halloween, but it was no big thing. We liked the candy and I can remember the shopping bags full of it—splitting and sorting it on the floor. Today, I can't tell you what costumes I wore—I can't connect to any great details.

By sixth grade (I remember it distinctly), sugar-dosing greed was exchanged for a tzedakah opportunity. Those were the years that orange UNICEF milk containers were big—we abandoned our quest for candy and roamed far and wide (further than I had ever even thought about going before) to gather gelt to make the world a better place. We did for others that which we would not do for ourselves. In those days, in that limited time before we knew better than to support UNICEF, Halloween taught me about self-sacrifice and the art of charitable fund raising. I made my first *tzedakah* appeals dressed in some thrown-together hobo costume on those October nights.

Soon after, UNICEF fell from grace—and in the void, Halloween greed made a big comeback. A couple of years later, we learned about the Palestinian math textbooks which were funded by UNICEF monies. A year or two passed, then we next heard the stories of razor blades hidden in apples. After that, we started taking our candy to the emergency room to x-ray. Halloween isn't all it used to be. UNICEF is out of favor. Greed is back, Casper the Friendly Ghost is gone, and Freddy Kruegger is now a really popular costume.

On the other hand, my family went crazy over Purim. Starting weeks in advance, my father became a seamstress. He spent weeks fashioning the best and most original Purim costumes for me and Judy. If you've ever seen one of those documentaries about what poor neighborhoods in Rio do to get ready for Mardi Gras—you know what my house was like. There were spangles and tinsel everywhere. My earliest memory is of a satin King Ahasuerus costume. It was purple on the outside, lined with gold satin. I had this studded and bejewelled cape which would have done Elvis proud. The coolest thing about it, however, was the crown. My father took an old baseball hat and made it into the center of a satin turban. It was encrusted in faux finery and then sewn onto the top of the turban. I used it for a couple of years and won some first prizes. Later, I had this great Haman costume with a long flowing black satin cape—lined, of course, in red satin. The three-cornered hat was a padded affair, sort of a giant *hamentash*, sewed around an old sailor's hat.

My sister's two best Purim costumes were even more creative. Once my father made her a gorgeous *grogger* costume. It was a huge cardboard box with a face hole cut out. It was covered in aluminum foil and had a mailing tube handle which was also covered in foil. The two amazing things about it were, first, that my father managed to glue down all of this foil with out wrinkling any of it, and second, that it had this great art deco border which took two nights to draw in three different colors: red, blue, and green. Judy became a deco version of the dancing cigarette box. However, Judy's best costume was as a Torah. My father, the seamstress, made her a white satin Torah mantle with this wonderful gold tasseled fringe. Her head went through the top where the roller handles would normally go. To go with it, he molded a tin breastplate, carved a wooden pointer (which was then covered in foil), and added a crown. It was really stunning.

The point here is very simple. Halloween was never banned—therefore, it never carried the enticement of a forbidden pleasure. It was a simple one-night affair which was enjoyed and forgotten. I didn't become Stephen King—it isn't one of my High Holidays. My family were Reform Americans; we only observed one day of Halloween.

When I compare the residual details in my memories of Halloweens and Purims past, I am amazed at how rich the detail is in my memories of Purim. In retrospect it has taught me that my parents' wisdom made real sense. They didn't waste the energy needed to fight Halloween; making Purim really spectacular was far more productive. Halloween teaches us that it is good and sometimes fun to confront our fears. It is a holiday which plays with evil in order to help us face fear. What concerns me about Halloween is not so much its pre-Hallmark origins in All Saints' Day and All Hallows' Eve, but its tendency towards meanness. It is not the treat that concerns me, but Halloween's validation of trickery. Purim is sweets, noise, and costumes, too. But it comes from someplace different. Purim is the story of how every Jew (even an inter-married Jewish woman who was only a "good enough" Jew at best) can be a hero—and that when we act together we are stronger than evil. I love "B" movies, but they don't direct my life. Halloween is Roger Corman's holiday—it is a George Romero epic. Esther is the kind of character Meryl Streep should play. It is Oscar material—it deserves a much bigger budget.

And now back to *Talmud 2000:*

a. **Should parents keep their kids from participating in Halloween?** My own feeling (not an authoritative response): Only if they can easily get away with it. I could do without Halloween—it is too subject to abuses—but fighting it too much only renders it too important.

b. **Is Halloween a valid reason for skipping Hebrew School?** Not on your life! There is plenty of time to make the rounds before or after class. I don't even recommend an early dismissal.

c. **Can Halloween defer Shabbat?** If you can make Shabbat more important and skip one year, do it. If you can't, consider: (a) running a Halloween event for your child and friends on Thursday or starting it with *Havdalah* in costumes on Saturday, or (b) do it early Friday night and then make Shabbat, or if it is a question of a dance or party (which can't or won't be avoided), apply the "Always make sure that Shabbat comes first" rule, and let them go (if you must)—after dinner.

d. **Would I let my child miss a whole weekend at camp because trick-or-treat might be missed?** No. (Unless it is a real fight—enough kicking and screaming and crying and door slamming and I would give in, but not until that point. Then, even if I lost, I would have won a moral victory, the importance of Jewishness would have been emphasized.)

Now, here is the hard question:

Must Purim costumes be exclusively Jewish? Real Jewish law doesn't speak to this question, but we need to:

Joel: What made Purim different when I was a child was that every costume affirmed Jewish identity.

Carol: When I grew up in a Reform congregation I thought all Purim costumes had to be Mordechai, Esther, Ahashuerus, Vashti and Haman. When I joined a Conservative one and learned that a Purim costume could be anything, I loved it. It was liberating.

Observation: When it comes to Purim costumes, some Reform congregations are stricter than more traditional congregations. Ironic!

Joel: Two years ago at my temple, the Jason in my class came to Purim in a *Friday the 13th* Jason hockey mask and Shane came dressed as Freddy Kruegger—is that Purim?

Carol: I don't know.

Comment: When you live in a mainly Jewish culture, Purim is a wonderful time to play with non-Jewish images (even Freddy Kruegger)—when you operate in a predominantly non-Jewish culture, the chance to enact Jewish roles and do Jewish play is really important. In other words, like most other truths, it depends.

Epilogue

There is a famous Jewish teaching pun in the Talmud (which really only works in Hebrew):

*"Yom **Purim** k'Yom ha-Kippurim."* "Purim Day is like Yom Kippur."
The Talmud doesn't explain this strange and inviting comparison.

Ask yourself, "How is Purim like Yom Kippur?" There are lots of right ideas you can find.

Playing with this idea, the Kelemer Maggid taught:

"On Purim, Jews dress up and masquerade as non-Jews, while on Yom Kippur they dress up and masquerade as pious Jews."

We can learn a lot from this lesson. Where classic Jewish wisdom saw Yom Kippur as the apex of the Jewish year and often began teaching about Jewish life with Rosh ha-Shanah, we can learn that it is equally valid to begin with Purim, to start with play rather than guilt.

13 | *Shelah Manot:* Try It— You'll Like It!

Shelah manot is the mitzvah of giving gifts of food to friends and family on Purim—it is an opportunity which should not be missed.

When it comes to mitzvot, *shelah manot* is a slam-dunk.

The Story: After Haman was hung, the Jews fought back and defended themselves against all the "pogroms" that he had planned for them. When the fighting was over, Mordechai, the new right-hand man of King Ahashuerus, sent a royal edict to Jews who lived everywhere from India to Ethiopia. In this letter he invented four new mitzvot and commanded Jews everywhere to follow them.

1. To tell the story of what happened—which is why we read the *Megillah* and do the *grogger* thing today.

2. To celebrate and have a good time—which is why we turn Purim into Mardi Gras with costumes, carnivals, parties and even acceptable public drinking.

3. To send gifts (of food) to their friends, which he called *shelah manot*—which is why we do our target mitzvah.

4. To give gifts to the poor—which is why Purim is such a wonderful *tzedakah* opportunity.

Following Mordechai's orders, *shelah manot* remains a mitzvah, a Jewish opportunity which is waiting for us.

The How To: (a) Make a list of family, friends and other people who are important to you. It can include both Jews and non-Jews. As you are working on your list, remember teachers, Jewish teachers, adoptive "grandparents" who are in your neighborhood or congregation, the crossing guard who always says hello, etc. As with any party list, you'll futz the number up or down depending on how much time and money you are willing to spend. (b) Prepare a package of "food" gifts for each person/family on the final list. The official rules state: "These gift packages must include at least two different kinds of food." Other than that, they can be as simple or as elaborate as you want. They can be of the scale of commercial food gift baskets or as simple as two cookies and a banana. It is traditional to include *hamentashen*—but this is not an obligation. (c) Prepare a special container for the gifts. Often this is just a paper plate which has been hand colored and labeled. But, consider a Chinese food container, a pint-size cardboard container (like the ones ice cream comes in)—or use your imagination. (d) On or around Purim hand deliver all the gifts possible (except where you have to resort to Federal Express, etc.) (e) Once this becomes a popular custom in your circle of friends, you can sit back and wait to sort your sweets the way other people do on Halloween—and the best part is, you won't have to have the stuff x-rayed for razor blades!

Remember to actively involve your children at every step.

The Point: First, this mitzvah is fun. Second, it involves food (often an end in and of itself). Third, it teaches a powerful lesson—we are not alone. Besides all the obvious Purim stuff, *shelah manot* is a radical celebration of connection. By making the list and then making the rounds, *shelah manot* helps us trace and celebrate the connections in our lives. In a way that is far more real and direct than greeting cards or obligation gifts, *shelah manot* celebrates connection and says, "We are not alone—we have friends, family, and 'significant others' in our lives." In the existential wasteland of 20th Century America, this is not a small lesson.

The Generalizable Lesson: All *mitzvot* (Jewish practices) are, to quote my mother's friend and teacher Rabbi Gunther Plaut, "opportunities." Some are easier to take advantage of than others. Some are more powerful or more immediate, or have more direct impact than others. A few of them are a lot of fun. A lot of them are rewarding. (And, as we know, some of them are a pain and a burden.) Which leads us to our next basic principle of Jewish survival:

> **Joel's Tenth Law:** Always score the easy *mitzvah* points. Be smart—at least rack up your Jewish continuity points on all the Jewish stuff which is inherently fun to do.

We know in our hearts that it is always better to perform a *mitzvah* than not to do it. Every Jewish tradition you observe is a check in the plus column. Your Judaism can certainly survive if you don't do everything. But, every time you skip one of the **fun** mitzvot or customs (like *shelah manot* or Simhat Torah)—it is a real waste.

Additional Purim Opportunities

1. Purim is a great time to do a "hands on" gift of food to the poor. (See **Number 24**: *Keep a Tzedakah Checkbook*, for examples and stories).

   A couple of years ago Kent Zeidman stood up at a Hebrew School assembly on *tzedakah* heroes and said, "How come adults only give healthy food to poor people? I bet poor kids would really appreciate a candy bar once in while—I know I would. I think that is something that we kids should do for other kids." The idea inspired everyone and we backed Kent's idea with a lot of quarters which had been collected weekly. There were plans to try to make a bigger thing, an organization called "Milk and Honey" which would include sweets among the necessities. It never happened, but the inspiration has lived on, at least with me (thank you, Kent). *Shelah manot* time, even though this mitzvah is officially called *matanot l'evyonim*—gifts to the poor—is the perfect chance to make it so, at least once a year.

2. When I was in college, Rabbi Saul Berman was running a college program at Young Israel of Brookline. It was a fun group. One year they ran The Purim Project. Something like ten thousand baggies were filled, each with a *hamantash*, a couple of nuts and a few pieces of cheap chocolate as well as a slip of paper which explained Purim and *shelah manot*. Then teams of Jewish college kids were sent all over the city to give them out. We went door-to-door in Jewish neighborhoods. We stood on city blocks and gave them to everyone who passed. We went to old age homes and preschools, and gave a little bit of Purim joy to all kinds of people. It was a mitzvah. It was a little bit of Jewish goodwill. It made the world a little happier in a lot of little ways. It was fun. Develop your own Purim Project.

3. If you are really in the Jewish In-Crowd, you already know about "Be Happy—It's Adar." I'll let you in on the secret. Adar is the Hebrew month in which Purim falls. The Talmud says, "When you enter Adar—joy increases." This is a great insight—that anticipation of a good time increases joy in the world. In the mid-sixties, hip college Jews started wearing "Be Happy—It's Adar" buttons, signing letters that way, and

even sending out note cards. I think a Boston underground newspaper called *Genesis II* started the practice, but I am not sure. However, if you can get your hands on a Jewish calendar, you too, can remind the world to increase its happiness quotient at the right time of year.

14 | When You Join a Synagogue, Make Sure to Ask: "Do Teenagers Come and Participate on Simhat Torah?"

Do not let Simhat Torah become a forgotten holiday. Do not let it decline into a minor event for old people and young children only.

Last night I got a message on my answer phone from Andy. He is 14, one of my former students, and he wanted to know if I wanted to go to a U2 concert. I was thrilled; he had remembered me. I felt connected. But, the sad part about that call was the fact that it was made at 8 p.m., just when our synagogue was beginning the celebration of Simhat Torah.

Obviously, he wasn't there. More depressing was the insight that he couldn't imagine that I might be there. He couldn't imagine that being in synagogue on Simhat Torah was something he or his favorite Hebrew School teacher might want to do. Here is the irony. Andy's family are synagogue-going people. His father, a former Sunday School teacher, now manages the temple cemetery. Personally, I think that the compassion Andy's father shows rates him as a moral giant. The amount of time he puts in as a volunteer marks him as a lay Jew of incredible distinction—especially since this is a private role, with only satisfaction as a reward. There are no *bimah* moments, just the knowing that you've helped people in need. He will be embarrassed when he reads this, but I am in awe of him. He is one of my heroes—one of my Jewish heroes. Andy's family is much more than a "good enough" Jewish family. The sadness, however, is that (while Andy's Jewishness is not at stake) in his life, in his family's life, Simhat Torah has become a lost holiday—a minor event—a High Holiday afterthought. That is a real loss and a real sadness.

Let's play another round of *Talmud 2000*. In the real Talmud, we frequently encounter the question: "After the Messiah comes and people only have to celebrate one Jewish holiday, which one will it be?" Our question is the same, but different:

> **TALMUD: Until the Messiah comes, and while most American Jews are only willing to really celebrate one or two Jewish holidays, which ones should they be?**
>
> **The Ghost of American Jewry Past:** Every Jew should come to synagogue for Yom Kippur. Kol Nidre is the "must" in the Jewish year—and *Yizkor* (on Yom Kippur), if you are obligated, is the other "must."
>
> **The Ghost of American Jewry Almost Past:** It should be going to a Passover Seder. Passover is where the extended family meets the most important story in Jewish history. Besides, there is good food (and good Jewish smells).
>
> **The Ghost of American Jewry Almost Future:** It should be Hanukkah. Hanukkah is a really positive Jewish holiday which celebrates Jewish courage and commitment. Besides, it is the moment in the year when we affirm that we are not Christians.
>
> **The Wisdom of the Refuseniks:** One should dance and celebrate Simhat Torah with great joy.

Just like "real" Talmudic debates, this is a good discussion, expressing conflicting views, each of which is partly right—while the one truly right answer (which is out of bounds) remains "all of the above." However, we need to reconstruct a Gemara in order to understand the richness here:

GEMARA: Why Yom Kippur? The conventional wisdom used to be that Yom Kippur was the most important Jewish holiday. After all, it was serious. It used to be, if you had to pick, Kol Nidre, the pinnacle of Jewish guilt, was the standout moment in the Jewish year. When Jewishness was all about obligation, Yom Kippur was when we affirmed who we were supposed to be, by stating that once again we had failed to meet those obligations.

The irony—and I do not believe that it is an irony which was lost, only not verbalized—is that Kol Nidre is all about saying, "I forgive myself, because I was 'good enough' even if I wasn't perfect." While the rest of the holiday is all about striving to try to be "perfect" next year, Kol Nidre is the one moment when we forgive ourselves for being human, and accept ourselves as "good enough"—then we start in on our breast beating workout towards spiritual fitness. Kol Nidre, whatever its real origin (and the scholars are unsure) is now explained by a Marrano myth (and we are pretty sure that the Marrano connection *is* a myth). We often explain the Kol Nidre's meaning by imagining that it was the prayer said by the Marranos as an apology for pretending to be Catholics and hiding their Judaism. They had to get that off their chests, and to relevel the playing field before they could even begin the Yom Kippur process. It is as if we imagine that they were saying, "We need amnesty from our worst sins, they are too horrible even to repent from, then we can start the Yom Kippur ritual." When we say Kol Nidre today, we absorb the Marranos' motivation. It is an emotional place we understand, because we understand compromise. It is an interesting choice for the most important Jewish moment in the year—setting the meter back to zero.

In picking *Yom Kippur*, we are picking God, synagogue and prayer as the center of Jewishness. Yom Kippur is the ultimate prayer moment—Kol Nidre, the ultimate show-stopping aria in the performance of the Jewish spiritual year. Observing Yom Kippur is the most basic, most minimal affirmation of synagogue culture. In a world of "at leasts," when you are "at least" a "revolving door Jew" (in at Rosh ha-Shanah and out at Yom Kippur), you've taught your family that you are "members." That is not a little lesson—though there are many more.

Why Passover? In picking Passover, we are picking the extended family. Even in the old days, Seder gave Kol Nidre a run for its money as the number one Jewish practice. In fact, as far as I know, the demographers always gave it the victory as the most observed Jewish custom. At worst, Passover is an ingathering of the family—real, extended. adopted, make-believe, reconstituted, or whatever—to commemorate an important Jewish moment and to underline its significance with food and festivity. Even if no Haggadah is opened, no questions asked, no Hillel sandwich made—even if it begins with a bourbon on the rocks, the way my Uncle Seymour's friend does—even if it is only matzah ball soup and brisket: *Dayenu.*

An Important Note: You've always been told that *dayenu* means "it would have been enough." That is a lie. It is a literal translation, but it is a lie. *Dayenu* actually means, "If that's all I'm going to get, I guess I can live with it—but I really want it all." Think about it. We say, "If God had taken us out of Egypt, but not sustained us for 40 years in the wilderness with manna: *Dayenu.*" I don't know about you—but I'm not that much into Outward Bound. Personally, I want to get to the last one on the list, I want to get Freedom, Torah, Shabbat, then pass "GO", then get $200, and then finish in the Land of Israel. I wouldn't have been too happy if God had taken the first *dayenu* seriously and stopped helping us after our initial escape. When I say *dayenu* to a family whose Passover observance is just an ethnic residue, a Marrano moment—you know what I really want.

Joel's Eleventh Law: Always say "*Dayenu*" to any positive expression of Jewishness. Remember, *dayenu* is aggressive-passive (the active inverse of passive-aggressive). It affirms what is as good—and then always seeks more.

Why Hanukkah? Hanukkah is rapidly becoming American Jewry's celebration of choice. It and Passover are presently slugging it out on the demographers' spreadsheets to see who is Number One. Hanukkah is an interesting choice—because it is so easy. First, and I think foremost, this is because Hanukkah has always been a place where the Jewish community has underinvested; a minor holiday, where the temporal real estate is underdeveloped. My sister, the MBA, would call it "an area of opportunity." Simply put, Hanukkah is easy, because it comes with very few rules and almost no expectations. In the past, Jews did very little with Hanukkah. For North American Jews, Hanukkah is our own new subdivision of the Jewish tradition—the place where *we* get to define most of the rules about what is authentic.

It is the one Jewish holiday where we can feel "better" than our parents, grandparents, ancestors, et al—it is the one place we have a chance to outdo them. At Passover, we doubt our ability to cook as well (because the true ethnic secrets have been lost to the jaws of the food processor and the inferno of the microwave) and we doubt our mastery of the inner meaning of the secret Hebrew Haggadah text which has now dripped through a Maxwell House filter. But, when it comes to Hanukkah, we can light more expensive *hanukkiot* (Hanukkah *menorot*), stage bigger and better parties, give electronic gifts, and stage those great tributes to the long forgotten druids where everyone in the neighborhood, *havurah*, or even their synagogue, lights their nine candles (or whatever is the maximum for the closest weekend night) at once, drips wax everywhere, and tells the sun, "Enough darkness, it is time to return!"

The **good news** about Hanukkah is that it celebrates positive Jewish identity, and allows us to transform our phobia about Douglas firs into an act of distinguishing between Jew and non-Jew. Hanukkah is the way American Jewry really makes havdalah. As by-products of that process, we celebrate all things Jewish, and gain a few comic book Jewish heroes—Judah "The Hammer" Maccabee & Co. *Dayenu.*

The **not-so-good news** about Hanukkah is that it really doesn't have much to say or teach. The real Hanukkah story was that of a civil war between two political factions. We celebrate because a religious party (which we would find oppressive were it around today) won a victory over a bunch of temple priests who wanted to go and work out between Temple services. When the rabbis got hold of the holiday (after they learned that, like Halloween, they couldn't get the people to *not* celebrate it) they tried to make it a celebration of "miracles." That is the reason that "the oil lasted for eight nights" is all that the Talmud records about the event. In the modern era, where miracles are not part of our everyday experience, we make it a freedom holiday, sort of a Jewish Fourth of July, and await the day when Arnold Schwarzeneggar will make a movie and play Judah. We really do want Hanukkah with biceps—an easy way to be proud to be a Jew and not envy the tinsel.

The rest of the **bad news** is that Hanukkah is a holiday for the nuclear family. You can invite gramps and grandma, but you don't have to. You can do stuff at the JCC or the Temple—they'll both stage major events—but it is just peripheral. In truth, Hanukkah is just five minutes and then back to homework or television. It is a very easy way to be proud to be a Jew. It is a nice little holiday; I simply doubt that it is the right place to step when we're crossing the stream. It is the wrong place to rest all of our weight.

Why Simḥat Torah? Because the Refuseniks in the former Soviet Union, who actually had to choose one holiday to celebrate, already chose this one.

One of my favorite passages in the Talmud is this argument. (*Bava Metziah 85b*).

Rabbi Ḥaninah and Rabbi Ḥiyyah were having a big fight.

Rabbi Ḥaninah bragged: "**If the Torah were forgotten**, I would bring it back by debating and arguing."

Rabbi Ḥiyyah answered him. "**When the Torah was forgotten** and it was up to me to bring it back, I planted a field of flax. I nurtured that field and later harvested the flax. I spun the flax and made a net. With the net I trapped deer. I slaughtered the deer and fed the meat to the orphans. I tanned the hide and wrote a Torah on the deer's skin. Then I taught Torah to five youngsters and Mishnah to six youngsters. Then I told them, teach each other what you have learned. This is the way the Torah was restored.

When we ask the question, "**Until the Messiah comes, and while most American Jews are only willing to really celebrate one or two Jewish holidays, which ones should they be?**", we are like Rabbi Ḥaninah; our question is rhetorical. We have choices, and we are imagining. When the Soviet Refuseniks chose to ignore the KGB and gather every Simḥat Torah outside the synagogue on Archepovoff street in Moscow, they were like Rabbi Ḥiyyah, actively rebuilding their Judaism. Their choice of Simḥat Torah was not made by any committee. No rabbis talked it over, no one voted—it was just collective insight, an instinctive and emotional response, and we can learn from it.

Instinctively they knew three things: Simḥat Torah is pure celebration, Simḥat Torah says that Torah is the center of our Judaism, and Simḥat Torah raises those two insights together into a community arena:

Simḥat Torah is the holiday that centers our life in the cycle of the Torah. It is the ultimate celebration of Jewish learning. For a congregation to lose its connection to Simḥat Torah is a great sadness—it loses the ability to make Torah a collective joy. To my way of thinking, the loss of Simḥat Torah as a spiritual heart reduces a synagogue community to a place to store blackboards. If the teenagers are missing, if it is only the entry level kids and the old folks who are there, then the very essence of Simḥat Torah is gone. It takes teenagers to dance with the Torah, to toss it high in the air, and then at the last moment, when the future of the scroll is at risk, use all their strength and dexterity to grab it out of the air, bring it close to their hearts, and continue the dance. We need the risk and the potential of teenagers in the mix, or the Torah will die (or remain in the ark as a museum piece).

My own synagogue, like oh so many others, has been losing its Simḥat Torah over the years. Were it not for the Reform practice of giving baby Torahs to the Consecration class, it would already be gone. To try to renovate the holiday, my Rabbi borrowed a nouveau ritual. He did what the professional slang now calls "a Torah roll." He unrolled the whole Torah around the whole sanctuary, letting everyone touch and look at it. He made the Torah belong to the whole community—sort of. **A Good Time Was Had By All**. Almost no one was there to experience it. Andy was home calling me to see if I wanted to see U2. His parents and brother were there with him. It was a secular night for them. Just about all of the other teens were missing too—or so I have been told, because in one sense, Andy was right. I had given up, too. I was elsewhere. I had gone looking for a better dance.

> **Snapshot:** When I was 17, I went to Israel for the first time. I spent a Shabbat with Rabbi Tuvia Ben Ḥorin, an Israeli Reform rabbi from the Tel Aviv area. What knocked me out was seeing his young son playing rabbi on Saturday afternoon. He had a play Torah, a play ark, and was having the best time imitating his father. I was never allowed to play Torah or play rabbi. When I was in kindergarten, getting my little consecration Torah was a big deal. I loved it. My father reached into the family *geniza*, (the traditional name for the place where Jews store no longer used Jewish ritual objects) his top dresser sock drawer, and pulled out his consecration Torah. He then fashioned a cigar box (remember cigar boxes?) into an ark which contained the two Torahs. It had velvet curtains which opened and closed with a pull cord. It was painted gold. There were sequins sewed onto the purple ark curtains. I think they were made of the satin which was left over from the King Ahasuerus outfit. My father was very handy. I loved it. I took it to Sunday School. My teacher was so impressed that she called the principal. The principal was so impressed that she sent for the rabbi. The rabbi was so impressed that he made a place for it in the temple museum. I imagine those two little Torahs are still there under glass in the downstairs display case. Never again was I allowed to play with them.

Snapshot: In graduate school I was an advisor for CFTY, the regional Reform youth movement in the Chicago area. That year, Reform Simḥat Torah was on Saturday night and the rest of the Jewish world celebrated it one night later on Sunday. Given the opportunity, we staged an all-teen Simḥat Torah event on Sunday. Nothing was planned. Just 300 teenagers and 6 Torah scrolls. Me telling stories and my friend Debbie Friedman leading the singing. It was at Temple Sholom. We did three hours of singing, dancing, and celebrating. Inside and outside. A great time was had by all.

I remember vividly that a teenager named Jane Wishner stood up holding a Torah during one of the pauses and told a story about Shraga Arien, (ל״ז) an important local Jewish teacher who had just died. She said, "In the Talmud, there is a story about Hillel and Shammai. A non-Jew came to each and asked to be taught the Torah while standing on one foot. Shammai drove him away, but Hillel said, 'Do not do unto others that which is hateful to you,' then added, 'Now go and study, because all the rest is commentary.' Shraga used to add, 'If that kid had come to me, I would have done it differently. Between the 'Do not do unto others that which is hateful to you, ' and the 'Now go and study, because all the rest is commentary,' I would have said, 'But first, let's dance together with the Torah.'" Debbie hit a chord, everyone jumped to their feet, and we danced and celebrated the night away.

The following week I went into my office and found an angry letter from the executive director of Temple Sholom, my friend Mr. Coburn, (ל״ז) who was just doing the board's will. He banned CFTY from ever returning to his synagogue, because of the disrespect we had shown their Torah scrolls. By dancing with them, by taking them outside, by letting everyone touch them, we had put their holiness at risk. The board's judgment was like that which had been made about the little ark my father had made—that Torah belonged under glass.

This is my final truth. We are Jews who only know one foot's worth of Torah. We need to learn all the commentary. For us, the Torah is all but forgotten, something under glass, that we are only allowed to control one day in our lives—the day we become bar or bat mitzvah. Otherwise, Torah seems to belong to the rabbi, who controls it every time its museum case is opened. Unless we return Torah to the people—and that is the meaning of Simḥat

Torah—it will age and die. It needs the risk and the energy. Jane Wishner is right. The wisdom she teaches from her teacher Shraga is truth. We need to let our teenagers dance with the Torah—we need to let them control Simḥat Torah, or with the best of intentions we will have put all their Torah dreams from childhood into the Temple display case. They need to dance with the Torah before they will learn all the rest of the commentaries. My synagogue needs to learn this lesson. They need to give Simḥat Torah over to the teenagers, to empower their leadership and involvement during this celebration, or the holiday will never return. Its lesson will be lost.

Deep in my heart I am scared of seeing Ḥanukkah become the "one foot" on which we learn Judaism—just because there is so little commentary to learn later.

I know that this is a hard one for this book—because as a parent, or as a congregant, you can't control what the synagogue does. But, you can influence it. Stand on one foot and make the call or write the note—then practice your Torah dancing.

A Final Recommendation

Celebrate every Jewish holiday like it is the only one you will get to celebrate, and pack all your Jewish feelings into it.

15 Visit Christmas

The best way to cure Christmas envy (a.k.a. The December Dilemma) is to start an exchange program where you visit your friends' Christmas celebrations and your non-Jewish friends join you for Shabbat, Seder and other important Jewish celebrations.

Hypothesis: Before we can stage an effective Ḥanukkah celebration we have to make our peace with Christmas. The way to do that is by making a big deal out of Christmas, with all its joys and delights, while at the same time pointing out: That is not where we live.

The first time I lived in Jerusalem I heard a great, probably apocryphal story. It seemed that a Christian *New York Times* reporter was living with his family in Jerusalem. Between Yom Kippur and Sukkot just about every family on the block built a sukkah. Every one of his kids' friends' families were building sukkot. All of their friends, their Israeli friends, were inviting them to eat out in the sukkah. As the story goes, the pressure built. Eventually, his kids asked, "Dad, can't we build a sukkah?" When the father says, "No," explaining "We're not Jewish," the kids respond, "A sukkah isn't really a Jewish thing— it's just a fun thing to do!"

Even if it never happened—the story provides lots of relief. It teaches us three lessons about how to deal with the December dilemma:

1. That we should regularly invite our non-Jewish friends to celebrate our Jewish holidays with us. Passover, Shabbat and Sukkot are great opportunities.

Joel's Twelfth Law: The best time to deal with the "problem of Christmas" is at any time in the year but the middle of December.

2. That as part of a "cultural exchange" we should visit our non-Jewish friends' holiday celebrations and have an opportunity to enjoy and appreciate them.

3. That we should make sure that we know and that our children know the difference between "visiting" and "owning."

To make this clear, a story from my mother's family:

Almost every year my mother got to decorate a Christmas tree. Often, she went to a Christmas party. My own family inherited the practice. It was always at the invitation of Christian friends. Once, when her brother, my Uncle Bob, nailed up a Christmas stocking on the mantle expecting gifts, my Grampa Charlie filled it with coal. He said, "That's what Santa does to Jewish kids who think they can celebrate a Christian holiday." When I was seven or eight, and thought about hanging a stocking, my mother's story about Uncle Bob stopped me.

Now that you've learned the basic principles of being a Jew and living through *The Attack Of The Killer Pine Trees*, let's see if you can apply them to some basic December Dilemmas.

Talmud 2000

1. **Your child sings in the school chorus. They decide to sing at the local shopping mall as part of the community Winter Solstice celebration. Their repertoire will include both "I Have a Little Dreidel" and "Joy to the World." You should:**

   a. Make a big deal out of the separation of Church and State, and see to it that the performance is limited to "Frosty the Snowman" and "Winter Wonderland."

   b. Tell your child to sing (if that is his/her desire) and to enjoy her/himself, but not to sing the words "Jesus" or "Christ."
   The *additional activity* which might be great would be to study the songs which will be sung as a family, to understand the difference between Judaism and Christianity. You can use Christmas as an opportunity to teach both what is good about Christianity and why we don't accept it.

   c. Tell your child to sing and have a good time, but to know that s/he is joining in a Christian celebration which is lovely and fun, and in which s/he is included only as a guest.

If you follow this last path, you can tell them that they can sing all the words, but not mean them. In the Talmud, the rabbis make a big deal out of *kavanah*. It means "aiming one's heart." They suggest that Jewish prayers and ceremonies have no impact without *kavanah*. Tell your child to apply this rabbinic insight to Christmas carols. They don't have to make a big deal out of singing them, as long as (1) they are not pretending to be Christian or denying or hiding their Jewishness, and (2) as long as they know not to "mean" them and intentionally point their hearts in a different direction.

2. **You are at a friend's Christmas party and the whole group starts singing Christmas carols. What should you do?**
   a. Enjoy the singing but do not join in.
   b. Join in, but do not sing the words "Jesus" or "Christ."
   c. Join in and sing, but always remember that you are there only as a guest.

3. **You are at a relative's Christmas party (one of your non-Jewish relatives) and the whole group starts singing Christmas carols. You should:**
   a. Enjoy the singing but do not join in.
   b. Join in, but do not sing the words "Jesus" or "Christ."
   c. Join in and sing, but always remember that you are there only as a guest.

4. **You are at a Jewish relative's "winter" party and the whole group starts singing Christmas carols. You should:**
   a. Chastise the group or the relative (either in public or private) and directly express your Jewish identity and values.
   b. Swallow hard and vow "Never again!"
   c. Apply the "God will forgive me" principle and feel that even though you hate it, "family is important, too."

Does it matter if you kids are there? Does it matter how old they are?

5. **You take your child Ḥanukkah shopping and run into the "Take A Photo With Santa" floor show. Your kid begs you.**
   a. You should "Just say no!"
   b. Allow your child to tell Santa what s/he wants for Ḥanukkah. But make it clear that s/he must be honest and "Tell Santa that you are Jewish." (Believe me, Santa hears this a lot. It is item seven in Santa training school—think who owns *Bloomingdales*.)

  c. Buy a copy of *Bubbie and Zadie at the North Pole*, the book that tries to establish the existence of "Hanaclaus."

6. **Your child goes into deep December Depression. You know that it is tinsel envy. You should:**
  a. Do a Louis B. Mayer, Busby Berkeley Hanukkah production that year. (Maybe even tell the story of *The Little Pine Tree Who Stood Up To Antiochus.*)
  b. You should confront the behavior, firmly establishing a boundary between Jew and non-Jew.
  c. You should listen with great empathy, even share the things about Christmas you like, but not shift your family practice one iota.

In order the find the right answers to these questions please follow these directions carefully. Find a group of thirty friends and form a secret cabal. Agree that for fifteen years, one third of you will try each approach. At the end of fifteen years you will examine your children's dating patterns, their involvement in things Jewish, and their overall attitudes—then we will finally have hard data, and have some semblance of an idea of what to do. Otherwise, trust your heart and your best judgment, and keep in mind that the best offense is (1) a strong Sukkot celebration and (2) friends who will let you help trim their tree.

Patti Golden is a genius. She is a friend of mine and the founder of the Jewish Holiday Workshop Series. I consider her one of my teachers. One important piece of torah she taught me was the story of a daughter who came home from college and told her about a "bull session" they had in the dorm.

> The daughter said, "Mom, I actually figured out that Hanukkah was one of the major reasons I never got involved with drugs or excessive drinking, and that I'm not involved in the promiscuous sex that is all around me. From having to celebrate Hanukkah when everyone else was doing Christmas, I learned that I could be different—and that was okay."

Extensions: Finding the Balance

Once we've accepted the idea of "visiting" Christmas as a way of establishing both appreciation and difference, two other pairs of opportunities come to mind. In each case, the members of the pair balance each other.

1. When I was a junior in high school, I was active in my temple youth group. And, my youth group was active in the regional youth group. And

the region was involved in some very *avant garde* interfaith dialogues. We had several one-day events with youth groups of other faiths. I will never forget that Sister Corita Kent (the artist who later left the Church and married Daniel Berrigan) began a meal by saying *ha-Motzi*. We Jews were surprised, and asked her about it. She said, "I bet that the Jews would understand and appreciate it. I figured the Protestants would assume that it was Latin and accept it. And, I knew that the Catholics would never question it." The year had been planned to culminate in an interfaith weekend retreat. In the last month before the event, it was canceled. Too many parents panicked. They assumed that it might turn into a dating opportunity. We protested. We argued that committed religious people were highly unlikely to abandon our faiths just when we were proudly presenting them. We lost. For twenty years I was confident that we were right. Now, more than twenty-five years later, I still suspect that we were right, at least about us.

We should expand these visits to a real "interfaith dialogue," appreciating and differentiating from not only stockings hung on mantles, but concepts such as "original sin," etc. It is important to bring back the idea of "tolerance"—the appreciation of difference.

2.   We should know more about our Judaism than we do about the religions we are visiting, and find more significance in it. This is the other side of "tolerance"—a living alongside, not assimilation.

In many ways Philip Roth's short story, "The Conversion of the Jews", is the ultimate expression of the angst of being Jewish in Christian America—where Christianity controls the horizontal and the vertical. At the story's critical moment, Ozzie—the protagonist—threatens to jump off the synagogue roof unless the rabbi gets down on his knees and admits that God is powerful enough to let a woman have a baby without intercourse, if that is something God wanted to do. We can unravel the story from there—because we know it. To prove that Judaism is better than Christianity, the rabbi had suggested that the prime Christian miracle— virgin birth—is logically absurd. Ozzie, grasping an opening, suggests that a God who could stop the sun and divide the Red Sea could certainly cause a few cells to switch from meiosis to mitosis without resorting to hitting below the belt. From that point on, neither side can back down. The problem is the imposition of the category of "have a baby without having intercourse." Even when we come to visit Christianity and appre-

93

ciate it, unless we have our own categories, their miracles will always obsess us. When their metaphors become the scale on which we understand and judge Judaism, a radical distortion will take place.

One logical extension of this essay is to go beyond Christmas and visit Easter, Palm Sunday, Ash Wednesday and the rest. If we're going to appreciate Christianity—we've got to go beyond the Santa on the Coke can. At the same time, if we don't know when and how to pull out and value our own religious tradition, Christianity can be a black hole, sucking away all our Jewish light. We need to tell "Ozzie" that God could do it, but we don't believe that God had any need to do it. Our God doesn't work that way.

3. If we're going to visit Christmas, we should "visit" more traditional Judaisms (and perhaps less traditional Judaisms) as well.

When I was fifteen, I was still on the swim team—thinking about "the gold." One day during an extra practice session I was giving myself, I wound up pacing this Orthodox kid whose name I have long forgotten. He was on the Maimonides Academy swim team and I made some stupid joke about a hydrodynamic plastic yarmulke for swim practice. We became friendly acquaintances and swam laps together a couple of times. Eventually he invited me to come to his shul, the Bostoner Rebbe's shul. He didn't cut his hair or dress Hasidic—but he did pray Hasidic. In return, I politely tried to turn the moment into a mini-*The Chosen* epic and invited him to come to Temple Sinai. He politely said, "No, thanks." I was a little hurt—having little understanding of "the rules" which prohibited his attendance. I felt slightly insulted—after all, I had been to Catholic masses and black gospel churches, and I was going with him on a Hasidic adventure. I had manifested "tolerance" and felt that he was being closed-minded. I didn't understand that his "tolerance" was different than mine—I knew more about Catholic dietary restrictions (it was Boston) than I did about kashrut. The Friday night I was to meet him, I dressed up really sharp, shoved my bar mitzvah *tallit* in my pocket (the first time it had been taken out since) and took the MTA to a block from where I was to meet him. That night was a big learning experience. I learned, for example, that "real" Jews don't wear *tallitot* at night. In my synagogue, only rabbis and *b'nai mitzvah* initiates ever wore *tallitot* (day, *minhah* event, or night.) And I learned that it was "a sin" for me to be carrying the *tallit* on Shabbat. Up to then, I had thought "sin" had to do with war, segregation, or perhaps murder.

That night was the beginning of a long journey from "Reform Jew" to Jew. My upbringing was highly parochial—parochially Reform. But the lesson is not an exclusively Reform lesson—just the opposite. If we want to live in a *k'lal Yisrael* universe, and not limit our children to an ideological as well as an ethnic gene pool, we need to visit and understand all the Judaisms. More and more, synagogues are becoming idiosyncratic places. All are inventing their own rituals and rewriting their own liturgy. More and more we are socializing our children to be Jewish in only one way and only in one place. We need to explore with our children the great diversity and richness of Jewish life. Not only should we take them to Jewish Museums and the Lower East Side, but they should have their chance to "shul-hop," stalking the wild Hasid and the righteously reconstructed, experiencing the living room *havurah* and the pageantry of "high church" classical Reform. If they are boys, they deserve their one shot at dancing with the Hasidim, and if they are girls they should experience the spiritual uniqueness of a women's minyan. Once we start visiting, we can teach them that there is more to Jewish life than their rabbi and their fifth-grade teacher.

4. If we are Reform and we visit Orthodox shuls, or "very" Conservative and we "slum" Reform, etc., we must do so with respect—just like our "Christmas visits." We have come to appreciate and "tolerate"—understanding that our family is different.

5. It would be great to take one year (maybe around the time your kids are 9-11) to visit all kinds of churches and synagogues. You could throw in a mosque, a meeting house, a tabernacle, and a Baha'i temple, too. Now *that* could be radical appreciation and differentiation, especially if each visit was punctuated with an affirmation of your own family's religious expressions.

16 | On Hanukkah, Tell and Retell the Things That Befell Us

To keep Hanukkah alive, you have to emphasize the task of telling and explaining the meaning of the celebration.

On Passover we know that it is our obligation to "tell the story" and make it come alive in our own homes. Hanukkah is a lot like Passover in that it is a home holiday—it is different because it is essentially a series of practices without explanation. Until you can answer this question without saying the word "Christmas" (and there is no official answer)—then the future of Hanukkah (and with it the Jewish people) is at risk.

Why do we give presents at our Jewish celebrations during the winter season?

In the real Talmud (*Shabbat* 21b-24b) we find this discussion of how much money a family should spend on their Hanukkah celebration:

If one only has limited resources...

The basic mitzvah is for each family to light one flame for each of the eight nights of Hanukkah.

A family who wants to enhance the basic mitzvah should light one flame for each family member, each of the eight nights of Hanukkah.

To maximize the mitzvah:

Bet Shammai (Shammai's school) believed that one should light eight flames on the first night, and one less each of the following nights.

Bet Hillel (Hillel's school) believed that one should light one flame on the first night and one more each of the following nights.

Bet Hillel won the argument based on their explanation, "In matters of holiness one should always expand and progress, not contract and retreat."

The essence of the mitzvah of Hanukkah is to advertise the miracle.

If we translate this to a *Talmud 2000* issue, it comes down to this discussion I bet you'll recognize:

A parent's basic obligation is to give each child at least one Hanukkah gift.

To enhance Hanukkah and make it better than Christmas, one should give at least one major gift per child as well as one minor gift per child for each of the other eight nights.

One school says the best gift should come on the first night, satisfying immediate desires—the other school says you should build up to the last night.

To maximize the Hanukkah experience one should give a significant gift on each night.

However, the children teach: One should give us one good gift on the first night, two good gifts on the second night, three on the third—until we receive eight spectacular gifts on the eighth night. Parents, however, should expect only one gift.

The essence of the Hanukkah mitzvah is to make children proud and positive about their Jewish heritage.

Hanukkah has suffered in the translation. In our celebrations and modifications we have given the Greeks the final victory. The cruelest irony of all is that we have used the foundation of Hanukkah to establish the *Maccabiah*, the Jewish Olympiad. But there are others:

> When I was a Reform rabbinical student in Jerusalem, we used to go to the Turkish baths every Friday afternoon. We didn't go for the ritual mikvah thing (spiritual purification); we went for the *shvitz*, to make the body feel good. Sitting in the *temperdarium* (the hot tub) one of the rabbinical students from the Seminary (the Conservative rabbinical school) who also made a practice of pre-Shabbat *shvitzing* said: "It's times like this that make you wish that the Greeks had won." We laughed. It was a guilty pleasure.

In the best truth we can reconstruct, Judah and Mattathias Maccabee, a.k.a the Hashmon dynasty, a.k.a. the Hanukkah heroes, came from a priestly family which was out of power. They were from a political faction who were angry at the priestly families who were in power. They didn't believe that the priests in power were holy enough. These Maccabees-to-be were upset that those other priests were trying to live Greek lives with the Jewish religion on the side. The Maccabee clan made it into a debate about "Jewish Greeks or Greek Jews." Bluntly, they wanted Jews to serve only The One Master.

Here is the rub: The Hashmon family were part of a political movement called the Hasidim. While they didn't wear the black and white of Polish nobles and speak with a Yiddish inflection, and they bear no connection to the ultra-Orthodox sect of our era—sociologically, they were the *Habad* (Lubavitch) of their day—they displayed the same intolerance. They knew that they alone were right. They didn't have Mitzvah Tanks and ambush other Jews with *lulav* and *tefillin*—but they did think of themselves as *Tz'va-os ha-Shem* (God's Army). They were like the rock-throwing Hasidim in Jerusalem today, who aren't satisfied with creating their own sense of Shabbat, but want to impose their level of Shabbat rest on every other Jew (you know, the guy all in black who says: "You vill not drive on the new highvay—you vill rest!"). They were "one way" Jews, fundamentalist fanatics who knew precisely what God wanted. Eventually, to preserve the peace, the other Jews called in the cops. In this story, we call the cops, "The Syrians—Antiochus' horde."

From that point on, the Hanukkah story is essentially that of a police riot. To control things, the Syrians and their crazed king tried to impose a neutral religion on Palestine—making both sides in this childish feud conform to *their* rules. When they forbade circumcision, Shabbat and Torah study, and imposed idol worship and the breaking of the pork taboo—most Jews got mad. It became something else then, the fight for religious freedom we like to affirm.

It would be very hard for us to celebrate the actual historic Maccabees. In our eyes, they stand for all the wrong things. Ironically, the Talmudic rabbis felt exactly the same way (though probably the Maccabees' use of violence and their political heritage bothered the rabbis more). When the Mishnah was compiled, circa 200 C.E., Hanukkah and the Maccabees were completely absent. (They were already missing from the Torah, because their saga started after its final publication date.) When the Bible's final edition was released (also circa 200 C.E.), the editorial committee rejected the Maccabees' work, too. Ironically, the Books of the Maccabees were preserved only in the Catholic Bible. The rabbis, the innovators who shaped the Jewish tradition we now live—the guys who tinkered in their garages and came up with Passover Seders, Friday Night Dinners, Saturday Morning Torah Services, etc.—ignored Hanukkah and hoped it would go away. It didn't.

By the time the rabbis were ready to release the revised and improved version of the Talmud, the one which added the Gemara (circa 500 C.E.) they knew that they had to say something about the Maccabees and Hanukkah. They had no choice—there was too much pressure. So, they were very careful. All they said was:

What is Hanukkah?

On the 25th of Kislev, Hanukkah is celebrated for eight days. You should not fast or mourn, because when the Greeks entered the Temple they defiled all the [holy olive] oil and when the Hashmon dynasty defeated them, they searched and found only one container of oil with the seal of the High Priest [indicating that it was kosher]. It was only enough to last for one day of lamp lighting. But, a miracle happened and it lasted for eight days.

That's all there is. Think about what is missing—just about everything. No heroes are named—Judah and Mattathias are missing, the nickname "Maccabee" is not authenticated. Antiochus, too, is never mentioned. All of the politics, all of the military brilliance, all of the courage have been deleted. That is the reason that all of us know almost nothing about the Maccabees—the rabbinic Rosemary Woods has struck. What we get instead of swords and swashbuckling (or religious fanatics) is just a little jar of oil. The little jar of oil gets the solo spotlight and that spotlight is focused on God's intervention rather than any human accomplishment. It isn't the classic warrior's "We give thanks to God..."—they give *all* the credit to God. In their version, God is no supporting actor.

When it comes to Ḥanukkah practice, they indicate only three things: (1) The saying of Hallel, the Psalms which praise God, (2) an insertion into *Birkat ha-Mazon* (The Grace after Meals) and the *Amidah* and (3) these directions:

> One has an obligation to place the *hanukkiyah* outside one's front door. If one lives on the second floor, one should put it in the window. If there is danger, one can place it on the table instead...the essence of the Ḥanukkah mitzvah is to advertise the miracle.

If we followed the original intent of the rabbis' Ḥanukkah, we would hire Walt Disney Enterprises to do the pyrotechnics for Ḥanukkah the way they do half-time shows for the Super Bowl—not to compare Ḥanukkah to the Fourth of July the way we often do in our "Ḥanukkah stands for religious freedom" rhetoric, but to help promote God—The Real Miracle Worker.

But in our culture, Ḥanukkah's meaning made a U-turn and came out in two different places.

Direction one: We have already seen that in secular Jewish culture the Maccabees have become the torch carriers in the Jewish Olympics—an absolute contradiction of the Ḥasidim's original intent.

Direction two: In American religious life, when we mixed Ḥanukkah with our pluralistic democratic ideals, we undid the Ḥasidim a whole different way. Listen to this American midrash (folk story):

> George Washington was at Valley Forge in mid-winter, ready to give up. It was too cold. He had been cutting off too many of his soldier's toes. Everyone was ready to quit. Before throwing in the towel, George takes one last walk around camp. He runs into the one Jew in the colonial army who is busy watching his *hanukkiyah* burn and singing *"Ma-oz Tzur."* George asks a few questions and in turn the Jew tells him the entire story of how the Maccabees fought for religious freedom. From this, George gets his courage back up, decides to continue the war, and even stands up in the boat the next day. After the war, the little Jew goes back to Newport and a few weeks later a gift from George arrives. It is a silver *hanukkiyah*, made by his friend Paul, with an inscription which thanks the Jews for teaching America how to light the torch of freedom.

100

It is a wonderful story, a perfect American Jewish myth—and even if you have never heard it before, it is the truth with which you have been raised. Even though Hanukkah was originally the story of fundamentalists who wanted to eliminate all outside influences from their Jewishness, when Hanukkah came over on the *Mayflower* it became the story of how all people are entitled to religious freedom. No one even noticed the transformation. Since then, Hanukkah—All-American Hanukkah, with its greeting cards and gift obsession—has been locked in a dogfight with Christmas. Your mission, should you choose to accept it, is to give Hanukkah its own meaning—something beyond being a blue and white reflection of their red and green celebration.

Let me give you a few pointers to help you out:

Why do we light Hanukkah candles?

The official Talmudic answer is: "Because the oil lasted for eight days." When we light the *hanukkiyah*, we are like the Maccabees who cleaned the Temple. We get to experience God—The Real Miracle Worker.

We have already learned that this is a made-up answer, a meaning which was retrofitted by the rabbis who contributed to the Talmud. Yet, it works, because it taps into our sense of truth—our deep, mythic, archetypal, primal core. Let me explain:

Not all repetitive customs are rituals—though many social scientists fail to make this distinction. They often define a ritual as any pattern of behavior which a group of people regularly repeats because it is comfortable and useful. The deep truth is that to be a real ritual, a practice has to act out a "mythic" (read "midrashic") script—otherwise, it's just a habit, even if it is a habit we love and revere.

Use this simple test: If you can't tell the story you are reenacting, then it is just a custom—what we've previously labeled Marrano practices. We have a lot of Jewish practices which are actually only customs. This week I lit a *yahrzeit* candle for my father. It felt right. I can attribute a lot of meaning to it—but I have no idea why I did it. I did it because I knew it was a responsibility and because it felt right. I wish I knew the story of its meaning. Most candle ceremonies are like that. However, the good news is, just as rituals can lose their stories, the wonder of the Jewish experience is that customs can grow new meanings—often more than one. Like salamanders, many Jewish rituals have lost, then regrown, many tales. (Sorry, the pun was irresistible.) Hanukkah and its practices are like that.

101

Think of rock concerts. Recently, I've been going to a few with my fifteen-year-old former students. (They invite me so their parents will let them go. I am a willing conspirator to see shows that most of my friends are too old for—besides, the kids stand in line for the tickets.) The last couple of times, on the way in to the show, the kids have stripped my car of the couple of disposable lighters I keep in the cassette box in order to light my pipe. Waving burning lighters in the air has become as much of a rock concert ritual as headbanging. Once, and I can remember the Dylan concerts where it started (the "After the Flood" tour), it was a political expression of solidarity with hope for the future. It wasn't about softer, slower music—it was about a commitment to peace. Now, the politics are absent, and lighter waving fulfills an aesthetic need—it is just a pretty thing to do.

Originally, Hanukkah started out as a ceremony to bring back the sun—it was a winter solstice observance. Because it was getting darker and darker, night was getting longer and longer, and we thought that the sun might disappear forever, we lit torches and showed the sun the way to return. Darkness is a mythic place. We all have our own "night terrors." That is the beginning of the solstice story, the fear that night will last forever. When we face that fear, we find another truth—the rest of the story. We remember that the "darkest hour is just before the dawn," and that we have to "rage against the coming night," and that "it is better to light one candle than to curse the darkness." These are truths that we all know, they are stories that we live from the inside out. That is the true foundation of Hanukkah. It is also why I lit a candle to confront the darkness around my dead father—even if I didn't know the full story.

From that *ner tamid*, that inner, primal sense of light, the Hashmonim found the courage to light their commitment. Then, when that story was passed to the Talmudic rabbis, they used the Maccabees' flame to kindle the lamp of God's miracles—their version of the *hanukkiyah*. By the time the flame gets to America, the torch is in Emma Lazarus' hands, a light unto all nations. It is a truth that grows and changes. That is the lesson we need to learn.

For a long time, Hanukkah has worked because it is so easy. Just light the *hanukkiyah* and the flames speak directly to our souls, the way that ocean waves do too. Flames are like that. The message that Hanukkah has fulfilled for us is not the intended message that "God does miracles" but the important understanding that "we can be proud to be Jews." As I have said before, Hanukkah has become our havdalah ceremony. The scary part of this story is that the differences (as we have noted) are disappearing. Unless Hanukkah speaks with its own loud and powerful message—it and everything that stands behind it will disappear. We need powerful, original, mythic answers to these questions (and others):

Why do we give Hanukkah gifts?

Why do we send Hanukkah cards?

Why do we gather in large groups to light our *hanukkiyot*?

These are all-new American practices—they need all-new explanations. We need to extend the Hanukkah story to cover them. Otherwise we'll all know, deep in our hearts, that our holiday is nothing more than a second-rate imitation of the Christmas celebration. (Let's face it, now that gifts have been given on Hanukkah, they are never going to be taken back—no one wants to be that much of a Scrooge!) So, our choice is to tell new stories about Hanukkah, to find inside our hearts the midrashim which make gifts and cards and the rest into Jewish truths. We know we can do it—because we have done it before. Get it?

All of this history and psychology boils down to this one simple practice—that of telling stories. When you are busy with your Hanukkah galas, in between the *latke* frying and the cleaning up of melted wax—tell stories about Hanukkah as it was, as it is, and as it will be. Some of these stories can be ones you have read and heard, but don't be afraid to grow them on your own. That is what Jews have always done. When you start in darkness—the light will come.

I know this is hard. I wish I could tell you what stories to tell. I don't know if:

a. When the Maccabee soldiers came home from the war, they brought all their children gifts, so that everyone could remember the reason they had gone to war to begin with. At Hanukkah, we are like Maccabean soldiers returning home victoriously and celebrating with our real miracles—our families.

b. After the Temple was retaken, the Maccabees reinstituted the practice of giving gifts to support the Temple, the one which had started with Moses and the Jews in the wilderness. The people were so generous that the Maccabees had much more than they needed. They sent much of the

103

money back so that families celebrated in the little sanctuaries of their homes—they turned the money, the "gelt," into gifts for their kids.

c. During the four years of the Maccabean War, no one could celebrate birthdays. (Or perhaps for the years preceding the war, Antiochus had banned birthday presents along with Shabbat and circumcision). Every parent promised their children twice the birthdays when the war was over. That first year the kids loved the eight presents—and made their parents promise that they would do it every year.

This much I do know—that the right stories will only be found in the laboratory of family practice. They are nothing I can create at my word processor. No matter how carefully reasoned and rehearsed, they will never feel true 'til they pour from a parent's heart and are confirmed by their children's widening eyes. I wish I could tell you what stories must be told—I can't. I just don't know. I only know that you have them somewhere inside you. This I can confirm: There is a light within you. That is Ḥanukkah's deepest, most basic message.

The Second Ending

About a month after I first wrote this essay, I came upon a better ending. I still don't think it is the right one, but it is much closer. It may be a starting point.

In 1966 a professor at UCLA, Maulana Karenga, synthesized a new African-American winter solstice holiday, *Kwanzaa. Kwanzaa* is a seven-day "harvest" holiday. It is celebrated by lighting one more candle each of the nights on a seven-branched candelabrum—three red, three green, and one black. Each day is devoted to a different theme—harvesting "values" rather than fruits.

It is easy to see the roots of this harvest festival in Sukkot (or in the common archetypal human heritage which was the origin of Sukkot) and in Christmas and in Ḥanukkah. If you have to sit down and think up rather than slowly evolve a holiday to facilitate ethnic development, this is a pretty good one.

Now here is the interesting point. As I was sharing this manuscript, Linda Kantor, the founder of Myriam's Dream, told me that more and more people are beginning to evolve a theme-of-the-day Ḥanukkah ritual. She was interested in that one night was usually *"tzedakah"* night. When she said it, I remembered a family in my friend Ron Wolfson's book *The Art of Jewish Living: Ḥanukkah*. They had a theme-of-the-night Ḥanukkah ritual which included an "earthquake preparedness gift" night, and a shoe night. When I saw a different list in Susan Abel Lieberman's *New Traditions*, I knew I was onto something. Her cycle was (1) big-gift night, (2) mommy night, (3) daddy night, (4) poem night, (5) small-gift night, (6) gift-of-self night, (7) giving night—their tzedakah evening, and (8) word night. Then, my friend Carol added in, "I used to take Rob and Geoff to the toy store, have them pick out something they really wanted, and then give it to some organization which would get it to Jewish children in need." When I saw the confluence, I got a flash....

> Try this Hanukkah story: After the good old Maccabees found the little jar of oil and lit the candelabrum, rather than just standing around with their hands in their pockets, they decided to organize a celebration. They said, "We will light an internal light—and hope that God will match it." Each day they centered the celebration on a different wish. They dedicated each day to renewing another important value, just as they had cleaned and renewed the sanctuary. As part of these celebrations they gave gifts to each other, to their children, and to those in need. After eight days of family, community, and commitment—the new oil arrived and the rededication celebration was over.

Now for your homework assignment. Look into your heart and discover the eight themes which were used for this first celebration. Get it?

17 Begin Your Passover Seder in the Kitchen and Finish the Second Half of the Seder for the Adults

It is important to actively involve children in the Passover Seder and make it speak to them. It is equally important that a Seder have an adult level which speaks to adult needs.

Here is another *Talmud 2000* debate:

One school says: "Passover should be for children. The Seder should be designed to hold their interest. If they get bored, the whole thing is pointless. Adults enjoy a Seder vicariously through the children's eyes."

One school says: "Seder should be an adult experience in which we make a place for children. We are the ones who need to learn from the Seder in order to effectively teach our children. A Seder experience is a model enacted by and for adults."

In the real Talmud they ask, "How long can a Seder be?" The famous answer is that Akiva and his friends once ran an all-nighter, a Seder which lasted till dawn. Our *Talmud 2000* question is: "How short can a Seder be (and still be legit)? After all, the *real* four questions are: "How much longer?" "Do we have to read it all?" "When do we eat?" and "You don't really expect to finish this whole thing, do you?"

We can already project part of this conversation in advance. The best answer is "Yes! We want it all. We want it both ways. We have two feelings about ambivalence! We want our Seder to play in Peoria, actively involving kids, and to be a meaningful experience for adults." If we know that is the best answer, let's talk pragmatics rather than philosophy.

I steal many of my best ideas from Cherie Koller-Fox. I always give her credit, I just write them down and publish them, which is something she just about never gets around to doing. She is one of my true inspirations—but even the nice things I write about her won't quell her justifiable anger at my sharing this secret before she can write it down. I am sorry about what I guess will be her hurt—but this is something I think you need to know.

Cherie teaches: "The best Seders begin in the kitchen, especially if you have young children." Cherie's vision is that you should make the things you need in the Seder with them, rehearsing the stories and the explanations as the egg is boiled, the parsley is spread out, the _haroset_ is food-processed, and the *maror* is tested. This informal telling and hands-on preparation turns the actual Seder service into a well rehearsed and anticipated performance.

I love this idea, and I hope one day she will write and I will publish the *Kitchen Seder*. I think she is absolutely right. I have added it to my "Doing Seder with kids" recommendations that the Torah Aura Productions Family has adopted for our adults-only Seder (of all over-age kids).

1. The wisdom of David and Shira Elcott: Have the Seder service on the living room floor on pillows, sofas and cushions. Turn the coffee table into the Seder table. Go into the dining room only when you are ready to eat.

2. Dorothy Grishaver: Make little Seder plates like at a model Seder so that everyone has one with everything on it already. It makes things go quicker and cuts down on the spills.

3. Jerry (ל"ז) and Sally Weber: Assign people to do things at the Seder in advance. Give Seder homework and make it very creative and participatory.

4. Cherie and Everett Fox: Turn the *karpas* part of the Seder into a big vegetable and dip appetizer thing. It fits with the traditional rhythm of the Seder, and takes the "hunger edge" off, giving you more time to do the service.

5. I will admit that I am less than convinced by the Conventional Wisdom perpetrated by the photocopy industry that the only meaningful kind of Seder is one that is cut and pasted from many sources into an amalgam of creativity. I don't oppose them—I just dislike the tyranny of the sense of obligation to have to write one. I think that a Storytelling Seder, a Question and Answer Seder, and even a Quiz Seder offer lots of opportunities. The real wisdom belongs to my friend, teacher, occasional coauthor, and mentor Ron Wolfson, who teaches: "The more you know about the Seder, the better able you are to make it work. You should learn something new about the Haggadah every year." Ron's Passover book, *The Art of Jewish Living: The Passover Seder*, is a great place to learn that one new thing for quite a number of years.

But, I think Cherie's plan is important in a whole other way—it contributes to Jewish survival by teaching hands-on Passover skills. A long time ago I wrote a draft of the *Ner Tamid* Award for the Boy Scouts of America. I don't know what happened to that material, but sometimes I try to fantasize what would happen if we had a real Jewish scouting movement. My father was a merit badge inspector when I was little. He specialized in "survival skills." When I was five and six I used to hear him test all these giant fourteen- and fifteen-year-olds on how to make a fire with wet matches and how to turn a blanket into a tent in a hurricane. Sometimes I fantasize equivalent Jewish survival skills, including Jewish knot-tying for *tzitziot*, the fringes on a tallit. Here are my top five Jewish Survival Merit Badges—the things which, if every Jew could still do them for him/herself, would put the Jewish people in much better shape.

Basic Jewish Merit Badges:

- Making a Friday night Shabbat dinner—both the food and the ritual.

- Leading Jewish services: morning, evening, afternoon, and Shabbat (Just being able to participate isn't good enough).

- Doing the Hanukkah routine: foods, ritual, stories, and gifts.

- Making and leading a Passover Seder.

- Reading Torah—not just learning one small portion from a tape, but having the skills to learn to read any portion.

When I play with my list, I have second-tier mitzvot like blowing a shofar, building a sukkah, and "bensching" etrog and *lulav*—and I have some non-traditional mitzvot like writing synagogue bylaws and running a fund-raising campaign. To be authentic, a real Jewish scouting movement would have to pass the test of owning the skills to keep Judaism alive when the *Minnow* is lost and they are castaway on a desert isle—or better yet, left in the wilderness for 40 years.

For Extra Credit: Design your own collection of Jewish Merit Badges. Then, write the manual and make sure that everyone in your family has earned each of them. It would be even better if you did this in a *havurah*. And, it would be beyond my expectations—and renew my faith in the universe—if some synagogue made it a bar/bat mitzvah requirement (rather than just a museum visit to 13 mitzvot). What a radical idea—the average (non-Orthodox) Jew having the capacity to live a competent Jewish life on her or his own! If you want to subscribe to this mad vision, the kitchen before Seder is a wonderful place to begin.

Regardless of your list's makeup, we all know that making Passover needs to be somewhere near the top.

So far we've talked about the need for Seder to work for kids—now we're going to focus on the other side of the equation, the adults. It is true that the adults at the table will "get off" on the kids' involvement—we love seeing and hearing the four questions mastered and the *afikomen* found. But it is equally true that we all feel a little childish in our understanding of Passover and most other Jewish experiences, and need to have some "adult" time on the task. (Too many of us last learned new Jewish stuff for our bar or bat mitzvah service.) The good news, the opportunity, is that the post-dinner part of the Seder is a perfect adult time. Once you do the Elijah thing—let the kids wander off if they want to. Use the last few pages of the Haggadah as adult time—call the kids back for the last bit of wine and the "Had Gad-ya" songfest. If you're having a good time, they'll love to join. If you know from family dinner parties, you're used to their running around during the post-dinner pre-dessert conversation—just file this under the same rubric.

Here is one of those unspoken truths. Finishing the Seder is an acid test of Jewish adequacy. If you don't get to the end, if you stop with the dinner, you know that you are just "getting by"—your Seder may be "good enough" but it won't approach "good." Even if you rush it, and don't do much, there is a symbolic victory in finishing the whole thing. It also gives you great adult time.

Joel's Thirteenth Law: Anytime your family goes back to the table and finishes the second half of the Seder, the after-dinner part, add 36 bonus points to your score.

18 Take the Matzah Challenge

Make a big deal out of "keeping Pesa<u>h</u>" all week. Make meeting the matzah-only challenge into a major accomplishment.

My twelfth Passover, which fell in sixth grade, was the first time I was ever allowed to take the MTA and go downtown by myself—actually Burton Rosenthal and I were allowed to go to the movies downtown, together. It was Passover, spring vacation, and a couple of days before my twelfth birthday. We carried sack lunches and plastic bags full of authorized Passover snacks. I was a dedicated "Reform" Jew but Burton was "Seriously Conservative"—two-sets-of-dishes-for-everyday Conservative. It was a horrifying experience.

In the morning we saw Joan Crawford in *Straitjacket*, the story of the Lizzie Borden axe murders. In the afternoon we saw Alfred Hitchcock's *Charade*—it was Cary Grant cool. We had the best time. We were proud of eating our sack lunches in the Boston Common.

We devoured all the snacks in our plastic bags and loved the movies. We were lost in the horror. On the way back to the MTA, we stopped and bought a slice of pizza each, continuing to talk about axe-murders and killing people by drowning them in claw-foot bathtubs and so on. Only when we got off the streetcar and started down Commonwealth Avenue in opposite directions towards our homes did the meaning of the pizza hit me. I shouted down the street to Burton, who was fading into the darkness in the other direction, that the pizza had messed up Passover for both of us—we hung our heads and staggered to our own homes.

Since that day, I've never talked about that moment with anyone. Burton and I buried it and never discussed it. It isn't so much guilt I feel about the moment—but a sense of failure. It wasn't that my parents would punish me. It isn't that I thought that God would hold it against me—it is just one of the two times in my life that I have failed the "Passover Matzah Marathon." It was myself that I had let down.

In the Mishnah there is a debate over how to say the Shema, though it is really a debate over the role Jewish ritual plays in our lives.

This is the debate:

One side (**Bet Shammaite**—Shammai's Gang) says: "A person should stand up every morning and recite the Shema, and a person should lie down every night, and say the Shema—because it says in the Torah to recite the words of the Shema 'when you lie down and when you rise up.'"

The other side (**Bet Hillel**—Hillel's Posse) says: "Wrong! You just have to say the Shema in the morning—the time when people get up. You just have to say the Shema in the evening—the time when people go to bed. Don't take the Torah so literally—it's teaching timing, not posture."

Then a **Bet Shammai** says: "Let me tell you a story. Once I was on a road trip. At sundown I followed the rules and laid down on the side of the road and said the Shema. I almost died. Some highwaymen attacked me when I was down."

The **Bet Hillel** Crew responded: "You deserved to die for your stupid, narrow-minded literal interpretation of the Torah."

This is what it means:

Bet Shammai thinks that Jewish ritual should stop ordinary life. You have to suspend what you are normally doing and change your posture—shifting into a Jewish ritual mode.

112

Bet Hillel thinks that Jewish ritual and ordinary life are "confluent"—they flow together. Most of the time you can work your Jewish stuff into your ordinary life. In other words, you could keep on hiking and recite the evening Shema as you move.

In other words, *Bet Shammai* wants "all or nothing" Jews. To follow *Bet Shammai*, Judaism gets to eat big chunks out of your life. To follow their wisdom (which in some ways is much easier—because there is one right way) you have to stop walking, lie down, and be Jewish. We are *Bet Hillel* Jews— we want it both ways. That is harder, because we are constantly looking for the right blend—walk too fast and you lose what the Shema is supposed to be.

The matzah challenge is good, because it gives you a Jewish accomplishment in your life. It's easy to do with kids—just think of all the charts on which you can paste gold stars. But, the matzah challenge is also good because it teaches us the *Bet Hillel* lesson. If you manage to get through a whole week—going to all the ordinary places you need to go, doing all the things you need to do—and bread (*hametz*) has not crossed your lips, you've proved that ordinary life and being a Jew can go together—that neither has to lose. That's a good annual lesson for you—and a great one for your kids. (Someone else can give you the recipes for *kosher l'Pesah* bagels which my mother used to make to get me through—you already know about my culinary expertise.)

That very night, my parents gave me my twelfth birthday present a few days early. It was an RCA transistor radio. A little thing for its day—it was about 10 inches long and weighed a couple of pounds. I fell asleep with the earphone in listening to Arnie the Woo-Woo Ginsberg play oldies. In the middle of the night I rolled over and the earphone wire pulled the radio off the shelf. It hit me in the middle of the back of my neck. I jumped up and dug my fingernails into the ceiling. I thought Lizzie Borden was after me with her axe. I spent that night sleeping between my parents—they couldn't get me out of their bed. Two days later I started having stomach pains. Two days after that my appendix exploded on the operating table as they were taking it out. I never believed that God was actually punishing me— because I don't believe in that kind of God—but I've often wondered what was in the pizza that caused the nightmare and the pain.

19 | Wear Canvas Sneakers on Yom Kippur

Through the absurd folk tradition of wearing canvas sneakers on Yom Kippur (thus avoiding leather) an important ethical lesson about priorities can be acquired.

A few years ago, I was at a break fast (the meal after Yom Kippur—not the thing with pancakes) where a woman said: "This year I didn't go to synagogue on Yom Kippur; I stayed home, called all my friends on the phone, and asked their forgiveness for the things I had done wrong."

There was silence for almost a minute. We were all quite puzzled. We were wondering, was this strange act of religious improvisation—this back-door violation of Yom Kippur in order to adhere to the essence of the holiday—a good or bad thing? Out of the silence somebody eventually asked, "Was anybody home?" I hadn't thought of that question—maybe I'm not naive enough to believe that everyone goes to shul.

The woman said, "No one was home—I talked to their answering machines!" The drummer in my brain sounded a rimshot—*b'dumb-bah!*

Our big question—a question for our New Age Talmud, *Talmud 2000*:

> **Does staying home on Yom Kippur, not going to services, (we'll assume fasting) and calling your friends on the phone to ask their forgiveness fulfill the Jewish obligation to observe Yom Kippur (to quote the Torah, "as a day of solemn assembly")?**

114

Does asking forgiveness from answering machines improve or degrade the process?

Isn't this just like the kid in *School Ties* who doesn't make the Sandy Koufax gesture, plays in the big football game on Yom Kippur, and then goes into the school chapel to say his prayers later that night—the night after Yom Kippur is over?

We'll collect your answers to these questions at the end of the chapter.

I wear yellow Converse high-top sneakers every Yom Kippur and I have been doing so for years.

> It is a custom not to wear leather shoes on Yom Kippur. It grows from a passage in Leviticus 23.27, the same one which gives us fasting. There it tells us to fast and afflict our souls. In the Talmudic tractate *Yoma* (11a), the list is expanded from fasting to include: not eating, not drinking, not bathing, not anointing ourselves with oil, not wearing leather shoes, and not having "conjugal relations." In other words, leather shoes were considered one of life's great pleasures.

I started wearing my yellow Converse high-tops as a hippie kind of thing. They look great with a grey suit. It was an act of authentic rebellion about which no one could complain. I used to get to give all kinds of sermons about my yellow high-tops—people would ask and I would teach:

> This is a story about a Hasidic rebbe: Once he auditioned two cantors to sing the High Holiday liturgy. One of them cried and moaned when he sang the prayers—and you could hear regret and suffering in every word. The other sang with great joy—you smiled with every phrase. When the rebbe picked the joyful cantor, everyone was upset. They said, "The High Holidays are solemn, you are not showing proper respect. You picked the wrong cantor. This is Yom Kippur, not Purim; we are supposed to be sad and mournful."

> As Hasidic rebbes do, this one said: "Let me tell you a story. Once there was a monarch who needed someone to sweep the royal floor. The monarch auditioned two janitors. One cried and sobbed when sweeping the floor—the other 'whistled while he worked' (and smiled a lot, too). The ruler chose sweeper number two, explaining, 'It gives me joy to see my chambers cleaned with such joy.'"

> Said the rebbe: "God feels that way, too. Repentance is a holy act. On Yom Kippur we sweep the sins out of God's chambers. It is holy work. There is joy in doing holy work, even if it is serious."

115

I think God finds joy in my yellow Converse sneakers. Even if God doesn't, I smile and find an inner joy which empowers my sweeping. I could have bought a black pair which would have fulfilled the "no leather" tradition and been discreet—but something spiritual would be missing.

> For six years now, I have led children's services at Valley Beth Shalom in Encino, California in my yellow high-tops—and I have told the story above, and other stories. Two years ago, a 13-year-old named Ethan walked up to me on Rosh ha-Shanah and asked: "Is Yom Kippur or Rosh ha-Shanah the holiday where we don't wear leather?"
>
> I told him, "Yom Kippur."
>
> He then said, "Great, I've got this radical pair of skateboarding shoes I want to wear with my bar mitzvah suit."
>
> I said, "If you mother doesn't believe you, tell her to call me. I'll confirm that wearing your Vans is a Jewish thing to do."

Question: If you were Ethan's parents, would you let him embarrass you by wearing neon sneakers with his suit on Yom Kippur? Or, would you be thrilled by the rebellion and his question? Which is the better Jewish response?

Last year my sneakers took on a different meaning. I wore the purple ones. (The color change was an inner, non-intellectual thing—connected to *When I Am Old, I Will Wear Purple*...and some other things). The color change wasn't the big issue.

> On Wednesday night, April 29th of last year, I watched on television and saw a picture from a helicopter which was hovering over my building showing the whole world pictures of a Footlocker store which was burning 12 floors below me. It was the beginning of the L.A. riots.
>
> The next day, on my way to the airport to make a speaking engagement, I got caught in the burning down and looting of a Fedco store. I wasn't scared. No one was the slightest bit threatening. It was too much of a party. Lots of people were stealing things, lots more people were cheering the thefts as an act of equal justice. It wasn't as much rage as it was celebration.
>
> It was then that I realized that the L.A. riots were about hunger, the wrong kind of hunger. Not a protein deficiency (though that is there,

too), but the need for $168 tennis sneakers—The Pump. It was a world of $408-a-month welfare checks—fulfilling its perceived need for $168 sneakers—Magic Shoes. It was the dark side of *Dallas* and *Dynasty*—too many desires delayed too long.

This year, my sneakers were an act of spiritual cleansing, a return to a simpler childhood where a T-shirt, a pair of jeans, and a pair of gym shoes were a functional, durable covering of my nakedness, not an accomplishment. They were a reminder to me that all desires are not needs—they pointed me towards my real hunger.

Right now, they are rebuilding the Footlocker store and I am slowly rebuilding my own sense of what is valuable and what is possible. The purple sneakers felt right. It was not a year for dress black, but I also couldn't go back to the yellow.

So here is the big question: Can you leave your petition of forgiveness at the sound of the tone? *Press 1* to atone for gluttony. *Press 2* if sloth is your sin. *Press 3* for lust...

Joel's Fourteenth Law: It is better to individualize your participation in Jewish communal practice than to practice Judaism as an individual.

In other words, let the kid wear the sneakers, and don't stay home and leave messages.

20 Sleep Out in a Sukkah at Least Once in Your Life

When you kids are young, spend at least one night (once) in a sukkah with them. If you don't have a sukkah, borrow one.

Joel's Fifteenth Law: Said in the name of Harlene Appelman: Never pass up a chance to combine a Jewish opportunity with something you ordinarily think is cool.

Havdalah is a cool ceremony. You have to wait for three stars to appear in the sky, then you light this great flickering candle, smell the spices, and drink some wine. But it is even better when you make havdalah at the planetarium after everyone has had a chance to look through a telescope, first. It is a great way to find three stars. That was Harlene's lesson.

Every father and mother looks forward to the day when each of their children is toilet trained. Let's face it, it's not publicly on the same scale as bar/bat mitzvah or a wedding, but it is a major opportunity to say *She-he-heyanu*. Only Harlene would find the Jewish side to toilet-training; she was the one who noted that Orthodox Jews give their sons their first pair of *tzitziot* as an incentive and as a reward for using the toilet. She uses it as a paradigm for a teachable moment.

Little boys often like the idea of lice and snakes and spiders. They often like the idea better than the reality—lice shampoo is no fun. The truth is, lice are everywhere. Every school, rich, poor, day school, or Country Day School has trouble with lice. But, if you send your child to a Jewish day school, lice is a double plague. Jewish mothers tend to think that lice are the stigmata of poverty. They forget that Irish setters and horseback riding are often the source. They blame it on *kippot* (ritual head coverings). Shared *kippot* may share the opportunity to experience lice shampoo, but they do not create it. Only Harlene would figure out that Passover was the perfect time to give Jewish parents the 800 number of a Lice Hot Line—teaching them that we are not alone.

This is the Torah of Harlene Appelman, her special insight into the Jewish cosmos. Harlene is a Jewish family educator *par excellence* who has developed all kinds of wondrous Jewish family events and activities. Harlene has an innate sense for what my teacher Dr. Bill Cutter made his five-year obsession, "confluence." Confluence is a big word which means "flowing together." Harlene is like one of those acupuncture specialists with their maps of the body and all its force lines. Time after time she finds the precise place where the richness of the Jewish tradition and the joys of growing up (American) meet. I've tried hard to internalize her vision and acquire her radar system. The sukkah is one of those places I've extrapolated on my own.

> Let's start with the vision. You know this scene: The kids take a couple of old blankets, and build a tent in the backyard. Then they run a couple of extension cords out to the makeshift tent, bring a light and a portable TV set and experience their first time "sleeping under the stars." We've all seen Dennis and Tommy do it—though I doubt that they said *she-he-heyanu.*

The sukkah is rooted in that kind of backyard camping spirit. The mitzvah is called *Ley-shev ba-Sukkah* "dwelling in the sukkah;" but conventional Jewish practice has converted that into food. When we "dwell" in the sukkah, we revive the sukkot that the Israelites camped in for forty years in the wilderness, we recreate the sukkot that Israelite farmers built alongside their fields to camp out in during the harvests, and we reexperience the sukkot which served as motels when all the Jewish people came up together to celebrate Sukkot in the Temple in Jerusalem. The *brakhah* says "dwell in the sukkah" and we generally fulfill it by eating our meals in there. Sleeping is considered a "nice" option, but having dinner under the electric light bulb that is plugged in inside the house is the essential way of making Sukkot actual.

119

The original *Invaders from Mars* was a 1953 cult film which dealt with the idea of "the enemy within." Like *Invasion of the Body Snatchers*, it dealt with the terror that Communists were hiding everywhere. When it was remade in 1986 with Karen Black and her son, Hunter Carson, it had less meaning. It isn't even worth renting the video unless science fiction B-movies are your thing. But there is this scene at the beginning where Timothy Bottoms (the Dad) and Hunter Carson (the Kid) are lying on their backs looking at the stars. The camera starts directly above them and we see them lying on benches, talking about constellations and stuff, and as we zoom in to the patio, the session ends in a tickling match. Then Mom brings the boys some hot chocolate. The movie isn't worth seeing unless you catch it on the Sunday Movie Special and nothing else is on, but this scene is quintessential Sukkot.

So is my unofficial taxonomy of Sukkot opportunities.

Maximum: Building you own sukkah, eating out in it regularly during the eight days of Sukkot, and sleeping out in it once or twice—along with at least one good sukkah party—is pretty close to the maximum. Oh yeah, Sukkot services should be included, too.

Minimum: Helping to decorate a sukkah (even if it is not yours) and eating out in a sukkah (which isn't yours) at least once forms a sort of minimalist Sukkot platform.

Place your Sukkot adventure somewhere in between.

Some Other Sukkot Opportunities

1. My friend Carol Starin taught me in the name of her teacher, Rabbi Ira Stone, that Sukkot is a wonderful decorating opportunity, that one can express all one's desires for tinsel, little flashing colored lights, and threading and hanging things through the sukkah. The number of Sukkot arts and crafts projects is infinite.

2. Carol also teaches that a sukkah is the perfect place to stage an obligations party. I didn't know what that was before she explained, but she assured me that you would. She condemned me for not being a housewife.

3. More than twenty years ago, the last time that ecology was big, I was teaching a fifth grade Hebrew School class in Lexington, Massachusetts.

We built a class sukkah as part of a hands-on historical project. When we talked about how to decorate it, the kids came up with the idea of *objet trouvé* (found junk). Rather than fruit and vegetables, our sukkah was hung with a rusted muffler, old cans shaped into decorations—and a lot of stuff like that. It was really striking, beautiful in a funky sort of way. Sukkot offers a lot of meaningful ecological, "Save the Planet" moments as well.

4. Then there is the X-rated sukkah. Anthropologists suggest that the sukkah probably started out as a consummation booth where couples demonstrated to the gods how to fertilize their fields before the winter rains. After the kids go to bed, consider reliving that piece of sukkah history. Even if you don't actually do it, enjoy that sukkah fantasy. All things that are good for the Jewish people are not "G-rated." There are adult lessons too. Put that in your sukkah and enjoy it. It could give *Ley-shev ba-Sukkah* a whole new meaning.

21 Keep Your Kids out of School on Jewish Holidays

The ultimate reinforcement of the idea that Jews are different (not better) than others is (1) keeping your kids out of school on Jewish holidays, (2) creating really positive holiday experiences on those days, and (3) then insisting that they do all the make-up work.

This is the suggestion which will separate the adults from the children. Let's start it with a *Talmud 2000* question:

On which Jewish holidays should a Jewish child be kept out of school? Is it different for elementary, junior high school, or senior high school students? What obligations go with keeping your child out of school?

Look at it this way. Which of these are good enough reasons to let your child take a day off from school?

a. Yom Kippur
b. A chance to be a one-day extra in *Home Alone III*
c. First day Passover
d. A family vacation to Hawaii which has to be tagged on to one of Mom's business trips
e. First day Sukkot
f. Flying down to Miami in order to go the Super Bowl
g. Grandpa's funeral

h. A chance to meet the President of the United States

i. A test for which s/he is not ready or a paper due which was not finished

j. An orthodontist's appointment

k. A chance to join an archeological excavation

l. The day that long-lost relatives from Riga fly into the United States

m. The child's birthday

n. Shavuot

o. A two-week trip to Israel

p. Hanukkah

q. To stand in line to get U2 tickets

r. As a protest over homophobia on the school board

s. The day before the bar/bat mitzvah

t. To see the opening of Malcolm X (per Spike Lee's invitation)

u. Purim

v. The last day of Passover

w. To go with you to a Renoir exhibit

x. Because s/he was up all night reading *The Hobbit* and really wants to finish it

y. Israeli Independence Day

z. Rosh ha-Shanah

I can't predict what your values are—but I had a good time with the list. I was surprised that I felt warmly towards staying home to read *The Hobbit*. Writing the list taught me a lot about my values. Interestingly, all of them are real reasons that I know families have used for letting their kids miss school.

> I had given a Hebrew quiz. Everyone in the room had failed it because not one of them had bothered to study. Andy then complained, when I made my nasty comment, that he didn't have time to study because of some science test. I remarked that it would only have taken fifteen minutes. He shrugged. Then I explained that as far as I was concerned, Hebrew school was more important than science, because here you learned the important things like ethics and the meaning of life. He laughed—not sarcastically—but with appreciation if not agreement. He muttered under his breath that he bet his parents wouldn't agree.

We keep our kids out of school for all kinds of reasons. The dark truth that we almost never admit is that except for reading and basic calculations, almost nothing learned in elementary school is of value—except a commitment to learning. The Jewish tradition wants up to 13 days a year—depending on when the holidays fall and your choice between Reform and Conservative practice.

a. 2 days of Rosh ha-Shanah
b. 1 day of Yom Kippur
c. 4 days of Sukkot (2 at the beginning and 2 at the end)
d. 4 days of Passover (ditto)
e. 2 days of Shavuot

The truth is, it's not obsessive, though it is a little challenging.

> I had it easy, and I know that we cannot generalize from my experience. I grew up in a school system where 90% of the kids in my grade were Jewish and almost all of them went to an intensive and demanding Conservative synagogue which was directly across the street from the public school. My town kept the elementary school open on Jewish holidays—but had to run alternative programs. My grade used to shrink from 125 to under 20. I always stayed out on the first day of holidays and always went to temple with my mother. After services we almost always got to eat out at Howard Johnsons and I got to order a milkshake. The big deal for me was that I was the only kid who went back for the second days—because we were Reform.

> It wasn't until I wrote this book, some 30 years later, that I even questioned the reality that my father had gone to work on every Jewish holiday except Rosh ha-Shanah and Yom Kippur. It would have been nice if the holidays were all-day, whole-family affairs, but what I did have made a major impression.

Things are probably much harder in your neighborhood. Both the parents in your family probably work. Keeping your child out of school for Shavuot (the Jewish holiday no one has ever heard of) is a much more daring thing to do—but it could be worth it!

a. It will teach the lesson that Jews have some special and fun things to do—especially if you, your friends, and your synagogue come together to make holidays an amazing experience.

b. It will also teach (with all the make-up homework) that Jews aren't better, just different. For your child, being Jewish will be hard—and rewarding. That is just the lesson we want to teach.

A final question, a *Talmud 2000 issue*: If Andy came home and told you that his Hebrew School teacher had said that Hebrew School is more important than "real" school—what would you say? How about staying out of school to have a Kodak moment with Hulk Hogan? (I know kids who did it for the Ninja Turtles.) Compare that to a morning of singing and dancing with the Torah on Simhat Torah.

P.S. Day school parents don't be smug—you'll probably have to cope with this problem when your kids hit public high school.

A Jewish Home

22 | Become an Inveterate Mezuzah Kisser

If you have a mezuzah on your door and you kiss it (with feeling) every time you come home—you are building the perfect foundation for positive Jewish family life.

My colleague Perry London (ל״ז) use to give a wonderful talk in which he presented the *mezuzah* as the quintessential element in raising children with positive Jewish identities. His explanation goes something like this.

A family hangs a mezuzah on the door. The mezuzah is a public symbol which says that this is a Jewish home.

As parents walk into the house they always stop to kiss the mezuzah. They also make a point of kissing the mezuzot on the doors of their friends' houses.

Note: For those of you who are not veteran mezuzah kissers—this is the procedure. First, touch your hand to the mezuzah, then bring your hand to your lips and kiss it. This precisely how we also kiss the *Sefer Torah* when we parade with it around the synagogue. The idea is that we are bringing its message to our lips. Some inner meditation on the meaning of the mezuzah (or Torah) should accompany the gesture.

Note: Notice that just hanging the mezuzah on the door is not good enough. Just hanging it on the door fulfills the mitzvah, the obligation to have one—and it fulfills the folk-magic need to have an amulet to protect the family—and it fulfills the cultural need to identify your house as a Jewish home—and it fulfills a social obligation by allowing you to have a _Hanukkat ha-Bayit_ (a mezuzah-hanging party)—but for the mezuzah to work its real magic, you have to rub it with your hand, your mind, and your heart. In other words, it is the kiss which activates the mezuzah to do its job.

Soon, Perry points out, your child will imitate your gesture. Mezuzah kissing will be part of the way she comes home every day—mezuzah kissing will be part of the way he visits all his Jewish friends. In this way mezuzot become a whole category of perception. By the way, it is often fun to make kissing the mezuzah a physical challenge for a child, so that gaining the height and strength to leap and touch it is the Jewish equivalent of an early childhood slam-dunk. Until that happens, being lifted to reach it by a parent is a nice moment of Jewish-flavored physical connection.

The next phase begins when the child begins to ask questions. First he will want to know what the box is called. Later, she will probably ask, "Do we have to kiss it every time we come home?" or "What will happen if we don't kiss it?" The concrete always comes first. Eventually they will ask the parents, "Why are we doing this?" Then, one of the great teachable moments in your child's Jewish life has opened itself to you. You get to sit down on the doorstep, or in a comfortable chair, or at the dinner table, or at bedtime, or anywhere that works and feels comfortable, and explain the meaning of the mezuzah.

The mezuzah tells two stories. First, the mezuzah is a way of protecting our homes and our families.

In the Torah we learn that before their last night in Egypt, the Jews smeared the blood of a lamb on the doorposts of their houses—it was a signal to the angel of death that this was a Jewish home which should be "passed over" on the night of this last and most fearful plague. While there is not a direct textual connection, we have the sense that the mezuzah is our asking God to protect our homes.

On the outside of every mezuzah is a single Hebrew word—one of God's names: _Shaddai_. The rabbis turn this name into an anagram: _Shomer Delatot Yisrael_, Guardian of Israel's Doors. When we nail up a mezuzah and when we reconnect with it every time we enter, a sort of non-verbal prayer for protection is pointed in God's direction.

From this story the mezuzah teaches us a wonderful lesson, "The best way to protect our families from the outside world is to proudly and publicly proclaim our pride at being Jews." We are safe, not when we hide, but when we label our homes as Jewish places.

The second story of the mezuzah comes from a different place in the Torah, the part of the Shema which reads: "You should write them (words of Torah) on the doorposts of your house and upon your gates." It is part of the same paragraph which makes it a mitzvah for us to teach Torah "faithfully to our children." This is a biblical passage which has become a prayer and turned Torah teaching into an athletic event: The Sit, Walk, Lie, and Rise. Here is where the mitzvah of mezuzah is actually rooted. With the mezuzah we literally nail the words of the Shema (and symbolically with it, the whole Torah) to our front door. My teacher and friend and personal *sofer*, Dr. Eric Ray, explains it this way:

> "Today when we nail a mezuzah to the doorpost of our house, apartment, or condominium, we still want to protect the place where we live and show that it is a Jewish home. A Jewish house is a place where people have respect for all human beings. It is a place where human life is valued and where people believe in treating others with loving concern. It is a holy home, not just a noisy place where no one has feelings for anyone else. A mezuzah is a reminder that God is part of our family life."

> The second story of the mezuzah teaches us that we have to make our house into a Jewish home, creating and protecting the things it represents. That is a way of living Torah.

There are many other mezuzah stories—but these two are the starting point.

> Next, according to Perry, it's time to go "hands on." It is time to get a new mezuzah, open it up and look at the parchment. It is time to learn the *brakhot* and let your child nail it up on his or her bedroom door.

> **Joel's Sixteenth Law.** Never let a rabbi or a more learned Jew hang up your mezuzah for you. Instead, make them teach you how to do it for yourself. Never do it for children, rather give them the resources to do it for themselves.

It is important that you take the responsibility for making your home a place where God is one of your neighbors. It is important that your child actively defines her or his room as a Jewish place.

It isn't hard, you just have to read the rules about where it goes and which way it tilts—and learn two basic *brakhot* (both of which you almost know anyway.)

Here are the rules:

a. Face the door from the outside. Touch the right doorpost. That is the side where you hang the mezuzah.

b. Place the mezuzah about two-thirds of the way up the door with the top of the mezuzah tilted into the room. If the door is not wide enough, it can go straight up and down.

c. Officially, a mezuzah should go on every door in the house except for the bathrooms. In common American practice, most families only have them on the outside door. Consider each mezuzah you add an opportunity.

d. Traditionally, Jews have mezuzah hanging parties. They are called <u>H</u>anukkat ha-Bayit, a "House <u>H</u>anukkah" (a home dedication). Consider the possibilities.

Here are the two blessings:

בָּרוּךְ אַתָּה יְיָ אֱלֹהֵינוּ מֶלֶךְ הָעוֹלָם
אֲשֶׁר קִדְּשָׁנוּ בְּמִצְוֹתָיו וְצִוָּנוּ לִקְבֹּעַ מְזוּזָה.

Barukh Atah Adonai Eloheinu Melekh ha-Olam
Asher Kidshanu b'miTzvotav, v'Tzivanu liK'boa Mezuzah.

Praised are You, Adonai our God, Ruler of the cosmos
the One-Who-Made-Us-Holy through the mitzvot
and made it a *mitzvah* for us to fasten a mezuzah.

This is an easy *brakhah* to learn. Say the Friday night candle blessing, stop before the "*l'haDlik ner*" and add in "*liK'boah Mezuzah.*"

The second blessing is the *she-he-<u>He</u>-yanu*, the "good time" *brakhah* that we do on holidays and at important moments in our lives.

בָּרוּךְ אַתָּה יְיָ אֱלֹהֵינוּ מֶלֶךְ הָעוֹלָם שֶׁהֶחֱיָנוּ וְקִיְּמָנוּ וְהִגִּיעָנוּ לַזְּמַן הַזֶּה.

Barukh Atah Adonai, Eloheinu Melekh ha-Olam she-he-<u>He</u>yanu
v'Kiy'manu v'Hi-giyanu la-Z'man ha-Zeh.

Praised are You, Adonai our God, Ruler of the cosmos, Who keeps us alive, Who keeps us going, and Who helps us come to experience this very moment.

The mezuzah is a perfect example of how Jewish rituals should work. First we do them and grow from doing them. We do them because they work for us. Then, as a way of imitating us, our children will inherit the practice. Slowly the meaning and details of each ceremony can be revealed and mastered. That is Perry London's lesson and it works for Shabbat candles and kiddush and Seder and all of the others.

I have a second lesson to teach. In order for a mezuzah to work, we have to rub it. It isn't enough just to have one. We have to touch it, use it, and constantly give it new meaning. We have to talk to our mezuzah and reconnect constantly with its meaning, or talk to God through the reminder the mezuzah represents.

> **Joel's Seventeenth Law:** Don't just hang a mezuzah. In order for it to work its magic, you have to rub it the right way. The same is true of all Jewish objects in your home.

Other Applications of the Mezuzah Principle

1. Every Jewish home should be a Jewish museum; it should be filled with objects that tell all kinds of Jewish stories. In **Number 26: Collect Jewish Stuff** we'll talk about all the different categories of "Jewish stuff" which you can use to color and flavor your home. Here, however, are a couple of guidelines.

    Especially when your kids are young, it should be a Jewish *children's* museum. It should be filled with things they can touch and manipulate. These need not be complex: a Seder plate, a _hanukkiyah_, a havdalah set, a kiddush cup, candlesticks, a *tzedakah* box, a dreidel, a *grogger*, little plastic letters on the refrigerator, Mom's tallit, Dad's tallit and tefillin, a few kippot, etc. make a really good start. (I didn't include women's tefillin because my women friends are mixed on the issue). It need not be Chagall, Shalom of Safed, Agam, Vishniac, Bill Aron, or Ben Shahn. (To cross-reference effectively, these are the kinds of objects we're talking about being part of the Jewish survival trunk mentioned at the end of **Number 26**).

    Yes, you have the right to keep important and valuable things protected—but ritual objects should not just "be there." Like the mezuzah, there should be ways of letting them touch you, by your touching them.

Museums can be about "life" or about "death." Your collection can either tell the story of who we are, or of who we once were. Do not fill your house with the mummies and sarcophagi of former Jewish life—it should not be a memorial, but rather a source of access, like the kids' museums where kids get to walk a few feet in fireman's boots and practice sliding down the brass pole. Remember, Jewish life is enriched by Jewish play.

You are allowed to have your ancient relics—your exhibits under glass. I encourage a collection of ancient oil lamps or great Russian saltcellars. Every family should have its own "Precious Legacy" exhibit to pass on. The past is an important part of the present. But, if we keep some neo-romantic lower east side Jewish art painted on a shellacked copy of the *Jewish Forward* on the wall, it ought to be balanced with the clay *hanukkiyah* that Shane made in third grade that the family still lights every year.

Now here is a great rainy day activity. Actually turn your home into a Jewish museum. Take a tour. Train your children to be the docents and explain the "Jewish stuff" to visitors. Write an "exhibit card" for each item, telling its story, both personal and universal. It should explain what Shabbat candlesticks are—and tell the story of your Shabbat candlesticks. Almost every item has both stories.

Next, plan a multicultural event. Have a home museum opening. Think of it as a great party—or the wonderful beginning of a series of field trips that Erika's fifth grade public school class can take.

2. Think *Auntie Mame*. At the beginning, there is a great scene where Patrick is brought into a wild party, given a notebook, and told to write down every word or expression that he doesn't understand. We should imprint on that scene.

It is common knowledge that if we own a great dictionary and use it aggressively to look up unfamiliar words we encounter, we establish a great (secular) learning process. I have friends who keep a dictionary on the kitchen table (between the plant and the napkin holder) for just that reason. The kids use it regularly to look up words that come up during dinner conversations—and the family sometimes winds up in some great games of "Dictionary" as well. In his new book on the chaos of management, Tom Peters (the *Search for Excellence* guy) explains that his life was changed when he decided to buy a stand for his dictionary (like the ones in libraries) and leave it out. He explains that proximity is the issue. By leaving the dictionary out, he's come to use it almost every day, and manages to learn a lot. We should introduce Tom Peters to Rosalind Russell, and have our Jewish Patrick and Patricia write down all the "Jewish things" which they encounter and then look them up together in the *Encyclopedia Judaica* (or in an atlas—because the news will give us lots of Jewish places). You know, Tom's dictionary is to general learning as a mezuzah is to a Jewish home—it will open up worlds you never dreamed existed.

3. Say *brakhot*. The unincluded 41st chapter of this book, which will be the first one in the sequel, will urge you to learn and say one-line *brakhot*. One-line blessings are not only for bread, wine, or candles, but for hearing thunder, seeing a wise person, encountering good or bad news, etc. They teach some powerful lessons. They (1) make a spiritual impact—connecting God to lots of ordinary places in our lives, (2) make a Jewish statement—bring religion out of the synagogue or dining room and into the backyard and the playground, and (3) provide an extensive foundation for learning Hebrew, by bringing a lot of Hebrew words, phrases, and even sound patterns into the aural vocabulary of our children. Someday I need to write that essay.

23 Make Bedtimes Jewish

By reading Jewish stories and saying the Shema with your child at bedtime, your are opening the potential for a powerful spiritual connection.

In *The Official Guide to Being a Good Parent*, the one published by Conventional Wisdom Press, the basic rituals of bedtime are carefully defined. We learn there:

- That bedtime should be quality time.

- That bedtime is a wonderful opportunity to read to your children.

- That bedtime is a moment when important conversations can best take place (though they will not happen every night, nor even most nights).

- That bedtime is a time for physical closeness.

- That (if you happen to be religious, and most people we know—except for Jews—happen to be) bedtime is a wonderful opportunity to share a prayer experience with your child.

However, if you are the kind of concerned parent who reads on, what you find in the small print is a lot of warnings. These were included to exempt the designer and the manufacturer from any liability. Go ahead and tell yourself that you can laugh—until they happen to you! The small print goes something like this:

- Warning! Night can also be a very scary time for children. It is sometimes hard for them to be left alone. The dark and the shadows can bring on many fears.
- If a child doesn't sleep the whole night through...
- If your child wets his/her bed...
- If your child refuses to go to bed...
- If your child refuses to sleep alone...
- If your child has trouble falling asleep...

Sound familiar? They should, because familiar is exactly what they are—part of what comes with being a family.

It is very simple to make bedtime Jewish. It is a bit harder to make bedtime profoundly Jewish. In the course of this chapter we'll talk about the difference. If you've bought *The Authorized Jewish Supplement* to *The Official Guide to Being a Good Parent*, you will find the following "bolt-on" additions which Judify (make Jewish) the generic set of good bedtime practices. They tell you precisely how to make bedtime Jewish—and in my self-important opinion, they are not bad.

- Follow all conventional good bedtime practices. All you need to do is add some Jewish "content" and some Jewish feelings.
- To do that, make sure that some of the stories you read or tell are Jewish stories.
  Know that Shabbat is a perfect time to always read a Jewish story, but it would be better if it wasn't the only time.
- It would also be really nice if Bible stories were part of the mix. Bedtime is the best place to first add Torah images to your dreams.
- Make the Shema (and perhaps an English prayer of your choosing) part of the everynight bedtime ritual. My parents were big on "Now I lay me down to sleep..." If it is your style, improvisational prayers, too, add something important to the mix.
- And, finally, be prepared to have some bedtime conversations focus on things Jewish. Every now and then, it will be something your child will want to talk about.

136

Don't Panic! When in doubt, the answer, "I don't know!" "I'm not sure!" or "I wonder about that too!" will serve to put the conversation on "pause" till you can regroup, rethink, or ask for help.

Now come on, you've got to admit that none of this is too hard. To do Jewish bedtime, all you have to do is blend in with the kisses, glasses of water, tucked in covers, tousled hair, and snuggles you are already doing, some Jewish stories, a one-sentence (six-word) Hebrew prayer, and a willingness to listen and share about Jewish feelings.

Profoundly Jewish doesn't ask much more. It just requires that you manifest a much deeper awareness. To understand that awareness, think about the bedroom of your childhood. I'll bet that it holds two different kinds of memories.

Some of them will be very warm and secure—like the kid gently wrapped into the blankets and sheets. It is all cuddly stuffed animals and sense of connection. Bedtime is stories and imagination—you know, the sugar-plum stuff.

Some of them are very dark—the monster in the closet, the monster under the bed, the scary shadow of the tree branch as it reaches across the ceiling toward you. Bedtime is also hiding-under-the-covers time—until the oxygen runs out and you have to emerge from your shelter to face whatever dangers are waiting.

Here is the truth hidden in those memories. Both the warmth and the fear come from the same place—the darkness.

Think of "Rock-a-bye, Baby" with its "If the bough breaks..." part. Think about the words to "Now I lay me down to sleep..." which you used to say without thinking about them—if you used to say them. It has its "If I die before I wake..." part. Think about why Jews say the Shema at bedtime. Here is the answer you have probably always known, but never admitted. We say the Shema at bedtime, because the Shema is supposed to be the last thing we say before we die. Bedtime is a rehearsal for dying—that is the deeper meaning of every bedtime ritual. The glass of water, the hair tousle, and the tucked-in blankets foreshadow a time in the far distant future when those things will again be done for a much aged and perhaps returned child. They, too, are a rehearsal. Stop. Do not think of any of this as morbid. There is nothing sad, or ugly, or fearful in any of this. After all, we are talking about "Rock-a-bye, Baby" stuff.

137

The purpose of bedtime ritual is to help us to learn the difference between that which is mortal and that which is eternal. Eternal things include laughs, hugs, jokes, hopes, dreams, stories and memories—all the real accomplishments—and the emotional bonds which make them possible. In all the warmth and fear of bedtime, night after night, we learn to face "the little death" which comes with sleep. In doing so, we slowly bury the fears which could come to immobilize us, and face the task of finding a meaningful direction to our life. Bedtime's message about dying is ultimately that love *does* conquer all. (The secret about cliches, by the way, is that before they became trite, they were once great conveyors of truth. That is why they got over-used in the first place.)

Let's think about some of the lessons that night teaches. Night holds many important moments.

- Our first experience of true awe often comes when we gaze up and notice the infinity of stars glowing in the eternity of the heavens. For me it happened during a drive back from a social at Camp Deertrees to Camp Mendota in the back of an open pick-up truck. I was 14, and we all got lost in the stars that hot August night. In that summer sky moment, all eight or nine of us had a "gosh gee" insight into infinity, mortality, eternity and humility. We scared and excited ourselves with our talk of endlessness. That is a nighttime experience. The Grand Canyon can work its own sense of wonder, but night is different.

- Many of life's most important conversations take place at night. We tend to say things in the dark that we can't admit in the light. Night time is like that. At night, under the shield of darkness, we often expose our insides, sharing things we'd never share in daylight. My friend Harlene likes to point out that car conversations are like that, too. She teaches that children often stage some of their most risky conversations with parents when they are being driven somewhere. Harlene thinks that it is the fixed time frame of the ride which makes the difference—they know that the end of the ride will come and they can escape if it doesn't go right. I think that the lack of eye-to-eye contact in the conversation has a lot to do with it, too. In my experience, phone conversations can have the same distant intimacy. While this lack of eye contact has something to do with night talk as well, neither car nor phone conversations have exactly the same quality as talking in the dark. When the veil of night hits, the mask of darkness falls, our inherent sense of mortality kicks in.

- Ever go to summer camp—or even camping for a weekend? If not, think sleep-over or pajama party—and remember the crazed antics or obscene joke telling sessions. You know that this too can only take place after dark. In those moments also, great truth is revealed.
- Because this is a book about parenting in which no child is likely ever to make it up to this page—we can admit to each other that while daylight sex has its own wonders, making love enfolded in the darkness offers a unique sense of connection.

The dual nature of night (its shadow and its connection to an inner light) makes it a time not only of great fear, but of amazing opportunity. Our job as Jewish parents is to put our kids to bed in such a way that Judaism has a chance to speak to all of life's great fears. Now in concept, that sounds terrifying. It sounds awesome. It is awesome, but is it anything but terrifying. Actually, it is as simple as blending Jewish stories, a one-sentence, six-word Hebrew prayer, and Jewish feelings with the kisses, glasses of water, tucked in covers, tousled hair, and snuggles. But it is doing all those things with an attitude—an attitude that it makes all the difference in the world. Not every single night, but just sometimes in the amalgam of childhood experiences, the bedtime repertoire should include awesome moments which rival profound star gazing, the deep bonding laughter of risky joke telling, and the deepest most revealing conversations. Some deep truths can only emerge when it is too dark to see eye-to-eye. You can't plan for these moments. You can't conjure them or make them happen. All you can do is run the regular pattern of authorized good parents' good bedtime experiences—and be ready to go with the flow when the universe opens and offers you an opportunity to make it something more.

So why is a great bedtime process so important to the Jewish people? It isn't just the simple truth that if you put your kids to bed Jewishly, they will in turn probably put their kids to bed Jewishly. It is great to think of Judaism as being passed on by a *K'ton-ton* story, the Shema, a kiss, straightened covers, and a "Sleep tight!" But, there is more to the story. Here is what we know and here is what it means.

We know that bedtime is childhood's most direct access to things spiritual. It raises the questions of life's meaning in a way that other holy spaces (such as synagogues) or other holy times (such as holidays) never can. Because death is always in the shadows at bedtime, it becomes a time to talk about true feelings, beliefs, concerns, and loves. Bedtime, especially when we are children, is the easiest time to feel that God is close on a regular basis.

We also know that if our children are to be Jewish in the future, it will only be because their Jewishness is useful and valuable to them. We are presently outlasting ethnic and culinary nostalgia. We've out-lived the time, at least in North America, when Jewish identity was an immutable determination; now it is just a preference. Therefore, to survive, Judaism has to be good for something. If Judaism teaches us to face our deaths with courage and meaning, to distinguish between that which is just mortal and that which can lead us to eternity—it has real value.

Great Jewish bedtimes, bedtimes which don't run away from the tough questions, can night-by-night build the foundations of a spiritually powerful Jewish life. If it works, we're talking eternal Judaism. Now, can I please have another glass of water?

Additional Activities

1. There are all these television commercials where the father is talking to the teddy bear or to the tombstone rather than talking to his kid about drugs or drinking, or perhaps about sex. We need to make one of our own, helping parents to realize the importance of talking to our kids about "God" and "death."

2. Another simple suggestion is to visit cemeteries. There is immediate value in introducing your kids to the "family plot" if mobility hasn't attenuated that connection. The cemetery is a great place to tell the stories of Aunt Felicia and explain exactly who Uncle Irving is related to—tomb-stones make good textbooks. Likewise, even if you can't go to a single place where the family remains are clustered, visit any cemetery. Read the inscriptions—do tomb rubbings—learn history. You can use any excuse you want—but do it. It will make death a lot less scary and a lot more ordinary part of life.

3. When I was working on my first master's degree at the University of Chicago, I did my student teaching at Akiva-Schechter, a Jewish day school. Rabbi Harvey Well was the headmaster, Millie was the school sec-retary—in reality they shared the administrative responsibilities. Near the

end of the year, Millie's father died and Harvey took Andy Shapiro, Jonathan Petzel, and the rest of the fourth grade to the *shiva* house. I was a little bit surprised, because to my "Reform aesthetic" fourth grade seemed too young, but Rabbi Well shared a little bit of Orthodox wisdom, which I now share with you. He said, "We practiced before we went." Teach your kids about life. Take them to the hospital—when you can get them in to see a sick friend or relative. Take them to retirement homes and old age homes. And, take them to make *shiva* calls and to be part of mourning minyans. But, before you do, take Rabbi Well's advice—and practice before you go.

This of course leads to another *Talmud 2000* question:

At what age should parents take children to *shiva* houses and at what age should they bring them to funerals?

24 Keep a *Tzedakah* Checkbook

Actively making the giving of family *tzedakah* a collective process, the subject of a monthly family meeting, will have a powerful impact.

When I was a little kid, one of the questions my parents refused to answer which bothered me most was—how much does my father make? It became a bigger deal than any of my unanswered sex questions. It felt like something dirty—it was in the "none of your business" category. I expect that I would have been quite satisfied to know how much my family gave to *tzedakah*.

The Recipe For a Powerful Lesson

Take a Jewish calendar and some markers—stickers are optional enhancements.

1. Write "pocket change" on every Friday on the calendar. On *Erev Shabbat* it is a tradition to put your remaining change in a *pushke* (*tzedakah* box) just before lighting candles.

2. Color in the days between Rosh ha-Shanah and Yom Kippur and write: "Ten Days of Repentance—Remember: *Tzedakah*, Prayer and Repentance can change God's mind and cancel a bad

verdict." You have just reminded yourself that this is an especially important time to give *tzedakah*.

3. Flip to Hanukkah and write the words "*Tzedakah* Bets." This is a reminder that some of the money you win at dreidel and more adult games should be allocated or even bet in the name of *tzedakah*.

4. In February or March you will find Purim. On it write "*Mattanot la-Ev'yonim*"—gifts to the poor. This is a reminder that Purim has its own kind of *tzedakah*.

5. Passover is only a month away. In the week before it, write down the words: *Ma'ot Hittim*. This is the name of the special *tzedakah* that Jews give before Passover to make sure that every Jew has the foods needed to celebrate the festival. Next to it you can also write: "New mitzvah: Don't sell *ha-metz*, give it to a food bank or homeless shelter."

    On Seder nights write: "Let all who are hungry come and eat."

6. On Shavuot write the words: "Story of Ruth = Obligation to Tithe."

7. Color in every other Jewish holiday, birthday, *yahrzeit* and write, "Give *tzedakah* as an honor or memorial."

8. If you child goes to Sunday School, on every school Sunday write: *Keren Ami*.

9. If any weddings, *b'nai mitzvah*, important anniversaries, etc., fall during the year, write "*Tzedakah* Opportunity" on the date.

10. Add in your own other *tzedakah* opportunities (like "Super Sunday") which should be part of your year.

So, what lessons have you learned? That the Jewish year provides lots of opportunities for giving. That giving is part of our life and year cycle. That... (fill in your own).

If you are a committed Jewish family, hoping to insure a Jewish future for your children and grandchildren, both the practice of *tzedakah* as a significant commitment and the chain of actual money given are important to you. This is the most powerful way I know to teach that lesson.

a. Start a separate checking account. I used to have one which read Joel's *Tzedakah Kupah*. (After writing this, I think I'll renew the practice). I learned the practice from some important laywomen in Rochester who actually wrote multi-thousand dollar donations on checks which read "Debi's *Pushke*" (or similar names).

143

Fill the checking account with the amount of money you wish to allocate to *tzedakah*. Encourage your children to do the same. You can even make donations in honor of good events (or in memory of a bad test score—etc.) You can charge *tzedakah* fines. Use your imagination.

b. Save all the "junk mail" which asks for donations each month, and all the other requests which have been brought to you.

c. Have a monthly allocations meeting. Slowly, a set of rules will evolve. And eventually you'll be able to contribute to a *Talmud 2000* chapter on *tzedakah*. It's long overdue.

Here are a few of the really good *Talmud 2000 tzedakah* questions.

1. The Jewish tradition asks for between 10 and 20 percent of your income, to be given to *tzedakah*. Should that be before or after taxes? What is the relationship between taxes and *tzedakah*?

2. The federal government will let you count synagogue dues as a charitable contribution. Should it be considered part of your *tzedakah* allowance?

3. How should you balance your Jewish and non-Jewish commitments?

There are many, many more.

Additional Activities

1. In his book, *Gym Shoes & Irises*, Danny Siegel, *maggid* of *menschlekeit*, the Guru of Giving, my teacher and often fellow traveler, tells the story of his mother's mitzvah. Every year at Seder they would host a collection of profoundly retarded and disabled children. While it took a lot of work and attention to make the Seder a success, it was well worth it.

2. I heard this story from either Dorian or Lonnie, two now college kids who used to help me run High Holiday Services at Valley Beth Shalom back when they were in high school. One of their families used to spend either a Rosh ha-Shanah afternoon or Yom Kippur afternoon (I don't remember which) working in a soup kitchen every year.

3. Every year the father of my friend Carol Starin has a caterer do Thanksgiving dinner and Carol in turn donates the money she would have spent to a school for homeless children, which uses it to provide a Thanksgiving dinner for their families.

144

4. Linda Kantor, the powerhouse laywoman behind Myriam's Dream (an organization devoted to intergenerational *tikkun olam*) has an annual family reunion. Among the reunion activities each year, they decide where to give a $1,000 dividend. She also reports that her friends have started making one of the eight nights of Ḥanukkah a time to give *tzedakah* gifts rather than gifts to each other.

4. Mazon, a national Jewish organization committed to fighting hunger in both the Jewish community and the world, works at getting people to donate 3% of the cost of life-cycle event parties or meals and holiday celebrations to help feed the hungry. Interestingly, this is based on an old Jewish custom—a traditional wedding feast always included a table for the poor and those in need. Mazon can be reached at (310)470-7769.

5. The Torah and the Midrash present Abraham and Sarah's family as one which performed lots of mitzvot, but was obsessed with one mitzvah: hospitality. Making strangers feel welcome was their thing—their family mitzvah. By legend, they even had a tent made with four doors—so that no stranger would ever have to look for a way in.

6. We'll speak of it in the chapter about bar and bat mitzvah, but in order to make birthdays a legitimate Jewish experience, we need to connect them to acts of *tzedakah*.

7. In *New Traditions*, Susan Abel Lieberman tells the story of a family who "fasts" every Monday night, skipping dinner. They have a family meeting, reading and studying world hunger, then they donate the money they would have spent to Oxfam (a world hunger relief organization). The nice part of this tradition is that the family gathers before bedtime for a simple bedtime snack—muffins, tea, jam—and a lot of closeness.

   Joel's Eighteenth Law: Taught in the name of Abraham, Sarah, Danny and his mother, Carol and her father, and either Lonnie or Dorian and whichever family: Find a family mitzvah and make sure there is one date on your calendar which is devoted to it every year.

Commentary: Some particular way of making the world a better place—whether it is working for the Heart Association fund, collecting used wedding gowns that the Rabbanit Brakhah Kappakh can provide to poor women in Jerusalem, working in a soup kitchen, or going all out on *Ma'ot Ḥittim* to make sure that all Jews can celebrate Passover—should be part of your family identity. It should be one of the ways your children will complete this sentence: **We are a family who....**

Tik·kun O·lam \tē-ˈkün ō-ˈläm\ *n* (Hebrew *tiken* correct, emend, repair, reform + *olam* world, universe, eternity): repairing the world. In modern Hebrew *tikkun ha-olam* is the term for social reform; for American Jewish activists *tikkun olam* is a guiding principle in environmental as well as social causes.

Tze·da·kah \tsə-ˈdä-ˈkä\ *n* [Hebrew *tzedek*] 1: justice 2: donations of time or money to charitable causes

G'mi·lut Ha·sa·dim \gə-mē-ˈlüt hä-sä-ˈdēm\ *n* [Hebrew *gamal* load, deal with, do good to + *hesed* kindness, benevolence]: deeds of lovingkindness

Ke·ren A·mi \ˈker-ən ä-ˈmē\ *n* [Hebrew *keren* fund + *am* people, lit., fund of my people]: money collected regularly from students in Jewish schools for donation to various (esp. Jewish) charitable causes and organizations

Bi·kur Ho·lim \bē-ˈkür hō-ˈlēm\ *n* [Hebrew *bikur* a visit + *holeh* sick, ill; a patient]: visiting the sick

He·sed Shel E·met \ˈhe-sed shel ˈe-met\ *n* [Hebrew *hesed* kindness, benevolence + *shel* of + *emet* truth]:

Lo Bu·shah \ˈlō bü-shä\ *vt* [Hebrew *lo* no + *bushah* shame]: to make certain that one does not shame, embarrass or degrade another person, particularly in the giving of charity

Pid·yon Sha·vu·yim \pēd-ˈyōn ˌshä-vü-ˈyēm\ *n* [Hebrew *pidyon* redemption fr. *podeh* redeem, ransome + *shavui* captive]: the mitzvah of redeeming or ransoming captives, now broadly interpreted to include monetary assistance and political action for the benefit of those who are "captives" under totalitarian governments that guarantee no individual rights and that strictly control or prohibit emigration

Ro·def Sha·lom \rō-def shä-ˈlōm\ *n* [Hebrew *rodef* pursuer + *shalom* peace] 1: a pursuer of peace 2: the act of pursuing peace

Hakh·na·sat Kal·lah \ˌhäk̠-nä-ˈsät kä-ˈlä\ *n* [Hebrew *hikhnis* bring in + *kallah* bride]: 1. escorting or welcoming a bride 2. providing for a bride's needs, e.g. foodstuffs or funds for a wedding feast, wedding clothes or trousseau

Ma·zon \mä-ˈzōn\ *n* [Hebrew *mazon*]: 1. food 2. *cap.* an American Jewish organization which uses charitable contributions to provide food for those in need

Ni·ḥum A·vei·lim \nē-ˈh̠üm ü-vä-ˈlēm\ *n* [Hebrew *niḥem* comfort, console + *avel* mourner]: comforting mourners

Ro·feh Ḥo·lim \rō-ˈfe h̠ō-ˈlēm\ *n* [Hebrew *rofeh* a healer + *ḥoleh* sick, ill; a patient] 1: a healer of the sick 2: the act of healing the sick

Hakh·na·sat Or·ḥim \häk̠-nä-ˈsät ȯr-ˈh̠ēm\ *n* [Hebrew *hikhnis* bring in + *oreaḥ* guest]: 1. welcoming guests 2. providing hospitality in general, especially for guests who are strangers

So·mekh Nof·lim \sō-ˈmäk̠ nō-ˈflēm\ *n* [Hebrew *somekh* support + *nafal* fallen] 1: support(er) of the fallen 2: the act of supporting those who have fallen

Mal·bish A·ru·mim \mäl-ˈbēsh ä-rü-ˈmēm\ *n* [Hebrew *lavash* wear, put on (clothing) *malbish* clother + *arom* naked]: one who clothes the naked

Pi·ku·aḥ Ne·fesh \pē-ˈkü-äh̠ ˈne-fesh\ *n* [Hebrew *pakaḥ* open (eyes or ears), remove debris + *nefesh* soul, person, in *Talmud, opening or removing (a pile of) debris (even in violation of the prohibiton of work on the Sabbath) for the purpose of saving a life*]: the saving of a human life

Tzar l'·Ba·a·lei Ḥa·yim \ˌtsär lə-bä-ə-ˈlä h̠ä-ˈyēm\ *n* [Hebrew *tzar* trouble, pain + *l-* to, for, of + *ba'al* master + *ḥayyim* life; lit. "pain of a living thing"]: in Jewish tradition, an abbreviated reference to the commandment to avoid causing pain to a living creature

Bal Tash·ḥit \bäl täsh-ˈh̠ēt\ *v* [Hebrew *bal* do not + *shiḥet* ruin, destroy] 1: an abbreviated reference to the biblical commandment not to destroy wantonly 2: among Jewish environmentalists, a general exhortation not to waste resources, based on a misunderstanding of the English term "lay waste," a synonym for wanton destruction as prohibited in 1

Ma·tir A·su·rim \mä-ʰtir äsü-ʰrēm\ *n* [Hebrew *hitir* release, set free, untie + *asur* shackle, imprisoned] 1: one who unfastens shackles 2: one who sets prisoners free 3: the act of doing 1 or 2   comp. *pidyon shavuyim* above

> Everyone has an English teacher somewhere along the line who tells them that the Eskimo have fourteen (or seventeen or whatever amazing number) different words for snow. They perceive snow in much finer categories than we do—and the vocabulary of snow both trains and expresses these perceptions.
>
> As snow is to the Eskimo, mitzvot which bring the world closer to redemption are to the Jews. Our vocabulary of commanded "good deeds" is definitional to what it means to be a Jew.

When "Negro" became "Black" the world changed. Likewise when "Latins" became "Hispanic" or "Chicano." Vocabulary has deep social and political ramifications. The term "spin doctor" has colored the way we see "political spokespeople." I spend half my life trying to figure out how to translate prayers and rabbinic texts without the use of he or she, his or her when God is involved. My constant verbal gymnastics daily reteach me important lessons about how women's needs have to be considered.

We know that language is a powerful way of transmitting values and culture, because it transmits unique perceptions in the distinctions it makes. A world with only "charity" is a very different place than one which contains all the mitzvot listed above. Second, we know that when we are forced to change our language or to be careful about the terms we use, this special attention to words teaches us an ongoing lesson and changes our perceptions.

> **Joel's Nineteenth Law:** Said in the name of Rabbi Yosi Gordon: Be an advocate of *Hebglish* (or if you prefer, *Engbrew*), the new "Yiddish" which is emerging around English rather than German. Use as many real Hebrew nouns in your English conversation as possible.

So let's talk about our version of "Eskimo Snow." While we know that all "Jewish" (Hebrew) words are good because they enhance identity and transmit culture, building a *tikkun olam* vocabulary is a triple whammy.

    a.   It does all the "cultural uniqueness" stuff. Having a Jewish language makes a difference. I remember being in my first year of Hebrew school and standing around in the public school playground with kids who were going to three different synagogues. Some non-Jewish kid asked if we had learned how to swear in Hebrew yet, and Andy Kushner looked at him and said, "You *boker tov morah*." We all laughed. The actual meaning made no difference. We shared a common bond and heritage.

b. These words go deep into the uniqueness of the Jewish people and help to teach a lesson about how we work to repair and heal the world which could never be taught exclusively in English—any more than I could really learn about snow without some loan words.

c. They help to shape your family identity in a way which lines up what you do with what the Jewish people are all about. Saying we are a family who is really concerned with *tzar l'ba'alei hayim* (keeping animals from suffering) makes deeper connections than either "Greenpeace Family" or "Matzah-eating Family"—it links two connections and two commitments.

I will admit that telling you that I just took the last draft of this book and dumped it in my *Bal tashhit* container is a bit much—we're into survival models here, not total obsession. But, it is a little piece of *tikkun olam*.

Linda Kantor: An Epilogue All by Herself

Linda Kantor is my telephone buddy—we've only met once, but we talk on the phone once in a while. Each one of those conversations is both inspirational and terribly challenging. When Linda and I were talking about this chapter, she said, "My advice is to buy a truck." To explain her insight, I'll need to fill in some background. Linda is one of the founders of an organization called American Friends of LifeLine for the Old. LifeLine for the Old was the obsession of a wonderful Israeli teacher named Myriam Mendilow who created a sheltered workshop in Jerusalem for old people to keep them from having to beg. She started with a book bindery, having the old fix the books that the schoolchildren tore—forging a connection between the two generations. She later added thirteen other workshops and a meals-on-wheels program, and blended in the handicapped as well as Arab, Christian, and Jewish elderly. She was an amazing woman. You couldn't say "No" to her. She would have a vision of some impossible but wonderful dream, and then ask your help—then you would find yourself doing it. Linda was one of the people who got caught in Myriam's gravity well, but she breaks all the laws of entropy—she keeps adding energy to the system. Now, Linda is busy organizing a new project: Myriam's Dream, an international foundation to provide for intergenerational projects to help the elderly and the physically challenged. She is busy drawing me into her gravity well. We talk, and she apologizes for taking so long to call me back—she was taping cardboard over all the windows the gangs broke in her "halfway house" because they used it to hold the first Neighborhood Watch meeting. We talk another day, and she wonders about how to find enough plastic to build greenhouses so that the seniors in the "halfway house" neighborhood can grow mums to sell to the people visiting the cemetery down the street. Linda is like that. She is not your basic suburban housewife. This year, her husband gave her a truck for a present. She says, "Until I had the truck, I never had any idea how many uses I would have for it." She reels off twenty errands she has just run, picking up x for y shelter, getting z to this or that food bank—it is an amazing list. I am in awe. I am embarrassed. I say, "Yes, I will work on Myriam's Dream and be a helper." My mother once nicknamed herself "the bulldozer" because she had the ability to keep going no matter what. Take Linda Kantor's advice. Get a truck. Be a truck. There is a lot of work to do. You could be the family who has a truck—your own version of a Mitzvah Tank.

P.S.
Myriam's Dream, Inc.
1500 Palisade Avenue
Ft. Lee, NJ., 07024

26 Collect Jewish Stuff

Filling your house with Jewish things—especially things which have meaning and stories—is a powerful modeling of your commitments.

I've taken it for granted that if you bought this book on your own (and it is not something your parents bought for you to try to influence the way you are raising their grandchildren) you probably already own the basic Jewish starter kit: 2 Candlesticks, 1 Ḥanukkiyah, 1 Kiddush Cup, 1 Seder Plate, 2 High Holiday Prayerbooks, 1 or more Haggadot, a Mezuzah, a Bible—and few other odds and ends, like leftover Hebrew School textbooks. (Come to think of it—if your parents bought this book for you they've probably given you the other stuff as well). If not, collect and use all of the above items first. This chapter is about moving to the next level.

We are what we collect. Just about everyone has a collection, and collections have a lot to do with how we see ourselves—and perhaps even more to do with the way other people see us. I've often thought that the major reason people collect things is to make it easier for people who don't know what to give them as gifts.

Jewish collecting opportunities are endless. In no particular order here are some possibilities:

Sefarim (Jewish Religious Books)
Jewish Books
Antique Jewish Books
Jewish Antiques
Jewish Antiquities
Jewish Art
Books about Jewish Art
Books about Jewish Collections
Jewish Photography
Books about Jewish Photography
Jewish Business Cards
Your Own Jewish Photographs
Jewish Sports Cards
Famous Rabbi Trading Cards (Yes, they really exist!)
Jewish Postcards
Jewish Stamps
Jewish Coins
Tzedakah Opportunities
Signatures and Autographs of Famous Jews
Jewish Periodicals
Jewish Ritual Objects
Memberships in Jewish Organizations
Photographs of Jewish Friends
Catalogs from Jewish Stores and Mail Order Houses
Jewish Recipes
Jewish Cookbooks
Kosher Wine (It is now possible to collect not bad Jewish wines—but I
    don't think you'd get very far with Jewish beer cans.)
Jewish Calendars
Jewish Toys
Jewish Games

Jewish Riddles
Jewish Crossword Puzzles
Jewish Advertisements
Jewish Trivia
Jewish Music
Jewish Records, Tapes, CDs
Books about Jewish Music
Jewish Dance Stuff
Jewish Clothes and Costumes
Bar/Bat Mitzvah Mania
Personalized *Benschers* and *Kippot* from Life Cycle Events
Jewish Pen Pal Letters
Menus from Jewish/Kosher Restaurants (Or, be the first one on your block to have a Jewish Matchbook collection. I have a toothpick dispenser from an Israeli Kosher Chinese restaurant on my desk.)
Jewish Films and Videos
Books about Jewish Films
Topic-centered collections—the whole range of Art, Media, Books, Artifacts, etc., relating to the Holocaust, or Israel, or Yiddish Theater
Oral Histories
Genealogies
Dreidels
Hanukkiyot
Mezuzot
Seder Plate
Haggadot
Jewish Amulets
Jewish Jewelry
Lists of Jewish Collections

Collecting is an easy and effective way to pass on a legacy.

Additional Activities

1. I just figured out that *The Swiss Family Robinson* is the "family education" version of *Robinson Crusoe*—"Robinson" and "Robinson", get it? So, some dark and stormy night when you decide to do away with television, why not play "Jewish Family Robinson"? The key to the Robinsons'

success was the trunk which floated in to shore carrying everything they needed—just like the castaways in *Mysterious Island*. So here's to you, Mrs. Robinson—imagine with your children what would be in your Jewish survival trunk.

2. Visit other Jewish collections and Jewish museums.

3. Make another list of more things which could be added to this essay as additional activities relating to collecting, using or displaying your Jewish stuff.

Jewish Nationalism

27 Play to Win at Jewish Geography or Be a Jewish Chauvinist

While it is a dangerous "two-edged sword" which can promote the worst of Jewish racist tendencies, the awareness of the presence and accomplishments of other Jews in the world is also a very positive factor in Jewish identity

Snapshot: I am little kid, in second or third grade, and my mother takes me into the voting booth with her. She pulls all the important levers, explaining all the key votes to me—and why the candidates are "good." Usually the word "liberal" is involved. When all the known candidates have been voted for, we begin a process of looking for Jewish names.

Snapshot: Jane and I are in London staying at a lovely bed and breakfast. We come down to a typical English breakfast (think sterling toast rack in the conservatory) and wind up playing Jewish geography with a couple from Chicago. Within five minutes we have identified three people we both know, exchanged the same gossip about the same rabbi, and shared the memory of our favorite kosher take-out place on Devon Avenue.

Snapshot: I am in sixth grade. I have never played little league in my life. I know the names of maybe four or five baseball players in the whole world. I don't get very far past Carl Yastrzemski, Ted Williams, Mickey Mantle, Yogi Berra, and Roger Maris. Yet I can still remember that hot argument at recess about Sandy Koufax choosing not to pitch on Yom Kippur. It is one of my very few baseball memories.

Snapshot: It is twenty-five years later. I ask my seventh– graders this question: "The midrash says that every Jewish person who ever lived or will ever live was at Mt. Sinai when the Torah was given. In the ten minutes before the program starts, what famous Jewish people would you most like to meet?" Sandy Koufax is on the list of every boy in the class (and about a third of the girls). They don't know from Hank Greenberg, but thanks to their parents, Sandy's refusal to pitch has lasted years more than any other detail of his career. He has earned his Jewish posterity.

Snapshot: I am watching HBO, and see a Neil Diamond Christmas special being advertised. Something in my stomach tightens. Even though no one else is there, I say out loud, "But I thought he was Jewish!" When they cut to show him singing "Santa Claus is Coming to Town," in front of a giant dreidel I'm nauseated. I've made my harsh judgment—Neil is now out of my will.

These are ethnic moments, like my automatic grimace every time my business partner Alan orders roast beef on white bread with mayonnaise. In my life, white bread is a judgment all by itself. It is a value statement—and I don't like it. It is a prejudice of which I am embarrassed to be honestly proud.

A Jewish lesson from ham: I've often thought that Jews should do what ham radio operators do. Every time a ham operator makes a contact with another operator they exchange "handles." They keep logs of everyone to whom they've spoken. They have these little cards (whose name I can't recall) printed up and send them to each other. It is a lesson we should learn—playing Jewish geography the way the ham radio operators do.

Vicky and Stuart Kelman (and Etan, Elana, Ari, and Nava) have a great wall in their kitchen. It is almost all cork and they have pinned to it photographs and cartoons and articles and other stuff from and about their friends and family. It is sort of the world's biggest refrigerator door—wall-sized. It is a collection of stuff that shows how they are connected in the world.

If I had kids, I'd have a Jewish contact board. On it would be a world map, a USA map, and an Israel map. I would pin up all the business cards of all the

Jews I'd ever met and add a flag to every city where I feel Jewishly connected. I'd add articles and travel flyers—anything which portrayed our ongoing involvement with the Jewish world. I'd make Jewish geography a world class sport. Not only does it make the world smaller—it makes the Jewish people larger.

My problem at the moment is that I am still searching for a truly clever Jewish "handle."

28 Subscribe to the *Jerusalem Post*

A simple and positive connection to the modern State of Israel can be built by reading the *Jerusalem Post* together weekly.

This is a really simple action with a really simple explanation—I couldn't figure out how to make this one more complex.

What to Do: Get a weekly subscription to the *Jerusalem Post* and make a point of reading some part of it with your children (until they develop a pattern of reading at least some of it on their own). You can make it a serious discussion of some article. You can choose to ignore the politics. You can make it a weekly game where they earn a "prize" if they can answer three questions about Israel that are answered in the issue. Hey—you can even just skim the ads. It doesn't matter. Just get the *Jerusalem Post* and open it every week.

Your Goal: The only real aim is to bring into your home a weekly reminder of the fact that Israel is a real, living, Jewish country and we are connected to it—and through it to Jewish communities around the world. This is the easiest single way of nurturing the national component in Jewish identification.

The Disclaimer: I do not work for the *Jerusalem Post*. I will get no kickback for mentioning it by name. I do not suspect that they will review this book—and including their name will not help its sales. This is the simple truth. The *Jerusalem Post* is the simplest, most dependable and available source of ongoing Israel connection I know. If you can find another source for your ongoing connection—like watching the Israeli News on a Jewish cable channel (if you have one) or monthly letters from your Israeli family or friends—that's great. But build a connection to the reality of Israel—today!

Equal Time: When my friend Elliot Spack read this chapter, he did his three favorite things (1) he wrote a note on a "Post-It" note, (2) he corrected me, and (3) he stuck something in my face to read. The note was attached to *The Jerusalem Reporter*, a magazine put out by a lot of former *Jerusalem Post* people, and the suggestion was that this would be a better choice for people who wanted to know about day-to-day Israel. I don't have a strong opinion. Why not pick up a copy of each and then choose the one you like best? Or make it a family event and involve the kids.

29 | Start the Israel Trip Savings Account—NOW!

A trip to Israel around the time a child is sixteen is potentially one of the most potent formative Jewish experiences available. It should be planned for and long anticipated.

For years I have wanted to do a documentary film called *"Summer Camp."* It would star sixteen-year-olds from all kinds of summer programs. They would be Jewish, Black, Anglo, Hispanic, Serb and Croat, Vegetarian, Irish, Scandinavian, Punk, Metal, Prep, Arab, Native American, Oriental—all the ethnic groups. They would be religious, secular, Howard Stern fanatics, fun-loving, self-helpers, football players, followers of the Reverend Moon and Junior Hasids of America, social action oriented—all the ideologies.

There would be kids from riding camps, computer camps, learn–to spray–paint–swastikas–on–the–wall camps, Outward Bound camps, Guardian Angel camps, ordinary camps—all the summer programs. And I would ask all of these sixteen-year-old campers what they liked best about their camp or program. I am convinced that every single one of them—black, white, Jewish, computer *nerd,* football player, communist, Native American and just plain ordinary—would answer, "My friends, man, there is nothing like my friends"—or something like that. It is something genetic—take sixteen-year-old, put in group, add sun and suntan oil, stir—and out comes life-changing and incredibly potent friendship. I bet you can tell me most of the songs which were on the radio when you were sixteen and who you were hanging with—right?

My friend Vicky Kelman has written a powerful think piece on Israel trips based on the extant research. She transforms all of the numbers and statistics into a powerful insight, "Israel trips work best when they are indeed pilgrimages." Simply put, every kid who goes to Israel at sixteen (or so) becomes Jason, Hercules, Sinbad and all those other Douglas Fairbanks characters. The trip to Israel is a quest for independence, identity, adventure, connection, sex (don't you dare leave out sex—we're talking about sixteen-year-olds—and don't panic, because "sex" need not mean "intercourse") and—in a distant, unrecognized sense—it is a quest to find meaning, by finding one's self.

Israel is the perfect adventure. One has to escape the luggage monster who wants to charge for overweight, survive the endless night of the El Al journey, make it past the riddle of the customs sphinx and more. There are physical challenges like the Snake Path. There is the excitement of intrigue—like sneaking past your guards to get out at night. There is no drinking age. There is a whole new money system to master—and a black market where you can get more of it. And, the best part of it is that while you are roaming in a country of relatives who all speak a different langugue and can't really understand you—your parents are thousands of miles away unable to complain about what you are wearing when you leave the house at night. Together with your friends, a team of strangers in a strange new homeland, you solve all problems—including dysentery—and make your own good time (despite all the careful planning which has gone into providing it for you). It is Indiana Schwartz time—a real adventure. It may even come with car chases—if you know anything about Israeli drivers.

We could go on and on about what a good thing visiting Israel is—and how perfect a summer trip at sixteen is—and how by making it Israel rather than New Zealand your child will imprint all this on a Jewish matrix—but you get the point. Let's face it, you've decided to make this happen, so here is what you have to do.

a. From the time your child is little, talk about what s/he is going to be able to do when s/he is sixteen and goes to Israel. Collect the folders and post cards—now. Build the expectation.

b. Even if money is no object, start the savings account now. Tithe birthday checks and bar or bat mitzvah gifts to contribute. Make the growth of such funds a collective *cause celebre* and involve your kid in contributing.

You want the kid really invested. You want it to become part of his or her targeting system—so that (a) there is no way of backing out even if s/he really wants to rebel against you, and (b) nothing but a good time is possible. Trust me; Suntan lotion, the Dead Sea, sixteen-year-olds of the opposite sex, Jerusalem, the discos in Tel Aviv and the sun setting over the Mediterranean will live up to expectations. Then, when s/he is ready to go, let him or her insist on being dropped off a block from the meeting point—so they won't be embarrassed. Don't push it. But, don't be surprised when they start to walk away and then run back and give you a huge ten-year-old's hug goodbye—and then walk the block without looking back. Sixteen-year-olds are like that. That is why this trip is going to work. Expect almost no mail—or a letter every day—then get ready to hear lots of good stories when they get back. But, know that there are a lot of other great stories you'll never hear, or not until years later. Enjoy their enjoyment. When they get back, they still won't make their beds, but things will have changed. Change takes time.

Jewish Education

30 Make Success at "Real" School a Jewish Priority

Classically, Jewish parents have been very concerned with education so that their kids could succeed in life. They often equated Torah with getting into Harvard. In this day and age, we have to care that our kids do well in regular school so that they have the skills to learn Torah—and we have to encourage our Jewish schools to participate in the growth of overall learning skills.

In talking about Noah, the midrash says, "In a land of blind men, a man with one eye is considered visionary." Our version of this has to be: "In a sitcom culture where most learning happens in soundbites, a person who reads *USA Today* has to be considered literate." It is within that greater culture that we are trying to perpetuate the study of Torah, Midrash, and (God forbid) even Talmud.

This is how Janice Alper once changed my whole view of Jewish education: I was visiting her at her Religious School office. We had set a meeting. When I got there, she was on the phone. She waved me in. The parent on the phone was complaining that the Hebrew school teacher had given her child homework, and was expecting the child to make academic progress (and not just feel good about being a Jew). They went back and forth. Finally, Janice said, "Well, I am sorry, that's our policy. After all, our last name *is* School."

166

It got me thinking. In seventh grade Sunday School I had a teacher named Mr. Temple. He taught us Bible. In real life he taught at the Boston Latin School. Sunday School was moonlighting for dollars until he earned an administrative position. I can still remember him standing in front of a class of 12-year-olds on the second or third day, writing the word "anthropomorphism" on the blackboard, and asking us to copy it into our notebooks, because it would be a good S.A.T. word. We did what he said. We copied "anthropomorphism" and then "took dictation" and wrote down the definition. Then, once he was finished, we asked him, "What is an S.A.T. word?" He told us. After all, our last name was School.

Even though I have no proof, there are two things I know to be true. I relearned both of them three years ago, when after a ten-year hiatus I went back to the Jewish classroom.

1. To learn what being Jewish really means—to understand the art of midrash and the logic of Jewish ethics, to master the regimen of Hebrew—takes what the regular schools call "good study skills."

    Good educations are no longer an automatic assumption, even for Jewish kids in suburban schools. When both parents work, it is harder to monitor progress, sit over a child doing homework, and show up at school for meetings. As money is cut and teachers' salaries don't keep pace, less and less attention is often paid to the individual child. We have to be on top of progress, because the schools often aren't. More and more, our secular schools are providing our students with less and less—reading, writing, problem solving, a sense of inner discipline, critical thinking skills and all the rest are declining.

    The simple end result of these realities is that unless a student learns how to learn in "real" school, it will be hard for us to teach her or him anything in Hebrew school.

2. If you look at Hebrew high schools, C.I.T. programs in Jewish summer camps, post-confirmation programs, and the kids who hang around to be in youth groups—you'll find that most (but not absolutely all) of them are the top students in their secular schools. There are Advanced Placement kids, the ones with 1400s and 1500s on their college boards. I don't know what is cause and what is effect—but real Jewish success and academic success tend to go together.

167

Our parents wanted us to be good students so that we could do better financially than they did. Our children have very little chance to outdo us economically—that is the sad truth in the post-Reagan reality. Learning as a means to economic advancement no longer feels true—just ask your kid. Learning is a necessity (to escape burger-flipping), but it is rarely seen as an opportunity. We want learning to come from a third place—we want it to be a joy. (My favorite expression of this is the philosophy of Brookline High School which says, more or less: "Learning is an acquired addiction—a preference for the tart rather than the sweet." They know that most great addictions, like cola and coffee, are "tart" acquired addictions.) Learning has to be a mitzvah, an end in itself.

Our grandparents took the Jewish value of Torah and spread it across to "getting into Harvard." They took, "it is a mitzvah to study Torah," deleted the "Torah" and made it into "it is a mitzvah to study."

We have to invert the process. We have to say, "because it is a mitzvah to study Torah, we are going to teach you how to study." I frequently tell that to Jewish teachers when I do workshops—now I've said it to Jewish parents in writing a book for them. My parents and their generation believed that children learned how to learn in "public" school, and then applied those good study skills to learn about Judaism a couple of times a week. My Hebrew School teachers assumed that I could read critically, take notes, write outlines and papers—all in seventh grade. Today, I can't make those assumptions with my ninth-grade students. If Jewish schools do their jobs properly, all students will be better students (as well as better Jews) for having studied there. We have to help them with the mitzvah of studying as well as with the mitzvah of studying Torah. We need to reconstruct.

1. We have to find the time to help our kids succeed and maximize their secular learning skills (not just their grades)—and know that their Jewish as well as economic future is at stake. We have to make all learning—Jewish and secular—co-equal mitzvot.

2. We have to encourage Jewish schools to be academic. To use reading and writing skills—to encourage critical thinking and creative interpretation—to demand accomplishment from our children and to encourage excellence—not only because it will allow them to enter the real depths and richness of the Jewish tradition, but because it will increase their overall competence as learners.

Today, I assigned an essay to one of my ninth-grade classes. I told them it had to be about two pages long. Their reaction: "That isn't an essay, that's a paper." I said, "No, a paper is eight to ten pages with at least three outside sources and footnotes." They winced. The essay was, "Give a coherent portrait of why Mishnah is an important thing to study."

A minute later I was remembering Mr. Temple as I wrote the word "coherent" on the board and dictated a definition. I justified the action with: "It's a good S.A.T. word." Unlike the kids who shared my Mr. Temple experience, they all knew what an S.A.T. was—they were already scared of it. Times change—less vocabulary and more anticipatory fear. I dictated the definition, twice, slowly, and then again for the little girl who was day-dreaming, then later felt the need to have it (because it might be on a test). After all, our last name is School.

Some Practical Opportunities

1. Go back to **Number 22: Become an Inveterate Mezuzah Kisser** and lift the insight about Tom Peters, Rosalind Russell and the dictionary—and place it permanently on the table you regularly eat dinner on. This idea, by the way, came from a suggestion my business partner Jane made.

2. Follow the example of the Zeidmans and demand a weekly in-house book review (of whatever the kids have been reading) at the Shabbat dinner table.

3. Follow the example of Sally Shafton and pick a child-of-the-week to study with you and then report on the weekly Torah portion at the Shabbat dinner table.

4. Do both 2 and 3.

5. Follow the example of Ira Lester Grishaver, who spent weeks "working" Filene's basement to find good clothes at affordable prices, who had to limit the toys and other purchases we could afford—but who had a basic shopping rule, "Books don't count." You could always buy books— though used bookstores were favorite haunts.

31 Take the Secret Pledge

The single most effective way to win the battle against dropping out of Jewish education after bat or bar mitzvah is to form a secret cabal with other parents and hold the line together.

This year I am teaching at the Los Angeles Hebrew High School. I consider it a privilege, especially because I get to teach parents on Sunday mornings as well as kids during the week. It is one of the most elite Jewish educational settings I know. It is a place where kids still go (all the way from seventh or eighth to twelfth grade) to a three-day-a-week, seven-and-a-half-hour after-school Hebrew program.

This year I learned that many of my parents feel bad about *making* their kids go to a Hebrew high school after bar or bat mitzvah. (Few parents question their right to make their children go up to bar mitzvah.) These parents were worried that their "doing the right thing" might Jewishly scar their children for life.

Most of the eighth-graders I teach at Hebrew High are there because their parents make them. Most of them kick and scream a little every now and then. But, by ninth grade and thereafter, just about all of our students give up the fight and admit that they like being there— maybe not all of the teaching, but at least being with their friends.

I realized that my students' parents need to learn this secret taught to me by my friend and teacher, Rabbi Larry Kushner. A long time ago he told me this story.

Once I took a group of families away for a *b'nai mitzvah* retreat. Late on Saturday night we wound up with all the kids off doing their own things somewhere, and all the parents sitting around the fire, drinking wine and talking. One of the parents said, "I don't want it to end. I don't want my kid to drop out of Hebrew School after her bat mitzvah. But," this parent added, "I am afraid to be *the* mean parent—I can't make my daughter continue if everyone else lets their children drop out." Then, everyone else spoke up. One at a time, all of them testified that they, too, wanted their children to continue—and all of them, one at a time, testified that they were also afraid to be the only one to draw a line in the sand. That night we continued to talk. We evolved an idea. We formed a secret cabal. That night, all the parents took a solemn oath that they would not be the first to let their kid drop out. It worked. Every year since then, I've told the story and added another year's worth of parents to our secret society. (In Larry's congregation, Confirmation, which is called *Siyyum*, is deferred to the end of eleventh grade—their percentage of retained students is not 100%, but it is close.)

Every time I think of that story, I start to hum "Alice's Restaurant"—that's because of the part at the end where Arlo suggests that the song could become a movement. He says that if everyone walked into their draft board and sang a chorus—the world would change. I feel the same way about Larry's secret parents' cabal—if we could get every family to join, all the Hebrew High Schools and all the Confirmations would be overflowing. It would be a problem we would love to solve. If there were no bad examples out there, if no parents would give in, then kids would give up more readily—there would be less fighting, and less guilt about making kids learn Jewish things against their will. All the guilt wouldn't go away—but there would be an awful lot less.

> **Joel's Twentieth Law:** Post bat or bar mitzvah education is a lot like the thank you notes which follow the ceremony. Few or no children will complete them on their own—that is why it is a mitzvah for parents to insist and even nag.

I know that we don't live in that kind of Jewish world right now—so start a conspiracy in your neighborhood, today.

> Remember **Joel's First Law:** Every year of Jewish education which takes place after bat or bar mitzvah is worth three or more years of anything which takes place earlier.

This, of course, leads us to another *Talmud 2000* discussion:

> What is worth fighting over? What Jewish things should parents *make* their children do? Which things should they recommend but consider optional?

I wish I had easy answers to this set of questions—maybe by the time I write the sequel... Here is what I do know.

1. That if we did set up a successful parental conspiracy—one where all parents would insist upon Jewish education until high school graduation (though I would accept Confirmation as realistic—much better in tenth or eleventh than ninth grade)—the struggle to make your own kid continue would be less difficult. This is a hard battle to fight when you feel that you are fighting it alone. Support is awfully nice. (That is the lesson the first half of this essay is trying to teach.)

2. That if communities could successfully package post bat or bar mitzvah "formal" education in a matrix which includes "youth group," "camp," and "Israel"—and overlay it with communal expectation and public esteem—that would help, too. We know that when post-pubic Jewish education succeeds, it is usually because the kids tolerate the education for the sake of being with their friends. Later on, they often admit that the education had some value, too. (That is the essence of the lesson found both in **Number 8: Do Not Make Them Go to Services, Create Reasons They'll Want to Go** and in **Number 37: Use Bribes to Keep Your Children from Interdating and Thereby Intermarrying.**

3. That if the expectation that children will continue their Jewish education through high school graduation is clear from the time they are in kindergarten, the resistance is usually reduced. Usually, fights are limited to individual sessions (Why do I have to go today?) rather than global—("Why do I have to go at all?") (**Number 3: Start a Jewish Expectations Photo Album**).

4. That if the Jewish communal culture didn't use "Jewish education" as a scapegoat, blaming it for their own ambivalence—it would take less flack from the average teenage autopilot. Jewish education is sort of the "military-industrial complex" of Jewish existence. (**Number 33:** *Never Suggest that Jewish Education is Caustic*)

Even if we did all these things, there would still be fights over Jewish education—as there will be fights over almost everything. Such fighting is the essence of being a teenager and of being the parent of a teenager. Even knowing that doesn't take away the pain. It hurts to wound your child—it hurts to have to say "No" or "You must"—when "Yes" or "That's great" is so much more rewarding emotionally for both of you. My teachers and colleagues the Wolins tell this story about their daughter. It has deep implications:

> Their seventeen-year-old daughter left for college in a huff of blame and chastisement. As she left home, she revealed to her parents all the ways they had limited, ruined, and devastated her life. Then she was gone. The next night they returned home from dinner out to find this message on the answering machine: "Where are you? I called and you were gone!"

Often parents are expected to be mean. Their meanness and lack of understanding is often the scratching post on which the teenager rubs off the skin of childhood. Often, limits are tested, just to see if they are important. Sometimes our kids want us to say "No." Other times, they are ambivalent about our saying "Yes." Remember, being a parent takes judgment. It is never applying a single rule—it is always balancing two or more commitments to fit the current situation. For lots of our kids, good kids, Hebrew school is a much safer place to rebel than drugs, or sex, or "real" school, or the rest of the litany of contemporary horrors.

> Years ago I ran a summer camp. I still vividly remember a twelve-year-old named Robbie. He was a leather-wearing, tough talking, Beverly Hills dirt-biker wimp. He started off tough, but cried when he fell down. These weren't sensitive tears, either. I remember one camp fire where he was messing around. I grabbed him from behind and put him in a tight, but not painful, bear hug. He struggled for a second, then turned to me and said softly, "I could get out of this if I wanted to." I said, "Yeah, I know." Then he rested his head back against my shoulder. For a second, a bear hug became a hug.

I have often thought post-pubic Jewish educational fights are like that, too—bear-hugs often turn into real hugs, if only for a second.

Joel's Twenty-First Law: Jewish education is not like date rape. When your children say "No," they sometimes do mean "Please make me."

The problem, (and I do not take date rape lightly) is that "no" is indeed sometimes playful—and "no" often does mean precisely "no." It takes a lot of love, a lot of listening, and a lot of checking out. When you assume that "no" really means "yes" you are taking a big risk. You can (and maybe should) do that if you're pretty sure—but, you'd better go slow and be really careful. What is true of a romantic relationship is equally true of parenting a teenager. Face value isn't always the true picture—but never forget that it can be.

What that means is that things which are worth fighting over—like bar mitzvah thank you notes and you must go on to Confirmation and you may not date the minister's son—are only worthy of so much fighting. Thank you notes aren't worth a runaway child. Confirmation doesn't equal driving a kid to drink. And even the minister's son is better than a teenage suicide. I've made these cases extreme on purpose—just to point out that I do know the danger.

> This is the truth. Permissive parents lose their kids to drugs, AIDS, suicide and the rest. So do overly strict parents. If you want perfect, get a photograph of your child at the last moment when she or he was perfect, and talk to the picture.

> If you believe in something, it is worth fighting for—but, you also believe in your child. Therefore, how far you will take a fight is a bigger question than whether you will fight. And that is something you'll have to work out.

My only wisdom is to start more fights than you finish—let them win the ones you figure you can afford to lose. Not to fight is to yield the point—to give up. To insist on victory, may lead to total devastation. In other words, the Torah of Kenny Rogers:

> "Know when to hold 'em—know when to fold 'em..."

Boy, parenting is hard. It is even hard to just write about. I am glad that I am the expert and you are the one who is going to get the door slammed in your face. I would even take my advice with caution.

32 | To Make Sure that Jewish Schooling Works— Continue Your Own Jewish Education

The single most powerful way of insuring that your children take their Jewish education seriously is to continue your own Jewish learning.

A story:

A man once came to the Kotsker Rebbe and complained that his son did not want to learn Torah. (Even though it wasn't Hebrew School he was talking about—we know those Sunday morning fights.) He asked the rebbe: "What should I do?"

The Kotsker Rebbe told him: "If you force your child to study Torah, he will study Torah as long as you make him do so. And, in fact, he will grow up and make his child study Torah in his time.

However, if you devote yourself to Torah study, soon you will find your child by your side, asking to study with you."

Get it? Do as I do! Scoobie Doobie Doo!

33 | Never Suggest that Jewish Education is Caustic or, Be an Advocate for More Jewish Learning

For Jewish schools to work for your child, you must break the cycle of "Hebrew School bashing" which has been imprinted on all of us. Likewise, you must join other like-minded voices and demand more, rather than less, from your Jewish school.

Jewish education appears to be locked in a cycle of apparent child abuse—and we are unwilling co-conspiritors. This scene reveals the problem.

Child: I don't want to go to Hebrew School today.

Parent: Forget it, you're going.

Child: Why do I have to go? I hate it—it's so boring!

Parent: Listen to me—you're going. I had to go and I hated it, and I survived. Now, you have to go. Even if you hate it, you'll survive, too.

Child: And I suppose you're going to make me walk six miles every day through the snow to school, too!

Over and over we have propagated the myth of the Hebrew School monster and convinced our children that dark, dank, and dangerous things lurk in the shadows of those late winter afternoons while their

176

teachers inflict upon them the horrors of Hebrew. We tell story after story about the Hebrew teacher from Hell, and have created a culture which has set up a profound expectation that Jewish education is actually caustic to positive Jewish identity.

You hear this assumption from parents—they keep on saying: "I don't want to force my child to go, because I want him/her to have positive feelings about being Jewish."

You hear the assumption in endless parent meetings where they ask, "Do we really need so many hours of schooling a week? After all, it isn't as if we are really teaching anything important." If the truth be told, we've lost a lot of the important things—like Jewish history, like Hebrew as a spoken language, like any sense of literacy with Jewish literature—because with the cutback in hours, teachers can't accomplish those tasks in the time that remains.

You hear it in the rhetoric of the American Jewish Communal Establishment (The Federated Universe) which now speaks of fostering "Jewish Continuity" or "Jewish Identification" and steers clear of the negative connotations of "Education" or "School." When they are deschooling the larger context of Jewish America, can you really expect your child's classroom to succeed?

You hear it in the underlying assumptions in lots of board and allocation meetings, where they cut funds to supplementary schools and rush to fund a growing slate of alternatives—looking to see if Jewish preschools can replace the horrors of Hebrew school, to see if Jewish Community Centers can transmit a Jewish identity free of the tortures of the classroom, to see if day schools can replace the angst of afternoon imprisonment. (Meanwhile, inside the day schools, parents often continue the theme—treating Jewish studies as a kind of "Hebrew School.")

And (because kids aren't stupid) you hear this assumption in almost every Jewish classroom where almost all kids already know the score—they know which side their parents will take.

The message has clearly been communicated: Don't take Jewish learning too seriously. It's bad but you can get through it—it won't bother you that much. That is a cycle of imagined and self-fulfilling abuse that only you can break.

Joel's Twenty-Second Law: If you can't say anything nice about Jewish education—don't say anything at all. (I do give you permission to talk about your worst Jewish schooling experiences if you also share your best times, too. That's only fair!)

Teachers, rabbis, boards of education, funding sources—all believe that most Jews want less. In my neighborhood, congregations are outdoing each other by seeing who can offer a bar or bat mitzvah in the shortest hours with the fewest demands. The scary part is that it seems to be working. My own synagogue cut a day a week of class and its school grew by more than ten percent. It is sort of, "I'll sell you a bar or bat mitzvah in four hours a week!" "No, I'll sell you a bar or bat mitzvah in three!" *USA Today* wins again. But if that is the game, they are all going to lose. Consider this ad found nailed on the wall at the University of Judaism, which appears weekly in the local Jewish newspaper:

> Jewish Bar & Bat Mitzvah Service: Bar & Bat Mitzvah Without Temple Membership. Bar or Bat Mitzvah Service in Location of Your Choice. One Year Preparation Program Taught in Your Home. Complete Party Planning. Brochure or Information: (818) 993-3980.

It is very simple. You can be assured that if you are not a voice for more and better Jewish learning, there will be less tomorrow. If you don't write letters, make positive phone calls about the good things, serve on committees or find the right people to do so, then the others, the ones who want less, the ones who are afraid that Jewish schools might work,will be the voices that are heard.

Remember, you do not have to be negative. A little praise goes a long way. Nice comments and notes to principals, rabbis, and teachers have an impact. A small thank you Hanukkah gift to a Hebrew School teacher takes away a lot of negative feelings. You don't have to be a radical—you just have to affirm and encourage the good.

However, one word to the wise, my personal warning: You'd better speak up now, or hope that there is very high quality in the "Jewish Educational Minute" which will be offered in the future. This one doesn't have a happy ending—unless you write one.

Take One More Step

1. There is a carpool game which parents call, "What did you learn in Hebrew School today?" Kids call the same game "Nothing." Develop your cross-examination skills. Work on your follow-up questions. Play aggressively. Don't take "Nothing" for an answer.

2. Adopt a Jewish teacher. Many (not all, and not even most) Jewish teachers are young and single, in school, or just out of school. They are often alone in your town. Have them to Shabbat dinner. Invite them to sit with you at Simhat Torah, and extend your family around them and thereby help to anchor them into the synagogue as well. Break the loneliness and sense of abandonment that teachers often feel when working in Jewish schools—and you can often change the world. Wonderfully, this is something only a family can do.

3. Become a classroom patron. Be a rebellious philanthropist. Ignore the building fund and the discretionary lines which get credited in the temple bulletin—give the Jewish teacher of your choice $50 to actually spend on his or her classroom.

4. Everyone else will tell you to volunteer to drive, or to lend your cooking or carpentry skills to a classroom project, and all the regular stuff—so go ahead and do that.

5. Watch the "Walt Disney Teacher Awards" and think both creatively and Jewishly.

34 | Learn the Curse of Joshua Mereminsky

To insure that your child has a quality experience in Jewish schools, s/he should start with the expectation of being a Jewish teacher someday (at least for some part of his/her life)—and to set a good example, you should be prepared to serve your time before the blackboard as well.

Ask any Hebrew school student—Ask any day school student—Ask any Jewish parent with a kid in school— Ask any Jewish educator—in fact, ask any Jewish teacher, and all of them will agree that the biggest problem in Jewish education has to do with Jewish teachers. What they won't agree on, is the kind of problem Jewish teachers have. They will all agree:

There is a shortage of well respected Jewish teachers who have outstanding ability.

We won't go into the disagreements (they all have to do with blame). What the statistical research shows is:

1. Most Jewish teachers spend less than three years in the classroom. Far more of them work at it for a few years than those who make a career out of Jewish teaching.

2. On the first day of school, up to 15 percent of classrooms in Jewish schools have not yet been permanently staffed.

3. There is a growing use of lay teachers in Jewish supplementary schools. These days, the in-jargon calls them "avocational" teachers.

4. As a way of keeping high school students involved, most supplementary schools (in-jargon for Hebrew schools) run programs for teenage teaching aides. Many of these programs use the term *madrikhim* for such teenage assistants (because "AIDS" has given "aides" a bad name). *Madrikhim* is the Hebrew word for counselor or leader—actually "guide."

Now take a deep breath. The next few things I am going to tell you may shock you. So relax and try to understand. Here we go.

First, you want to get your child to be a *madrikh* or *madrikhah* in a Jewish school. I will accept alternative service as counselor in a Jewish camp or leader in a Jewish youth movement—though the combination of summers working at camp and the year working in a Jewish school would be the best combination. (That wasn't too bad—the next one will be worse.)

Second, you want your child to grow into a Jewish teacher. It doesn't have to be a career. Jewish teaching isn't necessarily a profession—Jewish teaching is a life choice. In other words, for a few years during college, or perhaps after college, Jewish teaching is a great way of earning some money and paying back a debt. It is also a fabulous learning experience. (I know, this is a book about raising "good enough Jews," and being a teacher sounds like a major commitment. I told you this was going to be hard for you, but remember Jimmy Carter—he has a life *and* he's a Sunday School teacher. But now comes the hard one.)

Third, the best way of motivating your child to take Jewish education seriously, become committed to growing into a Jewish teacher, and do his or her part to preserve the Jewish tradition—is by setting an example and working in a Jewish school yourself. While you are catching your breath, let me tell you a story.

When I was a kid, I used to think of myself as the worst terror who ever refused to take off his jacket during Hebrew school. I held the world's record for the worst mutilation of a copy of *Ha-Yehudi Ha-*

Rishon. I put chalk in every eraser and was the president of the Drop-Your-Books-When-The-Clock-Strikes-4:51-p.m. Club. Even so, I had a very calm, enlightened principal who used to respond to each of my escapades with a simple curse: "I hope someday, when you become a Jewish teacher, your students will treat you as well as you treated your teacher."

I would laugh. Each time she cursed me, I laughed. I had absolutely no vision of myself as a Jewish teacher. It was the last of all possibilities, somewhere just after street sweeping. Immediately upon my confirmation, Esther Starr Grossman, the principal, offered me a job as her office aide. These were the dark ages long before teenagers were invited to work in classrooms. Mrs. Grossman also found me work as a Hebrew tutor. I was too flattered to say "no." Soon, with her help, I was working (as a high school student) towards my teacher certification at the Academy of Jewish Studies. Once I was in college, Esther found me additional Hebrew tutoring work—and when I was ready to teach, but still too young to qualify for *her* elite teaching staff, she helped to find me my first teaching job.

Over the years, her curse has come true. I have learned repeatedly that I was far from being a world-class disrupter of Hebrew school classes. One of the greatest terrors I have ever taught was a small, hyperactive, brilliant imp by the name of Joshua Mereminsky. In a group Joshua was just unteachable, but one-on-one I was taught much.

A couple of years ago, Joshua called and asked for advice. He was about to teach his first Hebrew school class. I immediately responded with that classic Jewish curse (taught to me so many years before): "May your students do to you that which you did to me..."

Over the next several weeks, I spoke with many of Joshua's former teachers, now all rabbis and educators throughout the country, and shared with them my perception of Divine justice. During that time, Joshua received a half-dozen phone calls from his former teachers, each welcoming him to the profession of Jewish teaching with a now-traditional folk curse: "May your students do to you that which you did to me..."

Jewish teaching is a legacy. It is a mantle passed on from teacher to student. Remember, every Jewish parent is supposed to be a teacher.

That is why it says in the *V'Ahavta*: "Teach them diligently to your children."

In advertising they call it "reason-why!" It is a hard sell. Without wasting time on being cute, here are six reasons why you want to spend some time working in a Jewish classroom and you want your child to do so, too.

a. **What goes around comes around.** The best possible Jewish teachers are caring, committed and dedicated people who are doing something they believe in. If you made it over a hundred pages into this book, you're dedicated—and the future of the Jewish people is important to you, and you want it to be important to your children. If you do it for somebody else's kids, someone good will be there for your kids.

b. **Good role models make a difference.** If you work in a Jewish classroom, you set a good example for your child. If s/he works in a Jewish classroom, you will have broken the chain of Hebrew school abuse. No longer will the words, "I went and I hated it, but I survived it. Now you'll go, even if you hate it, but you'll survive, too," be spoken.

c. **Teaching is the best way to learn.** This is true for the goose, true for the gander and true for goslings.

d. **Jewish teachers will only earn respect when respectable people do it.** This is not to say that Jewish teachers aren't respectable and that respectable people don't do it—but almost never is it considered a high-status job. Hebrew school has classically been a job for Rodney Dangerfield feel-alikes. In 1903, the first study of Jewish education was conducted in New York City. It reported that Jewish teachers were a crew of incompetent men who were paid a quarter per student per lesson—because they couldn't do anything else. Jewish teachers are not like that, but it often feels like they are still treated that way. When you and your friends enter the classroom, when everyone understands that they should put in their fair share of time transmitting Judaism, that status will change.

e. **It is fun and it is rewarding.** Trust me. Do it and you will experience some really frustrating moments—and some incredible instants of profound satisfaction. So will your kids.

f. **It's a mitzvah** (not just a "good deed" but one of those 613 traditional obligations).

I know you think I'm crazy, but I strongly believe this.

If every synagogue president thought of her- or himself as a Jewish teacher, because in some way s/he actually spent some time in the classroom as a Jewish teacher, the Hebrew school budget would get very different treatment.

If every kid who got into a carpool with a parent who had just been teaching a different class tried to answer the question: "What did you learn in Hebrew School today?" with the informative, "Nothing!"— the next follow-up question would almost always be different.

If every parent who complained about a Hebrew School teacher could do so out of his or her own experience in the classroom, the quality of both the complaints and the instruction would improve.

If every school board, every rabbi, every principal, knew that the kids who graduated from their Hebrew school had to know enough to become the next set of teachers in that school—the whole measure of their standards would change.

If every time a kid misbehaved in Hebrew school he or she was greeted with the curse of Joshua Mereminsky—the promise of a future as a Jewish teacher—then the whole universe would be a different place. All kids who go to camp anticipate being C.I.T.s, counselors, and then, if they are lucky, the camp director. If we worked at it, if we uttered the magic words, "I hope someday, when you become a Jewish teacher, your students will treat you as well as you treated your teacher," the whole meaning of Jewish education would be different.

Applications

1. Meet CAJE, the Coalition for the Advancement of Jewish Education—the one organization which celebrates and serves Jewish teachers. CAJE defines itself as an organization for Jewish teachers and it defines Jewish teachers as anyone involved in the transmission of Jewish heritage. CAJE includes professors, classroom teachers, avocational teachers, laypeople, rabbis, parents, and even teenagers. Take a membership in CAJE. Buy your teenager a teen membership in CAJE—and think about coming to their week-long summer conference.

   You can find out about CAJE by writing it at 261 W. 35th Street, Floor 12A, New York, NY 10001.

2. Both the Hebrew Union College-Jewish Institute of Religion (New York, Cincinnati, Los Angeles) and the University of Judaism (Los Angeles) run major programs for teenagers working in Jewish schools. So do many other Jewish colleges and a number of Bureaus of Jewish Education. Find out what is available in your area and offer your child a wonderful opportunity.

Bar/Bat Mitzvah and Teenagers

35 | Start a Child Exchange as Soon as Your Kid Enters Puberty

During puberty no parent can work with his/her own child. It is often most effective to trade off and deal with someone else's kids.

Here is my plan for parenting teenagers:

When your child begins to show the tell-tale signs of "the change" and you have to worry about the behaviors that will now be exacerbated by the full moon, you immediately sign up with the national Jewish registry. Shortly, they will send you a list of nine other Jewish families. All you have to do is write your name at the bottom, send a copy of the registry form to three other friends who are also raising emergent monsters, and then mail your child to the top name on the list. You will now be free of her or him for the next five or six years.

Don't worry, each child is sure to come back home and even talk to you when they are in college because they will need their laundry done. And, given current life cycle trends, they're even programmed to move back in with you and make you completely crazy sometime in their mid-twenties.

The only bad part of this plan is that twelve teenagers who belong to someone else are going to show up at your door, ask to raid your refrigerator, and demand that you listen to their problems with love and life for the next five or six years.

For those of you who have taken Parenting 101 and thought you had it all down, the transformation of your baby into a teenager can be an unnerving experience. For all of you who were good at car seats and carpools, who knew how to throw the best birthday parties, and who had a real knack for doing great bedtimes—puberty is a shock. All of a sudden, none of your best tricks work. You give up. Then, again all of a sudden, your 160-pound monster, the one with three days' growth of beard, crawls into your lap and wants to be cuddled again. Life is confusing.

This short essay is all about the things they don't teach you in Parenting 101—that having teenagers is a Zen process. To prove that it is a Zen experience, consider these three quotations from *The Art of War* by Sun Tzu. It is the Chinese edition of *Pirke Avot*.

So what kills the enemy is anger, what gets the enemy's goods is reward.

Force means shifts in accumulated energy or momentum. Skillful warriors are able to allow the force of momentum to seize victory for them without exerting their strength.

Persistence is not profitable. An army is like fire—if you don't put it out, it will burn itself out.

To apply these passages to your family life, just substitute the word "teenager" for "enemy" and "army" and understand that the technical term "skillful warrior" really means "parent." In other words. *"What kills your teenager's cooperation and spirit is your anger, what gets your teenager to do his/her best is rewards."* Get it?

I have often felt that if a thing is true, its opposite is usually true, too. In raising teenagers this is even more true (and then again it isn't true at all).

Take this example: Every teenager finds somebody else's house to hang out at.

Think about it. There are a couple of kids who just about live at your house and who are helping your child to devastate your refrigerator at this moment. Meanwhile, their parents would testify in court that your kid is always hanging out at their house. How these kids can always be in your house while your kid is always at their house—and the peer group is never apart—is an expression of the distortion of the time-space continuum in the universe; it is Zen physics and probability theory and all that stuff.

Yes, teenagers are confusing.

The midrash understands adolescent *angst.* It tells this story of the first bar mitzvah. I call this story "Abram Destroys His Father's Dreams:"

In *Pirke d'Rabbi Eliezer,* a midrashic collection, we learn that Abram was thirteen on the day that he smashed his father's idols. Now that's a myth that many thirteen-year-olds I know live. They could easily take Abram's Louisville Slugger and smash their father's most cherished obsessions to bits. Becoming a teenager is smashing all of your parents' false gods to bits—telling your parents that what they believe and what they stand for is nothing but meaningless trinkets and dust collectors.

To solve this problem, the midrash tells another story. I call it: "Isaac Abandons His Kids." In Genesis Rabbah, a different volume of midrash, we find this story of Jacob and Esau. Until they were thirteen, Jacob and Esau were sent to day school and their life was controlled by their parents. When they were thirteen, their parents set them free. Jacob, the one who would become "the God-Wrestler," Israel, continued his studies and remained true to the One God. Esau immediately left school and found a string of Canaanite women. He was the wild man. He followed them into idolatry and paganism and other addictions. When that happened, Isaac became the first Jew to say the bar mitzvah *brakhah*: **"Praised are You, Adonai, our God, Who has liberated me from the liability of being punished for** (the horrible things) **this** (kid does)."

When you put these two stories together you get a lesson I first learned on a *Star Trek* episode (whose plot, I've since learned, has mutated in my memory). Because of some accident, anti-matter versions of Kirk, Spock, and Chekov emerge. Suddenly, they know that if they are touched by their anti-matter equivalents—they will die. To save their own lives, and those of their suicidal anti-matter offspring, they form a circle, spinning so that each is always opposite somebody else's double. Parenting teenagers is a lot like that image. Our kids—at least for a few years—are our anti-matter offspring. During these years, our job is often to be good parents to somebody else's *angst*-ridden kids, while some other adult is serving in a similar role to the orphans we have raised. Both sets of parents, however, get to enjoy the few moments of respite—when your new moon monster, the one with breasts the same size as yours, still wants to cuddle.

a. You have to live with the Zen knowledge that you cannot remain in control. The rabbinic "Born Free" *brakhah*: **"Praised are You, Adonai, our God, Who has liberated me from the liability of being punished for** (the horrible things) **this** (kid does)," teaches the same lesson as Sun Tzu: *"An army is like fire—if you don't put it out, it will burn itself out."* You've done your best up to now. Now, recite the Serenity Prayer: "God grant me the serenity to accept the things I cannot change, the courage to change the things I can, and the wisdom to know the difference." As hard as it is, the only way to hold on is to let go. (I told you it was Zen!)

b. Teenagers will live a lot of their lives in a teenage subculture—a horde of wild children wandering *Lord of the Flies* style though the shopping malls and playgrounds of North America. It is better if they serve part of this time with and among other Jewish feral children with some guidance. Getting them connected to Jewish camps and youth programs before "the change" helps.

c. Even though they are teenagers, kids still need adults to listen and advise. In the technical literature they are called mentors. Barbara Zeidman calls me "Kent's adult friend," while Bruce Whizin labels the behavior "uncling." Work on the assumption that the universe is just. If you are a receptive adult—a good proxy parent to someone else's anti-matter child—another good soul is probably doing the same for your son or daughter.

This is the Torah of Stephen Stills, one meaning of the message he wrote as the chorus which began a cliche: "If you can't be with the one you love—love the one you're with."

In the old days, everyone had an uncle or cousin who had a ranch or a farm. The kids could be sent off to the wilderness to work out their aggression on horses and cabbage patches. These days, due to the technological advances we've acquired, we just have to do the best we can.

Just remember this (another lesson from Sun Tzu): *"In battle, confrontation is done directly—victory (however) is gained though surprise."*

36 | Joel's Bar/Bat Mitzvah Advisory

To make bar or bat mitzvah effective, for it to have a profound and ongoing impact on your child's Jewish development, it has to be set in context. To do that, you have to go against the conventional wisdom and help to reinvent the meaning.

Matt was twelvish when this story happened. Under much pressure, his parents decided to buy him a *Playboy* magazine. Mom objected—for all the right reasons, which she clearly expressed, about treating women as sex objects. Dad leaned towards giving in, not because it was "cute" junior machismo or the right "man-in-making" kind of growth experience—but because it was better coming from them than from "the street corner."

They bought the magazine and set all kinds of rules, like you can't show your friends, and you can't take it out of the house. A few weeks later, Matt went to camp, and Mom was busy helping him unpack his belongings and stow them in his cubby. Out of the trunk, Matt grabbed a metal box and tried to get it out of the way. Mom intercepted and demanded to look in the box. In it she found Polaroid pictures of the *Playboy*. She tried to confiscate the pictures, claiming that even though Matt had followed "the letter of the law," he had violated the spirit of the *Playboy* rules.

This case makes the perfect *Talmud 2000* bar/bat mitzvah test case:

> If so, should they have imposed the restrictive rules about its usage? Did those rules appropriately limit or undermine the magazine's function?
>
> And, given the situation, should the Polaroid pictures have been confiscated, punishing Matt for having broken the rules? Or should he have been honored for his "legal" insight, and allowed to keep them?
>
> Does any of this make a difference? Is there a long-run lesson and message here, or is this just a run-of-the-mill adolescent run-in?

A Hasidic teaching: To be a good person—one should have a pair of pants with two pockets. In one pocket should be a note with a quotation from the Psalms: "For me was the world created." In the other pocket one should have a different quotation from the Psalms: "I am nothing but dust and ashes." When one is feeling self-confident, one goes for the "dust and ashes" quotation. When one is down, one goes for the other slip of paper. It is a great lesson about *Midot Tovot*—proper balance.

Birthdays and the true meaning of bar or bat mitzvah represent this same balance.

- Originally bar mitzvah had no ceremony, it was just a legal status. The Talmud talks about the age of thirteen as the moment of assuming responsibility; there is no party. It was a lot like the draft. The Talmudic bar mitzvah says: "From this day on—if you do anything wrong, you will be punished." It is all "I am nothing but dust and ashes."

- Birthdays, on the other hand, are centered in "For me was the world created."
  I am in Cleveland, filling a guest sermon slot. I am to follow the bar mitzvah. Because I am *bimha*-sitting, I am part of the processional down the aisle, the *hakafah*, the circuit of the sanctuary made with the Torah scroll. In the process I notice something I have seen before, but never focused on or really understood. It is customary during the *hakafah* to use one's prayer book or one's *tallit* to kiss, then to touch the Torah (which the bar or bat mitzvah is carrying.) During that service in Cleveland, the bar mitzvah boy's friends—a lot of kids, and a few adults—were intentionally missing the Torah and kissing the kid.
  I'd seen it often before, but it had never registered. When I thought about it, I realized it conveys a wonderfully ambivalent message—

representing the best and the worst of American folk Jewry's Jewish contributions. It is a great statement of love and regard. In its best symbolism, it labels the bar or bat mitzvah initiate "special" and renders him or her a vessel for the Torah she or he is carrying. The celebration has created—the celebrant has become—a celebrity. It has gone heavily towards a "for me was the world created" moment. It also raises a serious question, suggesting that the Torah may well have been reduced to a prop. It seems quite likely that the "dust and ashes" message has been completely lost.

American folk culture has expanded bar mitzvah status from a stage in an evolutionary process, by transforming it into a poignant moment of celebration, a ritual which feels meaningful and true. A whole new branch of the Jewish tradition has been grown out of a minor legal statement. A legal status has ballooned into a life cycle epic. We have added a lot of good feelings, a simḥah, and a Kodak moment to the Jewish tradition. That is to our credit. Our task, now, is to put bar and bat mitzvah back into balance, bringing back the sense that Torah is central, the sense of personal obligation—and the balancing insight: "I am nothing but dust and ashes."

In America, bar and bat mitzvah seems to have been siderailed onto the birthday track. The more we make our b'nai mitzvah celebrations into birthday-melanoma, the more we will lose the sense of Jewish responsibility and continuity which they were initially intended to mark. Bar mitzvah has become all "For me was the world created" and almost no "I am nothing but dust and ashes." Perhaps, we should make our b'nai mitzvah candidates fast and stay up all night in the chapel—the way the ancient knights-to-be did. However, the single best path towards renewal is not to try to take the "bar" out of the "bar mitzvah"—the debate over "band" versus "DJ" is too well-ensconced in our folk traditions—but to go the other way and "Judify" each and every birthday.

This brings us back to a *Talmud 2000* question we first encountered in **Number 10: Make Kiddush and ha-Motzi on Thanksgiving:**

What could make a birthday a legitimately Jewish event?

What *brakhah* should be said on a birthday?

What famous birthday midrashim need to be created?

What obligations (mitzvot) should be assumed on each birthday?

What *tzedakah* custom should be developed as part of a Jewish birthday celebration?

Bar and bat mitzvah need a book of their own—I hope to be writing it myself in the next year or two. Until then, here are a few insights.

1. Bar or bat mitzvah is a *faux* ceremony, a Hallmark mutation, the transformation of what was supposed to be one step in an ongoing developmental process of escalating responsibility into a Kodak moment.

   Listen to one short sample text: **MISHNAH: One should not "afflict"** (with fasting, etc.) **children on Yom Kippur; but one should start to train them a year or two before** (they are thirteen), **in order that they become used to the practices. GEMORA: ...Rabbi Nahman said: "At nine and ten one trains them by the hours** ("Can you make it fasting to noon this year?" etc.) **At eleven and twelve they fast to the end of the day based on rabbinic teaching** (because the Bible doesn't prescribe it—but we think it is good for them.) **And, at thirteen they are obligated by biblical law to fast all day..."** (*Yoma* 82a) In other words, reaching thirteen was part of a process—not a photo opportunity. (Carol could take a whole sequence of yearly photos of Rob and Geoff fasting at eight, nine, ten, eleven and so on, to add to her album, but you wouldn't have to hire Jules Porter photographers to do a professional job. By the way, Uncle Jules *will* give me a kickback if you do happen to hire him!)

   Classically, thirteen was not seen as "manhood" or "womanhood" or "adulthood"—it was rather seen as an end to childhood, the beginning of some aspects of legal responsibility. It was analogous to a driver's license, which does not entitle one to vote, or reaching voting age, which does not allow one to drink alcohol (in almost any states anymore)!

2. Even though bar or bat mitzvah has grown beyond control, I believe there is little or no hope of—and therefore I have no strategy for— getting back to what it should be: a Thursday morning event, at which, after a six-month apprenticeship with the *minyan*, the child leads services for the first of many times in her/his life, and reads the first of many Torah portions that s/he will master. Then, after some honey cake and wine—and to show the significance of the day—the young person goes back to public school and probably fails a math test. That is not going to happen. So, we've got to go with the flow—folk Judaism ultimately knows best and wins again.

(I have heard the karate theory of bar or bat mitzvah. It is an "If you can't lick 'em, join 'em" approach which says, "Just as students of karate are trained to use their opponents' weight against them—we should use bar or bat mitzvah as a way of coercing families into more intense Jewish living." The idea is that, just as karate experts know that leaning or momentum in any one direction is a moment of weakness, and can use that weakness or that momentum against an opponent, especially a bigger opponent, bar or bat mitzvah is a time of leaning and momentum. The reasoning is that it is therefore our best chance to apply pressure. I find little merit to this notion (though I, too, am often caught in its flow). The flaw is that, while we win the fall, we also often train families never to lean in a Jewish direction ever again.

Everyone has already written to condemn Mitzvah a la *Gatsby*. I don't feel the need to do so. By the same token, you are an adult, you've bought this book and I can let you make your own decisions about videotaped invitations, laser tunnel smoke machine entrances for the Grand Mitzvahed Enfant Terrible, T-shirts which read "I Survived Jeremy's Bar Mitzvah Debacle" etc. It's already trite to tell you to downplay the "bar" and up the "mitzvah" quotient. Consider it said. If you want a good voice for all of that, buy a copy of Rabbi Jeffrey K. Salkin's *Putting God on the Guest List: How to Reclaim the Spiritual Meaning of Your Child's Bar or Bat* Mitzvah (Jewish Lights, 1992). (Go ahead, buy the book if you want—unlike Uncle Jules, they won't give me a commission.) Instead, I want to share a few other insights. Consider this bar mitzvah moment from my memory album:

Insight One:
Bar or bat mitzvah must make a change in your child's life.

In Darren's bar mitzvah speech he pointed out that all through his life his parents had used his bar mitzvah as a milestone, listing things he couldn't do until he was thirteen. He put them on notice that now he expected to begin doing those things.

Then his mother tried to respond: "Darren, over the past several weeks, while we were driving to your meetings with the rabbi, your practice sessions with the cantor, or your work with your tutor, you would ask me, 'What is the purpose of a bar mitzvah? Why do I have to have a bar mitzvah?' You said, 'I'd rather be home playing my guitar or doing architectural drawings on my drawing board.' I hope that someday you will understand why a bar mitzvah is important. (There was a big pause.) Maybe someday in the future you will be traveling abroad and you'll, by chance, find yourself in a synagogue and something will be familiar—and you will make a connection. Or maybe sometime when you are playing your guitar, you'll write an important Jewish song. Or, someday if you do become an architect, maybe you'll design a synagogue—and then you'll decide why a bar mitzvah is important."

The rabbi later commented, after the blessing, that having been at Darren's *brit milah* and at his bar mitzvah, he hoped to be at his wedding—and then he emphasized that there were things that he still wouldn't be permitted to do until then. It got a laugh.

Darren became a Jewish adult in the Marrano tradition.

Here is my first basic principle: **Bar or bat mitzvah must make a change in your child's life.** Darren sensed that, he just didn't know what the difference should be. His parents sensed that too, but didn't know what to suggest. The rabbi got a laugh—but didn't solve that problem on the *bimah* I want to make a real suggestion to explain to Darren the changes which bar or bat mitzvah makes. It starts with this insight:

Once, a father would say these words at a bar mitzvah: **"Praised are You, Adonai, our God, Who has liberated me from the liability of being punished for** (the horrible things) **this** (kid does)."

It is really a wonderful blessing. It acknowledges that thirteen-year-old boys and girls are nasty creatures—still awfully wolf-like. It sets the kid free, saying "I've done my best—now it is your turn to solo." It honors the boy in the emerging man—it acknowledges the girl in the emerging woman. It speaks to Matt and his Polaroid snapshots. It says, "There is a lot of trouble ahead—let's be honest about it," but also "I set you free to face it on your own—I trust you. If you want me—I'm here, but you're now on your own."

Today, most parents in most synagogues say this *brakhah* instead: **"Praised are You, Adonai, Our God, Who has sustained us, kept us alive, and brought us to this moment."** By itself, without the other *brakhah*, it is 180 degrees in the wrong direction. It takes the spotlight off the kid—it talks about the parents. It says, "Thank God, *we* made it to this point. Now we're all adults." Even the "we" of this *brakhah* is oppressive. It keeps the kid at home. The original *brakhah* which said "let the kid take the punishment s/he deserves" is a "nothing but dust and ashes" statement. It invites the growth-filled chaos which will be adolescence. The substitution of *she-he-heyanu*, the conjuring of the Kodak moment, makes it all "for me was the world created." We've sent Norman Rockwell an engraved invitation.

We are not going to take the *she-he-ḥeyanu* out of the bar or bat mitzvah process. No one is going to give up the "capture in the heart" record of this life cycle event. But, we can learn two other lessons from the original *brakhah*. We can restore the balance:

a. We must grant a post-bar or bat mitzvah child the ability to fail. We still have years to provide the safety net, but we will have to let them walk the high wire on their own.

b. Since the real meaning of bar and bat mitzvah is about responsibility and punishment (not privilege), bar mitzvah should be actualized as a change-point in the family's disciplining structure. In my mind, it would be the point where "grounding" and "getting busted" end— and taking responsibility for the consequences of one's actions begins. I would hope that from the day after bar or bat mitzvah, all "punishment" would end, and collective problem solving would take over— leading towards real solo responsibility in the college years. That is an insight which Darren and his parents might honor.

Joel's Twenty-Third Law: Say and mean the *brakhah*: *"Praised are You, Adonai, our God, Who has liberated me from the liability of being punished for (the horrible things) this (kid does),"* at your child's mitzvah event. Mean it, and let it change your relationship with him/her.

Insight Two:
Do not let your bar or bat mitzvah be a private event.

Twilight mitzvah events are a hallmark of the privatization of Jewish life. They are good because they can flow into a night "dancing" party—but they also are staged in a "gated community" where only those who are invited are part of the moment. More and more, privatization is the growing trend. (Think of the emergence of bar or bat mitzvah mills that now bring the training, the rabbi, the Torah, the caterer, and the photographer into your own home—all without synagogue membership.) This moves the coming of age in precisely the wrong direction.

My second basic bar or bat mitzvah principle is: **Do not let your bar or bat mitzvah be a private event.** It is the privatization which leaves the community out, and targets the kiss on the kid and not the Torah. Having been raised as a Reform Jew, I lack the experience of a daily minyan, which I've since learned about from my mother's new husband, Harold. Harold was raised in a Conservative universe I visited as a boy, but of which I was never part.

For him, and for a few of my friends, bar or bat mitzvah began with a six-month stint at the morning minyan. There, among the regular elders, and the elders-in-training who were putting in their time mourning for a parent, they learned by daily practice (or at least a couple of times a week) the regimen of the prayer service, the dance steps of the service's choreography, the art of wrapping tefillin, the ritual of the glass of schnapps at *simhah* times, a few good dirty jokes (which they regularly told in school) and that there was a circle of men who would always be there for them.

When I think about the life cycle of the morning minyan, I think of the robot grandmother in Ray Bradbury's story, "I Sing the Body Electric". (You can rent the tape; it was an after-school special called "The Electric Grandmother"—and it was also once a *Twilight Zone* episode with Billy Mummy.) She was built to replace the dead mother of a family of kids. She nurtures them through childhood and gets them to resolve their grief and find fulfilling lives. She leaves when they grow old enough to need her no longer . She returns when they are old and feeble, and again need someone to take care of them. It is a beautiful image of the Great Mother.

The minyan, as a corporate being, was classically there to celebrate a boy's birth and participate in his entry into the Jewish people, there to nurture a boy into manhood, there to comfort a man when he spent time in the ashes—mourning his parents and later perhaps his wife (or, God forbid, a child), there to escort a man as he aged towards the void, there to cry at his funeral, and there to remember him perpetually.

> Almost every non-Orthodox man dropped out of morning minyan right after his bar mitzvah. Harold did—my friends did. But they all came back later—drawn like iron shavings to a magnet—when their fathers, mothers, and wives died. From then on, each one's membership in this supportive circle of men was permanent. Each knew with surety that he would be back once a year, and that his son who would be his kaddish would follow in his steps.

This is a cycle of coming of age—to real maturity—which is all but lost today in non-Orthodox circles. The carpools killed it, the suburbs did it in, and sadly, the Reform movement never valued it at all. They never understood that the Jewish people needed a place for the old men to go. Once, the American bar mitzvah was legitimately an initiation into an eternal circle of elders who would always be there when life's real tests were faced. Unfortunately, it has now become something else.

Somehow, if a bar or bat mitzvah is to move your child toward the most positive Jewish future, it should not be a day which focuses exclusively on him or her as an end—a prince or princess for the day experience—but rather a move out of the home and towards the Jewish community. I can't tell you how (because I don't know your community), but a bar or bat mitzvah should move a child toward a real relationship with the Jewish people in an ongoing Jewish commitment—and not out if it.

Insight Three:
Do not let bar or bat mitzvah be overly important.

You should already know, "Do not make a bar or bat mitzvah into a wedding." I know it hasn't made it to Seattle yet, but in L.A. it is S.O.P.—three dances into the evening, the requisite hora medley is played, out come the chairs, and—just like the bride and groom at a traditional wedding—the bar or bat mitzvah and then all the other family members are individually lifted high in the air and danced around. It is celebrant as celebrity.

My copy editor, Carolyn Moore Mooso, says: "My theory is that parents do this at bar or bat mitzvah events because they've already given up on the expectation of celebrating a Jewish wedding with/for their kids, so they're just agglomerating the most picturesque wedding traditons onto a bar or bat mitzvah. Watch for the bar or bat mitzvah stomping a wineglass soon."

I therefore won't make abstinence from mints with the kid's name on them in icing one of my rules. If you're at all good at this, and on the right wave length, you will have already picked up on the thirteen mitzvot pattern, and added some "good deeds" and *g'milut hasidim* merit badges to your bar or bat mitzvah experience. So be it. It is good. And I assume that you already know that bar or bat mitzvah should not be treated as an exit from Jewish learning, synagogue going, or any form of Jewish life—it was engineered originally to be just the opposite.

Joel's third basic bar or bat mitzvah insight is: **Do not let bar or bat mitzvah be overly important.** What we need to do, is keep bar or bat mitzvah from being any more of an event than graduation from junior high school—which is precisely (more or less) what it was originally intended to be. It is just not worth spending years in preparation and recovery.

Insight Four:
Expect your bar or bat mitzvah experience to be rooted as much in rebellion as in acceptance.

One of my adult students, Cliff, told me this story:

> During one of my bar mitzvah lessons, the cantor told me to make sure that I did not go near the sanctuary when I was leaving the shul. He didn't explain. Being twelve, I headed straight for the sanctuary. When I looked through the stained glass into the sactuary—I saw all these naked women. There was a fashion show going-on, and the models were changing in the sanctuary. There were naked limbs and lingerie everywhere. Since then, there has always been this erotic edge to going to services.

Bar or bat mitzvah is all about being twelve or thirteen and a twelve-year-old state of being is all about rebellion and separation. Listen to what the Talmud understands about the Torah's law regarding the execution of rebellious children. (I have left this text in the masculine form—because that is the only way it makes sense.)

> **When is it possible to execute a son for being a stubborn and rebellious son?**
>
> He is liable for capital punishment from the time he first grows two pubic hairs to the time he first grows a beard.
>
> **The Torah teaches:** *"If a man has a rebellious and disobedient son...he shall bring him to the elders in the community's public place...and the men of the town shall stone him to death."* (Deuteronomy 21:18-21).
>
> Because the Torah says "son" and not "man"—an adult son is obviously exempted. And, any boy who is still a child—and is therefore not responsible for fulfilling the mitzvot—cannot be liable for his actions. (*Sanhedrin* 8.1/68b ff)

My friend Melanie Berman studied some of this material with her students, graduating high school seniors at the Los Angeles Hebrew High School. They came up with a very simple insight. Consider it a piece of *Talmud 2000*:

> **Why is bar or bat mitzvah at age thirteen?**
>
> Because that is the last time parents could make their kids go through with it. My parents could make me do it at thirteen, but I am a hell of a lot more rebellious now!

Let's consider a much more major shift in bar or bat mitzvah—at least in fantasy.

I would have the parents of *b'nai mitzvah* children drag them into the synagogue courtyard. I would have each elder stand with a cinder block in his or her hands as the charges against each of the rebellious children were detailed. I would have each parent admit that their child/ren was/were dangerous on some level. Next, the elders would lift the cinder blocks and get ready to pelt the kids—then at the last moment each parent would stop the action and say—"No, despite everything wrong with the kid, I want to keep him/her."

Then the *brakhah*: **"Praised are You, Adonai, our God, Who has liberated me from the liability of being punished for** (the horrible things) **this** (kid does)." would have lots of meaning. So would the process of bar or bat mitzvah as the beginning of a rebellion which leads towards adulthood. It is the beginning of pimples, masturbation, ugly loud music, slammed doors, and the two-hour shower. Enjoy them—even they won't last forever.

In Hebrew, the word *zaken* means beard. *Z'kenim* is the word for elders—the bearded ones. Bar or bat mitzvah is the time of an emerging struggle—real adulthood is its resolution. And so, my final basic recommendation is this: **Expect your bar or bat mitzvah experience to be rooted as much in rebellion as in acceptance.**

The Beginning

1. It is easy to find all kind of wonderful ways that schools and families have made the process of studying for bar or bat mitzvah meaningful. They all have to do with making Torah study more than "the tape."

2. Likewise, there is a wonderful list of mitzvah projects and *tzedakah* commitments which have been actualized to bring the coming of mitzvah into perspective. All of them make sure that the envelopes move in two directions and that the insights come out of both pockets.

3. And, many families have pioneered the return to the appropriately scaled "event" and have Torah to teach on that subject.

I have resisted being practical and useful in this regard because I don't want you to get lost in useful detail. There is a final, and more important, insight to be taught. To actualize the kind of bar or bat mitzvah you really want, know that it is nothing you can begin in seventh grade, or even sixth.

Final Insight:

Bar or bat mitzvah only expresses its full meaning and has its full impact when it has been a thirteen-year-old lifetime in the making—and can look forward to another hundred and seven years of Jewish living to fulfill its promise.

Even so, a Few Practical Suggestions

1. Rob Starin's grandmother was in the Jewish old age home. Rob had his bar mitzvah twice, once at the Jewish old age home and once in shul.

2. Cherie Koller-Fox spends an evening one-on-one with each bar or bat mitzvah child. Among the things which take place is a mitzvah-by-mitzvah review of the Jewish tradition in which student and teacher talk about the meaning and purpose of each and every one.

3. My synagogue has a long-lost custom called *Ben/Bat Torah*. Kids used to be invited to read Torah on the anniversary of their mitzvah events. I wish they would reinstate it. It was a good idea. Valley Beth Shalom, my other shul, keeps an active circle of teenaged Torah readers.

4. In L.A. we now have a bar and bat mitzvah trade show—the Expo. Twice a year the centerpiece and ice sculpture people, the laser-etched invitation people, and all the bands and DJs rent a big hall together, serve you sample hors d'oeuvres, and show you the latest technological innovations. Boycott the event if one occurs in your territory, just on purpose. You don't need to see the smoke machines and laser tunnel.

5. Make your kid, boy or girl, run a solo Shabbat as a home readiness test. Make him or her responsible for actualizing the Shabbat dinner for the family the Friday before or of the event. Make sure that it starts with menu planning, shopping, and cooking as well as *brakhot*.

Dating & Marriage

37 Use Bribes to Keep Your Children from Interdating and Thereby Intermarrying

Because it is so hard to threaten or forbid you child from interdating, go the other way and offer rewards for in-dating.

Establish a coercive and manipulative, but non-restrictive, **double standard** about dating Jews; however, do it years before your child begins to even think about dating. Then, consistently fulfill it once dating begins.

Here is the way it works. From the time your child is seven or eight, tell him or her regularly at bedtime (or in other convenient moments) that someday when s/he is old enough to want to go out on dates with boys (or girls), it's really important to you that s/he dates other Jews. You should readily admit that you can't *control* who they date—you want to concede this point immediately. Confess that if you forbid them to date non-Jews they could (and probably would) sneak around you and do it anyway. Then, testify that you do not want to encourage dishonesty in your family. Then reach your big conclusion and say (really dramatically), "I won't forbid you. I'll just tell you what I hope for you—that you will date and marry good Jewish wo/men. And, because that is important to me, I will support it every time you do. I will pay you (let's say) $10 every time you date a Jew—and let you use my car—as a reward for doing something I think is important. You can date any non-Jew you choose, but it will make me unhappy, and you'll have to walk and pay all of your own way."

Done early, this will probably start out as a family joke which conveys a powerful family value. Actually implemented, it will be a powerful statement of what you hope for the present and the future. And, practiced with consistency, it will have a profound influence. And all that time, it is proactive and nonrestrictive.

Here is the big fear (and we can talk about it). At some point, with gonads bursting over some blond with Viking genes and a *Bain de Soleil* tan, your kid yells at you, "You are prejudiced." At that moment you can smile and say, "Yes." The child may next yell, "You are trying to control me." With confidence, you can answer, "No, I'm just trying to manipulate you. You can still do what you want." Then, no matter which of the big three final spewings of fury your child chooses, you can end the conversation: "You still have your free will; you can still make any choices you want. I've made my choices, too, and that's to reward things which lead to the survival of the Jewish people—something which is very important to me." While this conversation is sure to end in an angry child walking out of the room and slamming some door, it is not the end of your family—and you can smile, knowing that it is also not the end of the Jewish people, either.

Extensions

The original inspiration for this practice came from my friend and teacher, Rabbi Shelly Dorph. It came from his famous Hebrew High School Parents' Orientation speech. He used to tell parents at those meetings never, ever to force kids to come to Hebrew High—instead, he advised bribing them to attend. "Personally," Shelly used to tell parents, "I suggest that you offer to buy them the car you are going to have to buy them anyway, if they go until they graduate." Then, he would continue, "And never keep them from going out and doing anything on Saturday night, just because they will have class early on Sunday morning—instead, just wake them up, shove them in the shower, and kiss them before they pile into the carpool." Being a good and creative parent, I'm sure you can figure out a number of proactive, positive Jewish uses of the bribe.

My friend and personal Czarina of Family Education, Harlene Appelman, builds upon the concept and explains, "In our house we paid for anything Jewish our kids wanted. For anything Jewish they wanted to do—there was always the money, no questions asked. Anything else they wanted to do, any other extracurricular activity, was fine, but they had to find that money on their own. But for anything Jewish, they just had to ask."

What is important in all of these cases is not so much the money as the message conveyed.

38 Some Jews by Choice are Great Jews

The future of the Jewish people will not be assured by a return to a kind of ethnic apartheid—where children fear involvement with non-Jews. Bluntly, Jews by choice and supportive non-Jews are everywhere in the Jewish community—they are even part of your family (unless you come from the small number of exception-families that prove my point.) To assure the Jewish future of your family, your child must feel that Jewishness is valuable and worth preserving; prejudice against involvement with non-Jews won't work—there is no stigma left.

At least once a week, Thomas Jefferson makes a contribution to my Hebrew School class. At some point in the Bible lesson, I'll mention something the famous French medieval commentator Rashi taught. At that point, Daniel will interrupt, and say, "Rashi was my relative." Without missing a beat, Yoni will pick up the cue, and say his line, "And Thomas Jefferson was one of my relatives." Yoni is telling the truth; his father is a Jew by choice. Even so, the family has lived in Israel, sent their child to a Jewish day school, and been active participants in Jewish life. When I teach, Thomas Jefferson and Rashi stand arm-in-arm in the back row.

In **Number 2: Always Tag All Four Bases**, I told the story of the kid who had the grandfather in the Klu Klux Klan. When I told that story to my friend, Dr. Joseph Reimer, who is in Jewish educational research, he said, "I was observing a school in Lexington the other day where one of the fathers at a ninth-grade family event said, "I'm not sure but my father was either in the S.S. or the Nazi Army." We have met the enemy and they are now members of our congregations.

In Washington adjacent Maryland, I meet Nicholas. His is another one of these new-age Jewish stories. A Jewish mother (who was deemed an unfit mother) loses custody of her son to the non-Jewish father. As a zinger in the custody fight, she gets the father to agree to continue the boy's Jewish education. The father is killed shortly thereafter in car crash. His parents inherit both the child and the Jewish obligation. Nick is brought to the *bimah* for his bar mitzvah by a wonderful pair of non-Jewish grandparents who have been his Jewish guardians.

In New Jersey I meet a wonderful Jewish teacher named Ron and his two children. He is one of the best classroom teachers I've ever seen. I take Ron and his kids out to dinner and hear an amazing story. The children's mother was a Catholic actress. Ron was a struggling Jewish actor. They were married in the Church and Ron took the pledge that the children would be raised as Catholics. The mother died suddenly and the priest came to visit Ron and asked him to change his vow. The priest said, "You are not capable of raising these children as Catholics; they need a religion, therefore you should raise them as Jews." Ron went Hebrew School shopping and found a synagogue which would take the kids without conversion. He drove carpool. Then, he volunteered his acting skill to play Moses in a school program. Soon, he was drafted to teach in the school. As long as he had to go—he liked kids, and was now a professional teacher—he agreed. The priest, who remained a family friend, went to Israel and bought the *tallit* that the son wore at his bar mitzvah. Ron continued teaching after the son's bar mitzvah—the son in fact, kept coming and worked as a *madrikh* in the school. Right after the daughter's bat mitzvah, the family dropped out of the synagogue and Jewish life (to work on after-school sports as a family unit).

In northern California I meet a non-Jewish woman (married to a Jewish man) who is the chairperson of the board of religious education of a synagogue. I look perplexed and it is explained to me: "She is one of the best Torah readers in the synagogue and keeps one of the few kosher homes."

Even more confused, I ask, "Then why hasn't she converted?" The answer: "She won't convert while her parents are alive. Her father is a minister."

There are thousands of these stories around today.

Now for the facts:

- The intermarriage rate is now over fifty percent. That is a factoid which is now fairly well known. Less well known is the fact that most converts (in either direction) are women—men are the ones who tend to refuse to change. (If you want to understand why, read Deborah Tannen's *You Just Don't Understand: Women and Men in Conversation*. It is a book about gender, not conversion.)

- Secular Jews are less likely to provide their children with a Jewish education than intermarried religious couples.

- Many, many former non-Jews, Jews by choice, are now active Jews and often serve as leaders in the Jewish community. There are now Jews by choice who are rabbis, cantors, educators, and an awful lot of synagogue board members. (Again, most of these are mothers.) Likewise, in a large number of homes where the mother has not converted, she is often the dominant force for providing Jewish custodial care.

- Many Jews by choice reject conversion at the time of marriage or even at the birth of their children. Often it happens when their children are of school age. That is the story of Barbara Zeidman whose wisdom is found throughout this volume. She is not only a Jew by choice, and a great Jewish parent, but a former synagogue president and a regional officer of the UAHC.

- At this moment, just more than 40% of Jewish children of school age are receiving a Jewish education. According to Steven M. Cohen's research, over 70% of Jewish children will be enrolled in a Jewish learning environment (formal or non-formal) at some point in their lives, but often this involvement will be too brief.

- There has been a lot of research into what "treatments" (schools, camps, preschools, etc.) are most likely to result in in-marriage. Don't let anyone fool you—we know just about nothing except: the **more**—the **better**.

- There is a famous essay called "The Ever-Dying People" by David Ravidovich. It points out that every generation of the Jewish people, starting with Abraham and Sarah, has worried that because of assimilation, they might be the last generation of Jews.

I hope, thus far, I've convinced you that the picture is confusing. There are no rules, only a collection of apparent truths.

1. Jewish is as Jewish does. A person's commitment to the future of the Jewish people is a better test of their offspring's Jewish future than any genetic or ethnic measure.

2. Cherie Koller-Fox, my constant inspiration, teaches children in preparation for bar and bat mitzvah in her school, her new mitzvah, "Make sure that by the time you get married, the person you marry is Jewish." There is a powerful realism in her mitzvah, therefore I'll make it one of my rules.

3. The single best way to preempt interdating (and therefore intermarriage) is to have your child committed to doing Jewish things with other Jews. This whole book is about how to try to effect that outcome.

4. If your child does interdate, interlive, or even intermarry—it need not be the end of your grandchildren's Jewishness. You want to constantly "invite" the non-Jewish signficant other into your family, and into things Jewish—otherwise you are likely to polarize the situation and drive them away. (How to do this is potentially the topic for another *40 Things You Can Do* book.)

5. The most critical years tend to be those the Jewish community forgets—the last two years of high school and the college years. Support 11th and 12th grade Jewish involvements, and most of all—because everyone else is abandoning it at the moment—support Hillel and other programs for Jewish college kids. Don't ever give the message that the end of high school and the years in college are time to take a vacation from Jewishness and devote yourself to other foci.

    Joel's Twenty-Fourth Law: Said in the name of Cherie Koller-Fox, "Teach your children that it is a mitzvah to make sure that by the time you get married, the person you marry is Jewish."

Don't worry, your odds aren't too bad. They're almost 50-50 and that's almost 20% percent better than Hank Aaron hit.

Final Wisdom

39 | *Illegitimi Non Carborundum* (Jewish Politics)

Belonging to any kind of group comes with its dark side, politics and disappointment (sort of like a family). To survive in Jewish life, you are going to have to "go with the flow" and endure the frustrations and disappointments of dreams deferred, delayed and dismissed. Those are the institutional realities.

> There is a classic joke about a Jewish Robinson Crusoe who is finally found after years on his desert island. He shows his saviors around the whole complex which he has built in his spare time. Among the accomplishments are two separate synagogues. When he is asked, "Why two synagogues?" he responds nonchalantly, "One I go to, the other I would never set foot in again."

I think it was Cherie Koller-Fox who first suggested the list, but a lot of us have contributed subsequently. It is a list of reasons that people drop out of communal Jewish living. These are the reasons people regularly give for leaving—when those of us who work with Jewish families welcome them back on their return. I'll bet they seem familiar.

a. I am a woman and there didn't seem to be a place for me. I didn't like feeling left out and hidden behind a curtain.

b. My rabbi was a hypocrite. He (choose one of the following) (a) slept with the Sisterhood president, (b) was a racist (and called the custodian a "nigger" in private), (c) was a snob and only dealt with the rich people (who lived on the hill), (d) ignored our needs when my family had a serious problem, (e) only talked about God and ignored the real issues in the world, (f) only talked about political issues and never talked about God, etc.

c. People pretended to be friendly, but they never cared about me/us. We could never be part of the real community.

d. It was too expensive.

e. God let us down. When _____ was sick, I prayed and prayed, but it didn't do any good.

These five reasons just about say it all. Jewish communal life lets us down. It always will. That is the nature of communal life. Let's face it, they spend their money (of which they demand too much) on the wrong things, they are not responsive, they stand for all the wrong things, and they have bad taste. Living in community means lots of compromises—and compromises always let us down.

Here is the final and ultimate truth—being lonely is worse. There are ways of living successfully and Jewishly as an unaffiliated single person, but it is just about impossible to do so as an authentic Jewish family—you either belong to an institution or establish a non-institutional community which meets your needs. Synagogues are a pain. *Havurot* bring their own frustrations. Both take many more meetings than you feel you have the energy to give.

Therefore, I'll give you my simple plan:

Once a month I write a letter of resignation from my synagogue. I tell my rabbi what he has done wrong. I tell my president how much of a hypocrite I think he is. I yell at the school and the youth group and the Sisterhood—and everything else which doesn't live up to my impossible, exacting, but absolutely correct standards. Then (this is the hard part learned after making the mistake a couple of times)—I don't send it.

I recommend that you do the same. Vent all you want—then burn the evidence. Remember that you have to land somewhere.

Rabbi Na<u>h</u>man of Bratzlav told this story:

> A king learns that anyone who eats of the next harvest will go mad.
> He also learns that there is enough food for him and his inner circle
> to skip this harvest and remain sane. He decides to eat the harvest
> anyway—he can't separate himself from the community. But, he and
> his advisors all paint a mark on their foreheads to remind each other
> that by staying with the community all of them have gone insane.

I think of that story as I burn my monthly letter of resignation. I suggest you
do the same. Remember, a synagogue is nothing more than a replica of the
Vatican, Carnegie Hall, Harvard, and Disneyland, built by a committee with a
limited budget.

40 Don't Try to Be Jewish Alone

Judaism is not just in your heart. And, even though family is important, it can't even be lived fully at home. To really get the most out of the Jewish experience, you need to do it in a group.

Judaism is a team sport.

You can play tennis up against the backboard but it isn't the same. Golf works just fine with one person and a bag—but it gets awfully lonely. You can hit the ball in the holes and blast out of the sand traps, but playing against yourself gets old fast—you miss the conversation. We've all played pick-up games of football with four or five people, and done the back-yard stickball thing with one friend and the little sister who gets to be the designated fielder. One-on-one can be a great game, a good way to spend an afternoon with a friend, but it isn't basketball.

When I was fifteen, I spent my last summer at Camp Mendota. Camp Mendota was what Shlomo Bardin called a "Jewish Indian Camp." Shlomo Bardin was the founder of Brandeis-Bardin Institute and I first met him and learned his wisdom through my friend Bruce Powell's stories. Shlomo died six months before I moved to L.A. and would have met him in the flesh. Camp Mendota was all Jewish kids and we had a Friday night service and bagels on Saturday morning, then a Tribal Pow-Wow on Saturday night. It was suburban Jewish kids living out a Zane Grey mutation of the Native American dream. Fifteen was the year I had decided to be a rabbi. It was also the year I got to be a C.I.T. I had emotionally outgrown Camp Mendota, but I had this need to finish the old dream, and be the C.I.T. It was a "both ways" choice. At Mendota, an Indian Camp for "two-way" Jews, Shabbat only lasted through bagels on Saturday morning. I arranged with Joe Schein, the camp patriarch (a warm bear-like grandfather figure) to have Saturday mornings off. I used to take my *Union Prayer Book* and my copy of Martin Buber's *I and Thou* down to this great clearing by the lake and pray and read. I can still smell the blanket of golden orange pine needles that covered the forest floor. It was a great time. I grew from it. To some great degree, even though it goes against the official reading of the Jewish tradition, I found my inner prayer voice and my personal philosophy of Judaism in that clearing that summer. The blanket of pine needles was soft and inviting. But, the power of those Shabbat mornings wouldn't have lasted and it wouldn't have been enough. It was a rehearsal, a kind of practice session where I hit my strokes against the backboard and walked the golf course alone. It was my involvement in Youth Group which had motivated my private prayers, and the expectation of the summer conclave I was going to after camp which gave them a sense of purpose. It was simple. For just those eight Shabbatot, I prayed with my imaginary community.

We've talked about this idea before, back with the story of *Birkot ha-Shahar* (how it's hard to keep exercising at home—despite all the devices those infomercials show you) in **Number 2: Always Tag All Four Bases.** Back then, we learned that cultural peer-pressure is a good and supportive thing. Judaism has always felt that way. I've already made this point, even though underlining it here is worth it—you'll practice more Jewish stuff if you're part of a practicing community. But I have a different point to make here—"hormones."

218

Let's talk about the wisdom of *The Blue Lagoon*, another trashy movie with one good insight. The brother and the sister do just fine on the desert island as children. They romp naked together and have a good old time. When they finally grow into Brooke Shields and Christopher Atkins, the art of coming between her and her Calvins becomes a big issue. Families can be like desert islands. Even if you make the best Shabbatot, light every single possible Hanukkah candle, in-gather all the errant horde for Seder every year, nail a mezuzah on every available door, capture every conceivable Kodak moment—your kids will still grow into the bodies of Christopher Atkins and Brooke Shields. If you care about whom they marry, then you have to care about who stars in their first erotic fantasies—not the movie stars, the actual fantasies that star their acquaintances.

Running the best Jewish home gets them started in the right direction, but it only covers the first part of the journey. Paying dues to a synagogue and sending them to its school (except when there is a conflicting soccer game) doesn't do it either, because odds are, your kids won't find a connection there, if you haven't. Ditto for sending kids to a Jewish day school without actively participating in Jewish life elsewhere. These are all Jewish *Blue Lagoon* childhoods.

The bottom line is this: To keep at it Jewishly in the hard moments, you need the support of a peer group—and so does your child. Otherwise, the storms afford many other warmer ports. The other part of the bottom line is that you can influence (but not determine) that peer group when your children are young. It is much harder once they can express wills of their own, and all but impossible once the state issues them driver's licenses.

> This is the true story of the minyan, the way one midrash tells it. Lot, Abraham's kid-brother-like nephew, has moved away because he's found his big-brother-like uncle oppressive. He leaves the countryside and the endless days and nights of shepherding for the Las Vegas of his times, Sodom. God gets ready to destroy the problem—Lot has found the wrong peer group.

> God talks to Abraham, and they get involved in the "Sodom Debate." Abe is plea-bargaining for Sodom's life. He gets God to agree to save the city if there are 100 good people in it. Next he gets God to drop the number to 90. It then goes to 80, 70, 60, 50, and then Abraham drops the number to ten. We get the minyan, the basic Jewish prayer community, from Abraham's minimal number. Why did Abraham stop at ten? What did he know?

Abraham counted on his fingers that Lot, Lot's wife, Lot's four daughters, and Lot's four sons-in-law all lived in Sodom and Gomorrah. That made ten. Abraham was sure that six of them were righteous and he hoped that the sons-in-law came up to the family's ethical standards—because he knew that less than ten wasn't enough. Noah and his wife, his three sons, and his three daughters-in-law were righteous and God didn't stop the flood for their sake.

A minyan is ten because God won't save the world for less than ten people who are trying to be righteous. Noah had a drinking problem. Lot was selfish. They were not perfect people—but they tried to be good. God respected their efforts. They were good enough people to be considered righteous. Righteous isn't perfect. (Unfortunately for Sodom and Gomorrah, Lot's sons-in-law weren't even good enough people.)

Next, two of God's angels visit Lot. On the way into the city, the men of Sodom try to rape them. (The Torah's meaning here isn't homophobia—as we'll learn later, the Sodomites are willing to rape anything that walks.) To provide adequate hospitality to these strangers (the part Lot remembers from Abraham's home) he offers the men of the city their way with his daughters—if they just leave the men alone. (This reveals the values he *didn't* remember when living among the Sodomites.) The story has an acceptably happy ending—most of them escape.

So what's our lesson? You can learn several. Among them are: It doesn't take 100 people to be a community. And, without the right friends, it is easy to lose who you are. Remember your needs. Remember your children's needs—one is silver and the other gold.

In *Care for the Soul*, Thomas Moore writes:

Loneliness can be the result of an attitude that community is something into which one is received. Many people wait for members of a community to invite them in, and until that happens they are lonely. There may be something of the child here who expects to be taken care of by the family. But a community is not a family. It is a group of people held together by feelings of belonging, and those feelings are not a birthright. "Belonging" is an active verb, something we do positively.

Joel's Twenty-Fifth Law: Don't just pay for a membership in a Jewish organization or institute—be a member. It is the only way to get your money's worth out of it.

Of all the students I teach this year, Zach is the most annoying. There is not a single angry or malicious bone in his body. He does nothing mean or intentionally disruptive. He just laughs a lot, often out of control. Zach also causes some disruptions because he is a youth group president and there is always some program to advertise or some phone list to distribute. It is hard for me to get angry. Here is the best part. The other day he brought a slide projector to class. He asked if he could have a few minutes to share something with the class. He was doing a project for public school. It was a slide-show autobiography. He was getting ready for his public-school performance (and I suspect he was a little anxious). He wanted to share his life with us, first—it was safer. That is the real meaning of Jewish community.

Applications

1. Carol complains that she shouldn't talk to me, because everything she says winds up in something I am writing. However, this is one more insight from Carol Starin. "When my kids were little, it was just a couple of couples. We called ourselves the Parents' Club. It wasn't anything formal, but we were there for each other."

2. More than 10 years ago we did a documentary on the Jewish community of Grand Junction, Colorado. It was a small group of about 20 families who rented a room in the local Lutheran church and set up the "Jewish Community Center of Grand Junction." In private, they call themselves *B'nai Lutheran*. We did a lot of interviews and learned a lot of interesting things. Almost all of the Jews in town had come from either New York or Denver. They had belonged to synagogues, but they hadn't been active members. They moved to Grand Junction without considering the Jewish consequences. Once they got there, they felt the loss (because Jewishness wasn't in the air the way it was in Brooklyn). They worked hard to seek each other out and then worked hard to sustain a synagogue with skills and accoutrements they had to acquire. There are a lot of them. My favorite was the desks in the classrooms. The whole Jewish enterprise in town was one classroom. Two fathers built custom furniture for their children to study on. Every desk and every bench had a Jewish star cut out of every leg.

The most powerful message about community is that you don't necessarily know it's there, until it is gone.

Epilogue: Become a Redemptive Name Dropper

Jews have always believed in stories. The <u>H</u>asidim in particular believe in the power of stories to do miracles. Take this story:

The old man was lame. He walked with great difficulty. One day he told the story of how his old teacher, his rebbe, had danced. Soon he was gesturing and moving with excitement. Before long he was up and dancing as he told the story. When it was over, he sat down and someone handed him his cane. The <u>H</u>asidim, when they tell this story, always end—"and that teaches us the power in telling stories."

As you've read this book you've probably noticed two things. One, that I tell a lot of stories, and two, that I've worked hard to tell you something about the people whose wisdom I have inherited. I've done it on purpose—both because it is a Jewish value, and because I think it is a good survival skill. If you've ever seen *All That Jazz* (a movie that is worth renting) there is a standing joke that Ben Vereen's character, a television variety host, introduces every guest as "A truly amazing performer, a great humanitarian, and my good friend..." The more he does it for people we know he hates—the more plastic it gets. I hope that has not been the effect in this book. I had a point to make. I wanted to show that Torah, real Jewish survival Torah, comes from scholars and 12-year-olds, from housewives and educators, from old movies and even from rabbis—that Torah is all around us when we make the right connections. The Talmud puts it this way:

> A person who teaches a thing in the name of the person who said it originally, brings redemption into the world.

That is why when we open the Talmud we are constantly running into: "Rabbi So-and-So said in the name of Rabbi So-and-So, that Rabbi So-and-So once taught...." Naming and honoring your teachers is an important value—especially remembering that your parents are your first teachers. But it is important to remember that naming one's teachers is also a way of telling a story and making the teachers dance.

About ten years ago I was handed a bootleg tape of a lecture by "The Rav," Rabbi Joseph Soleveitchik. He begins by explaining how he teaches:

> Whenever I start my lesson, the door opens up and another old man comes in and sits down. He is older than I am. He is my grandfather and his name is Reb Ḥayim Brisker, without whom I cannot teach Torah. The the door opens quietly again and another old man comes in. He is older than Reb Ḥayim. He lived in the seventeenth century. His name is Shabbatai ben Meir ha-Kohein, the famous "Shakh" who might be present when you study Talmud. And then more visitors show up. Some of the visitors lived in the eleventh century and some lived in the twelfth century, some in the thirteenth century—some even lived in antiquity. Rashi—Rabbenu Tam—Rava—Sashba. More and more come in. Of course, what do I do? I introduce them to my pupils and the dialogue commences. The Rambam says something; Rava disagrees. A boy jumps up; he has an idea. The Rashba smiles gently. I try to analyze what the young boy meant. Another boy intervenes and we call upon Rabbenu Tam to express his opinion and suddenly a symposium of generations comes into existence...

In writing this book, I've tried to do just the same thing. I've gathered around my word processor my teachers, from Rashi and Thomas Jefferson to my Nana Grishaver who once carried a bunk bed home on the MTA. I've told story after story and recalled teacher after teacher. For the past several months, all of these people have been gathered in my living room engaged in a conversation about how to best rear the Jews of tomorrow and give the Jewish people the brightest possible future. If you've ever seen *Return From Thunderdome* (*The Road Warrior III*) you'll know what I mean when I say we've been engaged in "The Telling." (It's worth renting, by the way, even if you're not into Mel Gibson, just for its vision of the power of a Marrano Seder to inspire even when the knowledge is garbled.) We've been busy with our *Talmud 2000* task—and I hope it catches on in your home, making some new Kodak moments for your family for many generations. I believe that stories have that kind of power—I believe that with all of my well and carefully aimed heart. I therefore put the whole future of the Jewish people in your hands.

Joel's Last Law: Collect, tell, and retell the stories of Jewish innovation and survival, passing them on to your children in the names of your teachers, for that is the surest path to the brightest possible future.

Appendices

Joel's Laws of Jewish Survival

Joel's First Law: Every year of Jewish education which takes place after bat or bar mitzvah is worth three or more years of anything which takes place earlier.

Joel's Second Law: The best way of making a child fulfill a Jewish obligation is by preempting the need to talk about it—to establish so clear an expectation that it isn't even worth bringing up.

Joel's Third Law: The *she-he-heyanu brakhah* is Judaism's way of saving "Kodak moments" in our hearts. Every time you want a picture to save the moment, whether or not you snap the shutter, say this *brakhah* and add it to the album in your heart.

Joel's Fourth Law: Said in the name of Ira Smith: Even when you feel that you can't be *shomer(et) mitzvot*, a keeper of mitzvot (Jewish actions), always be *zokher(et) mitzvot*, one who remembers (and teaches) that those mitzvot exist.

Joel's Fifth Law: Do not let your Jewish rituals become Marrano customs. Make sure they are not hidden and make sure they have meaning.

Joel's Sixth Law: It is always better to know that you are *compromising* an important Jewish practice because at the moment you "need" to do something else, than to *pretend* that the Jewish tradition consists only of things you want to do.

Joel's Seventh Law: Never do Jewish things for your children's sake. In the end, this will only serve to make Judaism childish and something all of you outgrow (years before dating and marriage come along). Rather, do Jewish things for yourself and then find a way to involve your kids.

Joel's Eighth Law: When you have to make choices, the Jewish tradition must never lose. It can compromise, but it must never lose.

Joel's Ninth Law: Give yourself permission to simplify your Jewish practice when you absolutely need to (trim "shell" not "spark"), but always try to make it taste authentic when you do.

Joel's Tenth Law: Always score the easy mitzvah points. Be smart—at least rack up your Jewish continuity points on all the Jewish stuff which is inherently fun to do.

Joel's Eleventh Law: Always say *"Dayenu"* to any positive expression of Jewishness. Remember, *dayenu* is aggressive-passive (the active inverse of passive-aggressive). It affirms what is as good—and then always seeks more.

Joel's Twelfth Law: The best time to deal with the "problem of Christmas" is at any time in the year but the middle of December.

Joel's Thirteenth Law: Any time your family goes back to the table and finishes the second half of the Seder, the after-dinner part, add 36 bonus points to your score.

Joel's Fourteenth Law: It is better to individualize your participation in Jewish communal practice than to practice Judaism as an individual.

Joel's Fifteenth Law: Said in the name of Harlene Appelman: Never pass up a chance to combine a Jewish opportunity with something you ordinarily think is cool.

Joel's Sixteenth Law. Never let a rabbi or a more learned Jew hang up your mezuzah for you. Instead, make them teach you how to do it for yourself. Never do it for children; rather, give them the resources to do it for themselves.

Joel's Seventeenth Law: Don't just hang a mezuzah. In order for it to work its magic, you have to rub it the right way. The same is true of all Jewish objects in your home.

Joel's Eighteenth Law: Taught in the name of Abraham, Sarah, Danny and his mother, Carol and her father, and either Lonnie or Dorian and whichever family: Find a family mitzvah and make sure there is one date on your calendar which is devoted to it every year.

Joel's Nineteenth Law: Said in the name of Rabbi Yosi Gordon: Be an advocate of *Hebglish* (or if you prefer, *Engbrew*), the new "Yiddish" which is emerging around English rather than German. Use as many real Hebrew nouns in your English conversation as possible.

Joel's Twentieth Law: Post bat or bar mitzvah education is a lot like the thank you notes which follow the ceremony. Few or no children will complete them on their own—that is why it is a mitzvah for parents to insist and even nag.

Joel's Twenty-First Law: Jewish education is not like date rape. When your children say "No," they sometimes do mean "Please make me."

Joel's Twenty-Second Law: If you can't say anything nice about Jewish education—don't say anything at all. (I do give you permission to talk about your worst Jewish schooling experiences if you also share your best times, too. That's only fair!)

Joel's Twenty-Third Law: Say and mean the *brakhah*: *"Praised are You, Adonai, our God, Who has liberated me from the liability of being punished for (the horrible things) this (kid does)."* at your child's mitzvah event. Mean it, and let it change your relationship with him/her.

Joel's Twenty-Fourth Law: Said in the name of Cherie Koller-Fox: Teach your children that it is a mitzvah to make sure that by the time you get married, the person you marry is Jewish.

Joel Twenty-Fifth Law: Don't just pay for a membership in a Jewish organization or institute—be a member. It is the only way to get your money's worth out of it.

Joel's Last Law: Collect, tell, and retell the stories of Jewish innovation and survival, passing them on to your children in the names of your teachers, for that is the surest path to the brightest possible future.

Joel's Bar and Bat Mitzvah Advisory

Insight One: Bar or bat mitzvah must make a change in your child's life.

Insight Two: Do not let your bar or bat mitzvah be a private event.

Insight Three: Do not let bar or bat mitzvah be overly important.

Insight Four: Expect your bar or bat mitzvah experience to be rooted as much in rebellion as in acceptance.

Final Insight: Bar or bat mitzvah only expresses its full meaning and has its full impact when it has been a thirteen-year-old lifetime in the making—and can look forward to another hundred and seven years of Jewish living to fulfill its promise.

Talmud 2000 Questions

Topic: When teenagers protest staying with the family on Shabbat...

"We know that it is good to have a family Shabbat together when the children are little, but where do we learn it is at all possible to keep the kids either at home or in synagogue when they become teenagers?" or "What things are worth fighting over?"

Topic: What is the Modern Jewish Life Cycle?

Figure out the ages of growth in your modern Jewish family. What are the stages of a modern Jewish life cycle? What privileges and what obligations are attached to each stage?

Topic: How do we make a birthday Jewish?

What *brakhah* should be said about a birthday? What midrashim should be written about Adam's birthday? What did Deborah get as a birthday gift? What did Bathsheba give Solomon?, etc. What should be birthday mitzvot? Is there a specific *tzedakah* custom which should be created?

Topic: What should Jews do about Halloween?

Should parents keep their kids from participating in Halloween? Is Halloween a valid reason for skipping Hebrew School? Can Halloween defer Shabbat? Would I let my child miss a whole weekend at camp because trick-or-treat might be missed?

Topic: Purim Nouveau

Must Purim costumes be exclusively Jewish?

Joel: What made Purim different when I was a child was that every costume affirmed Jewish Identity.

Carol: When I grew up in a Reform congregation I thought all Purim costumes had to be Mordechai, Esther, Ahashuerus, Vashti and Haman. When I joined a Conservative Congregation and learned that a Purim costume could be anything, I loved it. It was liberating.

Is Freddy Krueger an acceptable Purim costume?

Topic: Ritual Triage (Establishing holiday priorities)

Until the Messiah comes, and when most American Jews are only willing to really celebrate one or two Jewish holidays, which one should it be?

Topic: Hanukkah Gifts?

A parent's basic obligation is to give each child at least one Hanukkah gift.

To enhance Hanukkah and make it better than Christmas, one should give at least one major gift per child as well as one minor gift per child for each of the eight nights.

One school says the best gift should come on the first night, satisfying immediate desires—the other school says you should build up to the last night.

To maximize the Hanukkah experience one should give a significant gift on each night.

However, the children teach: One should give us one good gift on the first night, two good gifts on the second night, three on the third—until we receive eight spectacular gifts on the eighth night. Parents, however, should expect only one gift.

The essence of the Hanukkah mitzvah is to make children proud and positive about their Jewish heritage.

Why do we give Hanukkah gifts?

Topic: Seder Length

Is a Seder for the adults or for the kids? After you say "both," what is the balance?

One school says: "Passover should be for children. The Seder should be designed to hold their interest. If they get bored, the whole thing is pointless. Adults enjoy a Seder vicariously through the children's eyes."

One school says: "Seder should be an adult experience in which we make a place for children. We are the ones who need to learn from the Seder in order to effectively teach our children. A Seder experience is a model enacted by and for adults."

"How short can a Seder be (and still be legit)?

After all, the real four questions are: "How much longer?" "Do we have to read it all?" "When do we eat?" and "You don't really expect to finish this whole thing do you?"

Topic: Jewish Holidays vs. Public School

On which Jewish Holidays should a Jewish child be kept out of school? Is it different for elementary, junior high school, or senior high school students? What obligations go with keeping your child out of school?

Look at it this way. Which of these are good enough reasons to let your child take a day off from school?

a. Yom Kippur
b. A chance to be a one-day extra in *Home Alone III*
c. First day Passover
d. A family vacation to Hawaii which has to be tagged on to one of mom's business trips
e. First day Sukkot
f. Flying down to Miami in order to go the Super Bowl
g. Grampa's funeral
h. A chance to meet the President of the United States
i. A test for which s/he is not ready or a paper which was not finished
j. An orthodontist's appointment
k. A chance to join an archeological excavation
l. The day that long lost relatives from Riga fly into the United States
m. The child's birthday
n. Shavuot
o. A two-week trip to Israel

p. Hanukkah

q. To stand in line to get U2 tickets

r. As a protest over homophobia in the school board

s. The day before the bar or bat mitzvah

t. To see the opening of *Malcolm X* (per Spike Lee's invitation)

u. Purim

v. The last day of Passover

w. To go with you to a Renoir exhibit

x. Because s/he was up all night reading *The Hobbit* and really wants to finish it

y. Israeli Independence Day

z. Rosh ha-Shanah

If Andy came home and told you that his Hebrew School teacher had said that Hebrew School was more important than "real" school—what would you say?

Topic: Funerals and *Shiva* Houses

At what age should parents take children to *shiva* houses and at what age should they bring them to funerals?

Topic: *Tzedakah*

1. The Jewish tradition asks that between 10 and 20 percent of your income be given to *tzedakah*. Should that be before or after taxes? What is the relationship between taxes and *tzedakah?*

2. The federal government will let you count synagogue dues as a charitable contribution. Should it be considered part of your *tzedakah* allowance?

3. How should you balance your Jewish and non-Jewish commitments, etc.?

Topic: Parenting

What is worth fighting over? What Jewish things should a parent make his/her child do? Which things should they recommend but consider optional?

Topic: Bar or Bat Mitzvah

Can Matt transport the the Polariod pictures of the *Playboy Magazine* he was forbidden to remove from his room?

Why is bar or bat mitzvah at age thirteen?

Because that is the last time parents could make their kids go through with it. My parents could make we do it at 13, but I am a hell of a lot more rebellious now!

The age for formal Confirmation has changed many times. Should we change the age of bar or bat mitzvah? Older or younger?

Glossary

Afikomen/afikoman—from a Greek word meaning "dessert," the *afikomen* is the half matzah that is NOT eaten when one of the ceremonial matzot is broken early in the Pesah Seder, but is saved and distributed as the last thing to be eaten (hence "dessert") at the Seder's end. Traditionally, the *afikomen* is either stolen by a child or hidden by an adult for the children to find during the intervening steps of the Seder meal, and must be found and redeemed (usually with a cash payment) before the Seder can be finished.

Bar mitzvah—from Aramaic *bar*, meaning "son," and Hebrew *mitzvah*, meaning "commandment." The term *bar mitzvah* refers to a Jewish boy who has reached age 13 and thereby become "a son of the commandment," responsible for fulfilling his own ethical and religious obligations. The same term is used to refer to the synagogue service during which the boy is called to say the blessing for reading the Torah for the first time in public, a symbolic act that announces his new status. Usually the *bar mitzvah* boy will also lead some or all of the prayer service, read portions of the Torah and Haftarah, and give a short talk in which he teaches about the portion he has read. A boy who reaches 13 is technically a *bar mitzvah* whether or not he participates formally in such a service, and with or without a celebration. Notice: The celebration afterward is NOT a *bar mitzvah*—it is a party. See also: *bat mitzvah, mitzvah.*

Bat mitzvah (sometimes *bas mitzvah*)—from Hebrew *bat* "daughter" and *mitzvah*, "commandment." A *bat mitzvah* is a Jewish girl who has reached the age of 12 or 13 (depending upon the custom of the community) and

237

thereby become a "daughter of the commandment," responsible for fulfilling her own ethical and religious obligations. The same term is used to refer to the synagogue service during which the girl takes some formal part to announce her new status publicly. In liberal congregations and many conservative congregations, she may participate exactly as a *bar mitzvah* boy would (see *bar mitzvah*), but her participation may be much more limited in some conservative congregations and extremely limited if permitted at all in orthodox institutions.

The variant pronunciation *bas mitzvah* is Ashkenazic (Eastern European) and is becoming less common as American Jews increasingly adopt the Hebrew pronunciation used in Israel, which is Sephardic.

Bimah (*sometimes bema*)—the raised platform from which the Torah is read in a synagogue. In Ashkenazic synagogues the *bimah* is at the front of the sanctuary (usually on the eastern wall), while in Sephardic congregations the *bimah* is usually in the center of the room with the seats surrounding it.

Brit milah—the covenant of circumcision. Refers to the operation or to the ceremony surrounding it when done traditionally. The Ashkenazic pronunciation *"bris"* is still widely used.

Confirmation—a formal ceremony borrowed from the Christian community, in which young people of about 16 or 17 publicly affirm their commitment to the Jewish faith and the Jewish people. (Leaders of the early Reform movement believed Confirmation would be more meaningful than *bar mitzvah* because the young people would be older and more capable of understanding serious religious commitment. They attempted to establish Confirmation as a "modern" and "American" substitute for *bar mitzvah*, but were never completely successful.) Most Reform and Conservative congregations offer Confirmation programs. The ceremony is usually held during the festival of Shavuot, and is generally the culmination of two to four years of post-*bar* or *bat mitzvah* study.

Erev—evening, the eve of. Because the Jewish calendar dictates that each day begins at sunset and ends the next sunset, Shabbat and all festivals are ushered in on "erev ——".

Eruv—a "ritual fence" that Orthodox Jewish families and communities establish to mark an area within which the prohibition against carrying on Shabbat will not apply, since the area will be considered one's own domain. An *eruv* must be an actual physical boundary — string, tape or wire is usually used — and the *eruv* becomes ineffective if this is broken.

Etrog—a citron. This tart yellow citrus fruit is related to the lemon but is longer and thinner with a bumpy skin and a small knob, called the *pitom*, at the blossom end. The *etrog* is one of the "four species" that are blessed as a part of the Sukkot ritual.
An *etrog* is no longer considered kosher if the *pitom* has broken off.

Gefilte fish—the name means "stuffed fish," but *gefilte fish* is actually an Eastern European delicacy made by grinding fish with onion and other seasonings, forming the mixture into cakes and boiling them in fish stock. Usually served cold. In this book, "fish" (in quotes) means *gefilte fish*.

Gragger (also *gregger, grogger*)—a noisemaker used at Purim to drown out the name of the villainous Haman when the story of Esther is read. (The traditional *gragger* is a wooden case on a stick that is twirled so that a wooden tongue snaps against a toothed gear inside, making a loud clacking sound, but small metal and plastic versions are more common today. Any kind of noisemaker that turns up at a Purim celebration is likely to be called a *gragger*.)

Had Gadya—"One Little Goat," the Aramaic title of a very popular and very old song that is usually sung (among others) at the end of a Pesah Seder. Hundreds of different versions of *Had Gadya* have been collected from Jewish communities all over the world.

Halakhah—literally, "the way to go/walk." This term refers to the official legal rulings of the rabbinic tradition on the whole range of Jewish law and practice.

Hallah—a soft egg bread, usually baked in a braided shape, that is traditionally used for the blessing over bread (*ha-Motzi*) on Shabbat and festivals and at life cycle celebrations like wedding receptions.

Hamantash—a triangular pastry stuffed with a fruit or poppyseed filling, traditionally eaten at Purim. Plural: *hamantashen*

Hametz—literally, "leaven," but this term is used traditionally to refer to all food that is not fit for consumption during Passover. This includes all grain or flour products except those prepared particularly for Passover.

Hanukkah—an eight-day festival occurring in late fall or early winter, traditionally said to commemorate the rededication of the Temple in Jerusalem in 165 B.C.E., following the Maccabean wars.
The major home observance is lighting candles for each of the eight nights of the festival, and there are also traditional foods, songs and games. Small gifts of money for children are also traditional, but in North America Hanukkah has become a major gift-giving holiday because of its proximity to Christmas.

Hanukkiah—a candlabrum or oil lamp specially designed to hold candles or oil wicks for lighting the Hanukkah lights. The same item is called a *menorah* (Hebrew for "lamp") by many, and especially by non-Jews.

Haroset—a sweet mixture of fruit, nuts, spices, and sometimes wine or honey, that is one of the symbolic Seder foods. It represents the mortar used in the building the Jews did while enslaved in Egypt. The most common mixture among Ashkenazic Jews is apples and walnuts with wine and cinnamon, but there are many, many variations.

Havdalah—literally, "separation." When capitalized, refers to a ceremony that marks the end of Shabbat, separating Shabbat from the ordinary days of the week, in which blessings are said over wine, spices, and a multi-wicked candle, and good wishes for the coming week are exchanged.

Havurah—a group. Today this term usually refers to a group of families or individuals who gather for purposes of Jewish study or celebration in homes or other informal settings. Such *havurot* are now often sponsored by synagogues to foster social relationships and involvement, but the *havurah* model originally developed as an alternative to formal institutional affiliation.

Kippah—a skullcap, worn during waking hours by Orthodox men and boys, and by other Jews of both sexes who find it meaningful as a sign of respect for God and who may choose to wear a *kipah* at particular times—such as when eating, praying or studying—or all the time. Plural: *kippot*. The Yiddish word for the same item is *yarmulke*.

Kosher—literally, "proper." *Kosher* is a term most often applied to food and meaning the food is permissible according to the Jewish dietary laws. These laws of *kashrut* (*kosher*-ness) cover preparation as well as ingredients. In American slang, *kosher* has returned to its original meaning, as in "There's nothing going on here that isn't perfectly *kosher*."

Latkes—pancakes. To most American Jews, *latkes* are the crisp potato pancakes traditionally eaten at H̲anukkah.

Lulav—a palm frond, with leaflets bunched together and bound to make a long, straight, flat object which is then bundled together with branches of myrtle and willow. The term *lulav* refers either to the palm frond or to the entire bundle; *etrog* and *lulav* together make up the "four species" that are blessed as part of a Sukkot ritual. The symbolism of both the "four species" and the waving of the lulav are explained in a variety of different ways.

Maccabees—a nickname for the H̲ashmon family, whose patriarch was Mattathias of Modi'in, later applied to their followers as well as to the family. They led the guerrilla war against the forces of the Hellenized Syrian ruler Antiochus, whose desecration of the Temple and prohibition of basic Jewish rites caused the general populace to support the zealously observant Maccabees after a long period of popular Hellenizing. The Maccabees' eventual victory and rededication of the Temple is the occasion commemorated by the festival of H̲anukkah.

Madrikh—a guide. In North America this term is used for teenagers assisting teachers in Hebrew school or Sunday school, and also in some Jewish camps and youth programs to refer to counselors or other leaders. In Israel, however, a *madrikh* is usually a tour guide. Feminine: *madrikhah*.

Maggid—an itinerant popular preacher. This title was applied to such preachers from the 11th or 12th century through the 1800's in Eastern Europe. During much of this time, rabbis did not preach to their congregations very often, and *maggidim* were paid by communities to do so.

Ma-oz Tzur—The title of a traditional H̲anukkah hymn, which means "How Strong a Rock." This tune is often used to chant some of the prayers of the regular prayer service during H̲anukkah as well.

Maror—the "bitter herbs" that are one of the symbolic Seder foods. Horseradish is the food most often used for *maror* in North America, but any hot or bitter food can be used. It symbolizes the bitterness of slavery.

Megillah—Hebrew for "scroll." When capitalized, *Megillah* usually refers to the scroll of the Book of Esther, which is read in the synagogue at Purim.

Mensch—Yiddish for "human, person." A *mensch* is a person of character and integrity, an admirable example for others. The adjective is *menschlich*, while the quality of being a *mensch* is *menschlikeit*.

Mezuzah—a small case containing a parchment scroll upon which are written some key verses from the Torah. *Mezuzah* is Hebrew for "doorpost", and a *mezuzah* is fastened to the doorpost of a Jewish home. A modern development is the miniature *mezuzah* worn on a chain as a necklace/amulet.

Mitzvah— from the Hebrew root meaning "command", a *mitzvah* is literally a commandment. In Yiddish and English usage, *mitzvah* has taken on the more generalized meaning of "a good deed." In this book, *mitzvah* is defined as "a Jewish act." Plural: *mitzvot*

Muktzeh—something inappropriate for use on Shabbat that should therefore not even be touched on Shabbat.

Ner Tamid—"eternal light," the light before the ark that burns continuously in every synagogue, recalling the one that also did so in the ancient tabernacle, and later in the first and second Temples in Jerusalem.

Pesah—the eight-day festival that commemorates the exodus from Egypt, known in English as Passover, observed primarily by celebrating ceremonial meals (*Seders*) on the first two nights at which the story is recounted, and by eating no leavened products.

Pesahdik—appropriate for Pesah; usually applied to food and indicating that the food in question contains no leaven nor any other ingredients not kosher for Pesah. See *hametz*.

Pirke Avot—literally, "Chapters of the Fathers." *Pirke Avot* is also known as *Avot* and is one of the 63 tractates of Mishnah. It is a collection of pithy ethical teachings of notable rabbis who lived from the end of the prophetic period through the end of the second century C.E.—most of the same people whose discussions make up the Talmud. *Pirke Avot* appears in its entirety in traditional prayer books because it is recited on Shabbat afternoons between Pesah and Rosh Hashanah.

Purim—a festival occurring in early spring that commemorates the bravery of Esther, a Jewish woman who used her status as a wife of a Persian ruler to save her people from slaughter. Her story, the biblical Book of Esther, is read and the holiday is marked by noise, drunkenness, feasting, the giving of gifts and of charity, costume parades and carnivals.

Pushke—Yiddish term for a box or other container used to collect charitable contributions of money; a *tzedakah* box.

Rebbe—the Yiddish form of the Hebrew "rabbi," which literally means "my teacher." This title of respect is applied primarily in Hasidic circles, and identifies one whose leadership is rooted in holiness and spiritual power, whether or not halakhic scholarship accompanies these qualities.

Rosh ha-Shanah—literally "head of the year;" the Jewish New Year. Rosh ha-Shanah usually occurs in September or October.

Sefer Torah—although it literally means "book of the Torah," this term refers to an actual Torah scroll, as opposed to a printed book or any of the more general uses of the word "Torah."

Shabbat—the Sabbath; the seventh day of the week; a day of rest. In the Jewish tradition, Shabbat begins at sundown Friday and ends at sundown on Saturday.

Shabbesdik—characteristic of or appropriate for Shabbat.

She-he-heyanu—A one-line *brakhah* that praises God for having sustained us long enough to reach this time. Said at *simhah* events by the celebrants, at the beginnings of festivals, and on the occasion of doing something good for the first time (or the first time in a year).

Shiva—the Hebrew word for "seven." Because the traditional period of deep mourning immediately after a death is seven days, this time has come to be called *shiva*. The mourners are said to be "sitting *shiva*," the home is a "*shiva* house," and the community enables them to pray without leaving home by coming to them and conducting a *shiva* minyan.

Shvitz—Yiddish for "sweat," refers to either a steam bath or the sweaty experience of having one.

Simhah—a happy occasion. Most often used to mean a joyous life cycle event such as a wedding or a bar or bat mitzvah.

243

Sofer—a scribe; specifically one who is trained in the laws and calligraphic techniques of writing Jewish sacred texts such as the scrolls inside mezuzot and tefillin, and the Sefer Torah. In addition to the requisite skills, a traditional *sofer* must also be an observer of the commandments.

Sukkot—the eight-day (seven among Reform Jews) festival of "booths", observed primarily by building and "dwelling in" a *sukkah*, a temporary shelter with a roof of branches through which one can see the stars. A *sukkah* is usually decorated with fruits and vegetables to signify the bounty of the harvest. *Sukkot* is both a harvest festival (at which prayers for rain to insure future harvests begin to be offered) and a reminder of the Jewish people's wandering in the wilderness for forty years.

Tallit—frequently translated as "prayer shawl," a *tallit* can actually be any piece of cloth with four corners that is large enough to wrap around the shoulders, and to whose corners are attached *tzitzit* (see below). The commonest type is about 6' x 2' and is worn draped around the neck with the two ends hanging down in front; a larger square tallit more like a woolen cloak is becoming increasingly popular.

Tefillin—small leather cases containing passages from the Torah. The *tefillin* have long straps by which they can be tied to the arm and around the head, in literal fulfillment of the commandment to "bind them (words of Torah) for a sign upon your hand and let them be a symbol before your eyes." Traditionally observant Jewish men and some women wear *tefillin* during morning prayers daily except on Shabbat.

Torah—literally, "teaching." When capitalized, the Torah is either a printed book that includes the first five books of the Bible, or the actual scroll of these books handwritten in Hebrew (also called a *Sefer Torah*). Without the definite article, Torah may have a much more general meaning, including the whole range of Jewish texts, teachings and traditions.

Tzitzit—fringes or tassels, specifically the tassels on the four corners of a *tallit*. The wearing of *tzitzit* is a commandment in the Torah. Plural: *tzitziot*.

V'Ahavta— The section of the Shema which immediately follows the line "*Barukh Shem k'vod malkhuto l'olam va-ed.*" This paragraph is found in Deuteronomy 6:5-9, and consists of commandments about continual awareness and teaching of the words of Torah.

Yahrzeit—literally, "year's time." In Jewish tradition, a person's *yahrzeit* is the anniversary of his or her death, the time when surviving relatives remember the deceased loved one by burning a special 24-hour *yahrzeit* candle and saying kaddish.

Yom Kippur—the Day of Atonement, a solemn day ten days after Rosh ha-Shanah which is marked by a 24-hour fast and a full day of repentant prayer and meditation in the synagogue.

ז"ל—the Hebrew abbreviation of the phrase *"zikhrono/ah liv'rakhah"*, used after the name of one who is deceased when mentioning him or her in speech or in writing, which means "May his (her) memory be for a blessing."

Joel Lurie Grishaver is a founder, co-owner, and creative chairperson of both Torah Aura Productions and Alef Design Group. He has degrees from Boston University and the University of Chicago, and has completed coursework for additional degrees at both the Hebrew Union College and the University of Southern California. His articles appear regularly in Jewish periodicals including *Jewish Spectator, Jewish Family*, and *Hadassah*. He has written more than 40 books and countless other educational materials including: *Shema is For Real, And You Shall Be a Blessing,* and *Learning Torah.* His serious writing is well respected and his cartoon characters (with two eyes on  the same side of the nose) are known wherever children are engaged in studying Torah. Joel is an adjunct faculty member of the University of Judaism, a regular instructor in their Department of Continuing Education and a fellow of the Whizin Institute for Jewish Family Living, and was a founding board member of CAJE. He also does penance for having been a menace to Temple Sinai's Religious School, by teaching afternoon Hebrew school classes.

This is a Hollywood book, and the sequel is already in the works. We are already planning **40 More Things You Can Do To Save the Jewish People.** And, in good *Tze u-L'mad* fashion, we want you to write us. To mail your best Jewish parenting suggestions or to get an Alef Design Catalog for other publications, send to:

Alef Design Group
4423 Fruitland Ave.
Los Angeles, California, 90058
Or fax your ideas to us at: 213–585-0327
Or call: 800–845-0662 • 213–582-1200